PRAISE FOR *BAGHDADDY*

"In the air force, it's often said that 'every airman has a story.' Bill Riley's story is extraordinary: intensely personal, raw, candid, searing, insightful, and inspirational. Flashing from a tough childhood to challenging service in our nation's defense, Bill's narrative demands close attention but rewards it with nuggets of great value. Whether he's talking about living, life, the limits of knowledge, or the drive to overcome obstacles, Riley has painted a compelling picture of what it means to lead—in combat and in fatherhood—and to love. You'll want to meet him after reading his story."

—Lt. Gen. Chris Miller (ret.), USAF, Former Air Force
Deputy Chief of Staff, Strategic Plans & Programs

"Lt. Col. Bill Riley's nightmarish childhood would have destroyed most people. A mother hurting her child is perhaps the ultimate betrayal in human experience. It is said that sometimes the finest steel is forged in the hottest fire. This memoir of Riley's military career is interwoven with thirty years of the most violent clashes our world has ever seen. From firsthand involvement with the brutality of cultures that use their own children as weapons and teach them to decapitate prisoners, his writing moves effortlessly to descriptions of overwhelming tenderness and the nobility of the human spirit. Riley gives us a glimpse of the brilliant intelligence warriors who orchestrate our military. I didn't know they existed, but I am glad to know they are on our side. *Baghdaddy* would make a very good movie—and it's all true!"

—Jim Nicholson, MD, USMC (ret., Korean War), Silver Star
and Purple Heart Recipient, Author of *George 3-7th Marines*

"*Baghdaddy* is raw, insightful, and a powerful read. Detailed accounts and memories of Riley's early years are both heartbreaking and profound. He somehow turned abuse into a valuable life lesson about how inner strength can keep you alive under the most dangerous and hostile conditions.

"The book is vivid in its storytelling—I could almost feel the shrapnel, rocks, stones, and bricks hit my skin as the author detailed accounts of multiple attacks by enemy forces. *Baghdaddy* is a story about love, loss, friendship, invisible enemies, and, at its core, a man who found solace through sharing his story."

—Hope Manna, Writer/Producer

"This was more than a read; it was an experience. Riley's story could have easily been told in two separate offerings—both his upbringing and his later military experience could each have filled volumes and stood alone on its own merits. But told together—a more complex undertaking for the author—the stories weave the fabric of how this man was made and how the childhood was utterly necessary for the final product of the adult.

"Although I did not serve with Lt. Col. Riley, ironically, I did deploy to the places he takes us in this book. Not only are his descriptions of the areas dead on, but I also appreciated his explanations of the cultural challenges, his interpretations of Middle Eastern attitudes, and the 'rest of the story'—often untold—regarding the history of the goings-on as well as the US military's involvement."

—Tammy Seley Elliott, Command Chief
Master Sergeant, US Air Force (ret.)

BAGHDADDY

BAGHDADDY

HOW SADDAM HUSSEIN TAUGHT
ME TO BE A BETTER FATHER

Lt. Col.
BILL RILEY (Ret.)

BROWN BOOKS
PUBLISHING GROUP

Baghdaddy
How Saddam Hussein Taught Me to be a Better Father

Brown Books Publishing Group
16250 Knoll Trail Drive, Suite 205
Dallas, Texas 75248
www.BrownBooks.com
(972) 381-0009

A New Era in Publishing®

Names: Riley, Bill, 1965- author.
Title: Baghdaddy : how Saddam Hussein taught me to be a better father
   / Lt. Col. Bill Riley (Ret.).
Description: Dallas, Texas : Brown Books Publishing Group, [2019]
Identifiers: ISBN 9781612542928
Subjects: LCSH: Riley, Bill, 1965- | Retired military personnel--United
   States--Biography. | Abused children--United States--Biography. |
   Fatherhood. | LCGFT: Autobiographies.
Classification: LCC E897.4.R55 A3 2019 | DDC 973.931092--dc23

ISBN 978-1-61254-292-8
LCCN 2018960370

Printed in the United States
10 9 8 7 6 5 4 3 2 1

For more information or to contact the author, please go to
www.BillRileyAuthor.com.
Facebook: @BillRileyAuthor   Twitter: @BillRileyAuthor

To the men and women we know, and the people we don't whom we'll never meet, in uniform and in the intelligence service who protect us and keep us safe. A long line of military and intelligence professionals fought for and continue to preserve the freedom and liberty we enjoy today. They sacrifice much. They are patriots.

To Lucy in the Sky and Johnny Be Good. I love and miss you guys. If there's a heaven somewhere up there for spies, I hope you're finally back together again, in a state of bliss, doing happy things that make the angels cringe and envy.

Last, but not least, I want to thank my sons, Xander and Sam, and my wife, Jodi. You make me a better man, and you mean the world to me. Jodi didn't want any part of this book. Some of my childhood bothered her more than it did me, and while I love her for that, a long, loud argument ensued when she ripped out all the scenes with her in the draft. Especially since a big part of this story is about the struggle to become a father, I kind of had to talk about her and about becoming a father. In the end, she grudgingly allowed me to write how we met and about the birth of our boys. I was able to sneak in a few more vignettes, but then she caught me, and I had to stop if I wanted to stay married.

CONTENTS

DISCLAIMER

After my final debriefs in and around DC, I'm finally done with polygraph tests and travel restrictions. My goal is to never have another classified conversation, time-sensitive target, cryptic meeting in a vault, or background investigation that includes everyone and anyone I've ever known.

In fact, I don't intend to do anything worthy of debriefing ever again.

In accordance with the Office of the Director of National Intelligence (ODNI) Instruction 80.04 / my nondisclosure agreements, this manuscript has completed ODNI prepublication review. In coordination with several other agencies, *Baghdaddy* was cleared for public release on February 28, 2018.

The views expressed in this publication are the author's and do not imply endorsement by the Office of the Director of National Intelligence or any other US government agency.

This work is a memoir, not a transcript of history. These stories reflect my subjective observations of events, memories, and experiences. Most of the names and personal identifying details in this story have been changed. Additional changes were made to protect operations. Other changes were made out of respect for the dead.

To tell this story more concisely while preserving the impact of the events described, a few of the people depicted in this story are hybrid characters. That means conversations I had with more than one individual, and our interactions, were condensed into one character. This was necessary to help ensure nonattribution and privacy. This approach also allowed me to streamline this memoir while preserving its heart. Finally, events in this story do not always flow in chronological order, and the timeline was compressed in several areas for pacing.

I don't want anyone or any operation to suffer from my sharing of this story, so this manuscript went through significant vetting and prepublication review. Despite that, I don't believe the changes made to this memoir take anything away from the things I saw or did or from the lessons I learned. This cross section of my life made me who I am, and it's been one hell of a ride. Any flaws in the telling of this story are mine alone.

Seize your days.
Bill Riley

PREFACE

On the one hand, writing a memoir is a foolish endeavor. I was trying to make a swirl of memories into a coherent story that someone else, who wasn't there, would get, while my friends kept saying, "This must be *so* cathartic for you." Plus, in a memoir, if the protagonist is an asshole, I'm an asshole. There's no shield or place to hide.

Writing this story meant reliving things I'd built tall, thick walls around so I could live like normal people. Unlocking that door was pain, and I feel everything.

On the other hand, some stories are important enough to share, and revisiting the past from a more mature, detached place let me examine raw, emotional things more objectively than I could as a kid or as a young airman in a firefight. That was cathartic. It forced me to look hard at how I became me. I knew I had strong friendships, but I didn't realize, on a rational level, how wrong my life would have gone without them until I started connecting the dots.

As I sorted through the stories I wanted to share about my military and intelligence experiences, I noticed patterns, and I focused on cause and effect. What I did and saw in survival school helped me realize the similarities between preparing for war and what my father tried to prepare me for in life.

I remember when, after fighting through an ethnic riot in Yugoslavia, the gunfire suddenly stopped, and I woke to an uncomfortable silence. Then I felt Lu warm against me. She was breathing softly, and I relaxed. I thought, *That's ironic.* My mother had created a brutal make-believe world full of secret organizations for us when I was a kid, and there I was all grown up, an intelligence analyst, covered in cuts and bruises, and in bed with a spy.

Sometime later, as I examined what I did in Kuwait, it seemed to lead directly to what I found in Iraq. September 11, 2001, changed everything. Then, after my father died, I fixated on what he tried to teach me, but it wasn't until after my first tour in Iraq that it finally all made sense.

The last piece of this story fell into place after I was a father, when I realized there really wasn't much difference between surviving childhood, fatherhood, and combat. That led me to this story of what happened and why, friendships and battles, my war, and the journey home.

PART I: GROWING PAINS

To see a World in a Grain of Sand
And a Heaven in a Wild Flower
Hold Infinity in the palm of your hand
And Eternity in an hour
A Robin Red breast in a Cage
Puts all Heaven in a Rage
A Dove house filld with Doves & Pigeons
Shudders Hell thr' all its regions.

—William Blake, "Auguries of Innocence"[1]

---

1   William Blake, "Auguries of Innocence," lines 1–8, https://www.poets.org/
poetsorg/poem/auguries-innocence.

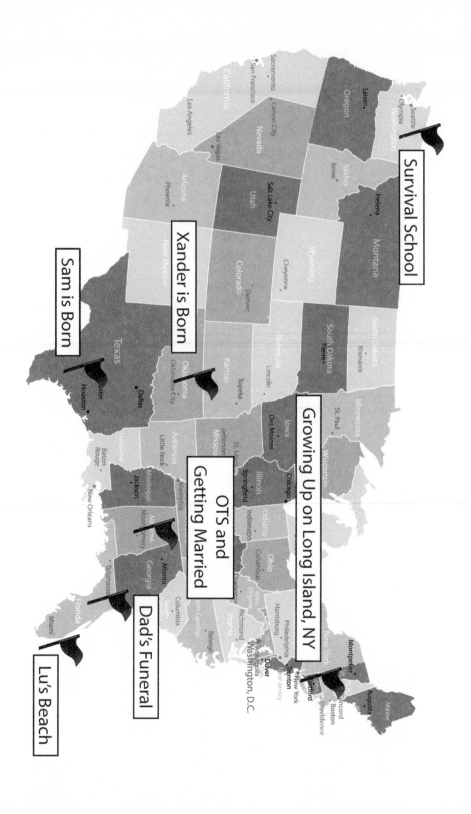

CHAPTER 1

September 11, 2001—Hampton, Virginia

It didn't register as America. I couldn't look away from the jagged image of that second Boeing 767 hanging in the air, advancing frame by grainy frame, and penetrating the South Tower of the World Trade Center. They played the explosion over and over again.

United Airlines Flight 175 was lost with sixty-five souls onboard.[2] There wasn't a single thing I could do but watch as terrorists used a civilian airliner as a weapon in a religious war that many Americans didn't really believe we were fighting.

In a fiery instant, hundreds of men and women at work were murdered for ideological reasons that could be distilled down to: you are infidels who keep us from destroying Israel, you exert political and economic power in the Middle East because you're the devil, and this is the only way we could hurt you, so we did.

Americans died that morning because our enemy believes that those who think, act, or believe differently from them aren't human. If history has taught us anything, it's that regardless of where, or when, or how, dehumanizing a people inexorably leads to atrocity. The people on that plane and in that tower were businesspeople, travelers, employers,

---

2   "United Airlines Flight 175 List of Crew and Passengers," York County Williamsburg Professional Fire Fighters, last modified November 20, 2018, http:// iaff2498.org/news/united-airlines-flight-175.html.

employees, and families. They were murdered because they were free, worked together as equals, and held different interpretations of God. They came to work, a lot like you and me, and they went about their business the way we do, any given day of the week. Some arrived at the World Trade Center early. A few raced to make it in by nine in the morning. By 9:03 a.m., so many lives had ended.

It was a terrorist attack. It was chaos. It could have been you, or me.

It was a tough day to be a father or mother. Kids asked, *Why?* And the adults didn't have good answers. Reporters interviewed each other; they commented and speculated, but they didn't know. By 9:04 a.m., we did know the world would never be the same. Osama bin Laden sent us videos. He claimed they didn't hate us for our freedom, and that if we just stopped interfering in the Middle East, our own security would be guaranteed—but those were lies.

I grew angrier the longer I watched. Those knife-sharp images stabbed into my brain, but I couldn't look away. It was important to remember every detail of that moment because I grew up in New York, I was in the military, and I knew a reckoning would one day come. But those pictures were a different kind of shrapnel. Each fragment was a fléchette—of migraine, suffering, disbelief, and rage—that pinned us to September 11, 2001, as it was burned into us.

Two thousand nine hundred ninety-six lives were lost.[3]

We were a nation united; we held our collective breath; and together, we watched.

It was the flame to which a moth is drawn.

---

3   "September 11 Terror Attacks Fast Facts," CNN, September 3, 2018, https://www.cnn.com/2013/07/27/us/september-11-anniversary-fast-facts/index.html. This total includes nineteen hijackers.

That was the day we went to war. I'll never forget it, or the things I had to do afterward. That morning, I was chief of plans for the Air Combat Command Inspector General in Hampton, Virginia—part of a livid, blue-uniformed throng, clustered around a large flat-screen television in a leased facility a short drive from Langley Air Force Base (AFB). Together, we watched the world change.

Pressed next to me, a young blonde staff sergeant stared at the same monitor. She hadn't noticed the tears streaming down her cheeks.

My hand involuntarily went to her face, and I wiped the wet away with my sleeve. Under other circumstances, I might have gotten a fist to the face or a trip to the social actions office for harassment, but she just offered a sad smile and let me dry her tears. Then she wiped a tear from my cheek that I hadn't noticed either.

She'd just transferred in from a different base, and in the flurry of activity that followed, I never even got to know her name, but I'll never forget that raw moment of mutual helplessness and anger. I could finally appreciate how my parents could vividly recall every detail from where they'd been the moment they heard that President John F. Kennedy had been assassinated.

Previously, I'd understood. After 9/11, I knew.

That afternoon, I was in a briefing, waiting for our general to give us our orders. In a headquarters, death comes slowly, slide by PowerPoint slide. I was staring out the window and daydreaming instead of paying attention to a long briefing that, after two hours, had managed to convey very little real information. It was a tough audience on the best of days. The topic was obviously overcome by the escalating attacks, and everyone was lost in their own thoughts as the monotone briefing washed over us.

I noticed the door open, but it didn't immediately register that our general was standing there. When my brain finished processing it, I stood up so fast I knocked my chair over and said, "Ladies and gentlemen, please stand for the inspector general."

The general offered a brief smile that was gone by the time he reached the podium and motioned for us to take our seats.

"President Bush is now at Barksdale AFB, and in a few minutes he will address the American people. He will tell them what has happened, what we are doing to stop anything else from happening, and that we will hunt down and punish those responsible for these attacks. Many people were killed, many more were injured, and we don't yet know if the attacks are over or if more are still planned. As this is not a hardened facility, we will disperse. Department chiefs will release all personnel to close telephone standby after the president's broadcast is complete. Your family and friends and neighbors will be frightened and outraged, and some of us will find we have family or friends who died or were injured in these attacks. Now is the time to hold your loved ones. Now is the time to let your family know you're safe and to reassure those around you who are scared. This is the time to be there for the people who need you, because we will call you soon. When we do, be ready."

"Yes, sir," we said, standing in unison. Then the president's broadcast began.

Hampton Roads sparkled, and we bristled with anger and anticipation. Across that dappled steel-gray waterway in Norfolk, the docks were chock-full of aircraft carriers and their support ships, several of them already making ready to get underway.

It took a few days, but we canceled every inspection we had scheduled to free up fighter, bomber, reconnaissance, and special support units for combat deployment.

Everyone understood it was our Pearl Harbor.

We speculated on where we would go as details became available. Fifteen of the nineteen 9/11 hijackers were Saudi Arabian citizens; it made sense that there would be some reckoning, and the Kingdom of Saudi Arabia would have to account for at least a few things.

Sometime later, I asked our general why we were going to Iraq. I had firsthand experience with the game Saddam Hussein played with the US and international weapons of mass destruction (WMD) inspectors, and I understood how ruthless he was from my time in Kuwait. I was there when we unleashed an all-out assault on his chemical, biological, and nuclear research, production, and storage facilities. I remember like it was yesterday, preparing for those attacks and working with the Kuwaitis in the aftermath of Saddam's rape of Kuwait during the Gulf War. But there was still a lot about going to Iraq that didn't make sense. Our general was patient with his young captain. We reviewed what facts we knew, and he let me vent for a while before he reminded me of three important things: I was only a small, squeaky wheel in the great machine; our leaders assured us that, despite evidence to the contrary, Riyadh was our friend; and the military existed to uphold democracy, not to practice it.

I understood it to be a serenity prayer.

The campaign for Iraq didn't live up to its shock-and-awe moniker. How could it? It was an exercise in déjà vu. President George W. Bush urged the Iraqi people to rise up, throw off Saddam's yoke, and greet our forces with open arms, but the Kurds and Shi'ites remembered all too well our resolve to liberate Iraq in 1991. Then, they followed the call of his father, President George H. W. Bush, to topple Saddam with a spectacular uprising. The Kurds quickly took the north, and the Shi'ites revolted and seized the south.

But winning the hearts and minds of people living in the middle of a war is a complicated thing. In Iraq, it came down to a situationally unique mix of trust, security, and opportunity for the Iraqi people that the commitment and overwhelming force provided by our occupation couldn't always guarantee. Over time, we did tremendous good, but in 1991 we also instigated a revolution in Iraq, and then we abandoned the two communities with the most to gain from Saddam's fall. They answered our call to revolt and took a righteous stand against real tyranny, and they were winning. Saddam lost his grip on city after city. Then, we withdrew our support. We didn't just go home; we relocated to just across their border to observe the obvious outcome.

Out in the open and cut off, the Kurds and Shi'ites had no choice left but to withdraw and go into hiding as Saddam focused all his resources on quelling that civil war. A few got away. But many freedom fighters and inconvenient Iraqis were hanged on Saddam's palace walls. Liberators fled where they could, and the free cities fell one after the other.

Torture was again the tool of governance. Rape rooms became a Ba'ath Party franchise. Hunted refugees fled as Saddam's war on terrorism purged all opposition and Ba'ath rule was restored. It hit the northern and southern cities hard. That was the winter of 1991 in Iraq.

The Gulf War was also an absolute success. Kuwaiti rule was restored, families were reunited after living through atrocities, oil field fires were extinguished, and coalition force casualties and collateral damage were the lowest of any conflict, ever. Saddam Hussein's war machine was curbed, and his chemical and biological weapons capability was in disarray and hobbled more than we knew. For more than a decade, stability was maintained in the Middle East. Regular unleaded gas dropped to just over one dollar a gallon. All good things.

Even if we were committed this time, we had a long history together that the Iraqis we'd have to fight and work with wouldn't soon forget. But our world was unraveling. Anthrax was in the mail a week after the 9/11 attacks. Anthrax is an infectious disease commonly found in the ground and primarily transmitted through contact with infected domestic animals. It occurs naturally, and veterinarians and wool workers are routinely vaccinated against it. But anthrax can also be weaponized. Weaponized anthrax is specifically designed to spread quickly and invisibly and cause mass casualties. You inhale it, you go about your business, and if you're not treated quickly enough, you die. That's what was in the mail after 9/11, and those letters went to political offices and news outlets across the US. People forget that in addition to Senators Daschle and Leahy and the State Department, employees at NBC, ABC, CBS, and the *National Enquirer* were attacked and injured, including one producer's seven-month-old son.[4] According to the CDC, the spores loaded into those letters caused twenty-two people to get anthrax. Five were killed. Twelve of them were mail handlers just doing their job.[5]

---

4   "Timeline: How the Anthrax Terror Unfolded," NPR, February 15, 2011, https://www.npr.org/2011/02/15/93170200/timeline-how-the-anthrax-terror-unfolded.

5   "Anthrax," Centers for Disease Control and Prevention, last modified August 1, 2014, https://www.cdc.gov/anthrax/bioterrorism/threat.html.

Saddam Hussein threatened to destroy us with WMDs, and he wasn't allowing inspectors into his WMD facilities, again. After repeated attempts directly and through the UN to get him to honor the terms of his Gulf War surrender, he still stonewalled inspectors. Congressional offices were closed. The media speculated on what else might be in the mail and about where we might be vulnerable to other WMD attacks.

After Saddam's last "fuck you," we attacked.

November 2003—Baghdad, Iraq

The road from 9/11 to Iraq wasn't a clear path. I understood how we got to Iraq; even if the logic was bent, I got it, and my orders were clear: support coalition operations across Iraq; support Coalition Provisional Authority activities to create a stable, working government so Iraqis could govern themselves again; resolve longstanding communication issues; and help the Iraqis rebuild their communications capabilities wherever possible.

When I arrived in Iraq, I found myself at the crossroads of who I could be and what I would be, and my time was running out. It was still hot mid-November. Heat radiating off the stone buildings made them appear to waver in the convective air. I blinked a few times to get the salt sting out of my eyes. We were in an unfamiliar place, slowly moving through a thick, enthusiastic crowd along the broken pavement and dirt of a large plaza. Clusters of dead trees and low, smashed structures were all that remained of a city park hemmed in on four sides by multistory concrete buildings divided by congested alleyways.

We could smell the crowd before we saw it. A sharp assault of un-washed humanity, overflowing sewers, and years-deep layers of refuse that had never been collected. The stench was overwhelming. Children played on debris piles the size of small hills composed of broken concrete and garbage.

After weeks of terrorist bombings in government buildings, cafés, and popular meeting places across Iraq, there was finally a lull in the violence, and the souk markets were open again. Within the square grew a thriving bazaar filled with the sound of merchants hawking their wares and shoppers bargaining for deals. We drove around men in long, white shirts holding hands as they leisurely walked the market. We passed through tendrils of charcoal smoke heavy with the scent of roasted meat that began to abate the harsh stench of the plaza.

Diners balancing plates on their laps and drinking hot tea from small Styrofoam cups sat together on a raft of carpets under the colorful tarps of shops selling kebabs and grilled chicken stuffed with fruit. The pent-up frustration of curfews and caution and fear was giving way to laughter, commerce, and song. It was nice to see people being people again. More of that would mean we were winning.

The men who lined the edge of the square leaned against the shaded walls, their Kalashnikov rifles slung casually over their shoulders as they joked and argued, traded information, and scanned the square for opportunities. As we drove by them, the graybeards looked away, young men watched us with mild curiosity, older boys waved, and a few hard men glared.

Our Humvee slowed to a crawl as a swirl of humanity opened and closed around us.

It was our last mission of the day.

We were trying to find a fire station.

Baghdad never had an effective 911/first-responder system. After years of corruption and intimidation followed by recent fighting, looting, and bombing, the fire stations we did find were left damaged, abandoned,

11

or unusable. It was still impossible to make a phone call across Baghdad, so firemen relied on smoke, family, or neighbors to lead them to the fires that broke out every day. Very few fire stations responded quickly. Most didn't respond at all.

Then it happened. In that crowd, framed by buildings I'd only seen on CNN, I recognized someone walking toward me in a sweat-stained suit that had seen better days.

It had been a while.

As my driver negotiated the central market stands and rubble piles in the plaza, I concentrated on that familiar face. After I made eye contact, and before he turned away and disappeared into the crowd, I was sure of two important things: I knew him, and he knew me. I squinted through the sweat dripping in my eyes to see where he'd gone, but the crowd had washed away all trace of him. *Small world. How long had it been?*

I didn't realize then, but I'd been preparing for Baghdad for a long time. Learning to cope with uncertainty and insanity started when I was just a boy. My military career as an intelligence analyst began in the mideighties, during the tail end of the Cold War. Since then, I've specialized in communications and worked with intelligence and special operations professionals from every service, virtually every intelligence agency, and several friendly foreign governments during surveillance, combat, and combat support operations.

My moments of true clarity always seem too few and far between. In Iraq, by the time all the pieces finally fell into place, it was almost too late for me. Afterward, who I had been when I got there finally made sense, and I was able to figure out who and what I really wanted to be. Maybe I'm a slow learner. Perfect clarity only comes to me in flashes. That day, clarity came to me in the muzzle flash of enemy gunfire.

When the trap was sprung, the souk was torn apart by the distinctive sounds of AK fire and explosions. Our Humvee had ground to a halt, and we were caught in a web we couldn't break through. The gunfire was close, and bullets cut indiscriminately through the market. Shots and cries. Shouts and prayers. Screaming people who had been smiling and laughing just moments earlier. Some dragged others away; most fled as fast as they could run. A mound of debris provided us some cover, and the incoming rounds hit short and long. They dug into the gravel in front of us, and they ricocheted off building walls behind us, but we were stuck and couldn't move.

Dozens of children mobbed our Humvee. They embedded themselves into every vehicle opening, wedged under our tires, and formed a ring around us. We couldn't drive them away or move forward or backward without crushing them, and we were out of time. Shots hit closer and closer. We had to go but couldn't move.

One boy looked down the alley in fear, and I found a man there frantically dialing numbers into a cell phone. He was trying to detonate the bomb and kill us—but his call wouldn't go through. As I pushed through the children to get to him, I thought, *Why do they always use kids?*

. . . But I'm getting ahead of myself. I'll circle back to where and how this mission began. I promise. If I start at the beginning, everything will make more sense.

What you must know now is that there are striking similarities between growing up, fatherhood, and going to war. It seems obvious when you think about it. Each one is about how we navigate conflict to overcome obstacles to achieve a goal. Whether that goal is adulthood, successful, well-prepared offspring, or victory. Each tests us in a different way, and each one absolutely helped prepare me for the others. Although, my order was a little off, and for years, that one question haunted me: *Why do they always use kids?*

CHAPTER 2

1971–1974—Farmingville, New York

My mother was a natural and gifted storyteller. Mother had that voice and way of saying things that made us desperately want to believe in what she said, even if we knew otherwise. Even adults were swayed. It was a powerful voice when we were children, and then for a while longer. For a time, it was impossible for me to see where truth ended and the lies began. It was all I knew. For years, I accepted everything at face value without question.

After all, Mother told us it was true.

From an early age, I understood there were monsters in the world, but, at the time, I didn't realize how fast they could creep up on you. I found myself surrounded before I even noticed they were there. Monsters are part of the power of storytelling. They come in all shapes and sizes, but the worst creatures by far might be called the "doppelgangers." Doppelgangers don't have to wait to go bump in the night. They don't need to wait to be invited in. They're fiends who wear the faces of the people you know and love the most.

Familiarity gives them the power to hurt you, bad.

Mother always said that, except for my arrival, she was a good Roman Catholic girl. I didn't understand it at first, but over time, it became her under-the-breath mantra, ultimately her catchphrase. Eventually, I understood that I was the reason my parents married.

It was a common enough tale. Youth. Romance. Pregnancy. Do the right thing. Get married, for better or worse, and then raise a family. It was the way it was—a roll of the dice.

On days my father wasn't home, Mother would shut herself in her room and smoke until she had to come out and make dinner. We always put out plates and silverware with a place set at the head of the table for my father in case he came home. When we were little, it was usually the four of us—Mother, my two sisters, and me—for dinner with an empty chair at the head of the table. Most nights, it was like waiting for Elijah.

While we ate, Mother would smoke and tell us about the important work she was doing for the government in secret labs disguised as common places, like the A&P grocery store. We were a family on the "inside," part of the select few who knew that WWIII started right after WWII, that battles were fought every day at labs, control centers, and information collection points hidden in plain sight all around Farmingville, New York. Secret to everyone except the agents of the organization, who knew which shelf would slide back if you touched the produce just right.

If you were on "the list," you knew. If you weren't on "the list," you were just a civilian oblivious to the war being fought, battle by battle, at the post office or gas station or in that shady spot just past the hedges in the town park.

The name of the organization changed over the years, as Mother was assigned different duties, until almost all the agencies responsible for prosecuting the war were absorbed into "the" organization—although she was often called back to work for "the" CIA when her talents weren't in demand elsewhere.

As our awareness of computers grew, her stories became more elaborate. She told us of how she was detailed to the Burroughs Corporation, where she helped develop cutting-edge computer processors for sensitive areas within the government. After that, she worked for "the" NSA until a random encounter with enemies of the state while she was getting her tires rotated blew her cover. She was sacked even though her team thwarted a nuclear attack during "the" fast-food incident at the McDonald's that wasn't really a McDonald's. Because her cover was blown, she could never work for "the" NSA arm of "the" organization ever again. It didn't matter that her team caught the saboteurs and sent them to "the" reeducation facility in Iowa. Mother could never return.

To fill her time after "the" NSA, she did piecework for a dozen different agencies until she finally settled on traveling as an inspector for the Long Island Railroad, "just until things cooled off." She told us she left for work after we went to school and always returned just before we got back. That was what they had to agree to if they wanted her help. It was her one inviolate rule, and once she got home, she would smoke in her room to unwind until dinner.

When we were little, we asked her nonstop questions about her day, and her eyes sparkled as she told us the details she could reveal. We were sworn to secrecy, and we took it seriously, hanging on her every word. Then she'd ask about our day, nodding her head as she chain-smoked until it was time to pick up the dinner dishes. Something always happened when she stopped to take my plate. Her manner would change, her enthusiasm would drain away, and she'd look at me with empty eyes and say, "You know, everything was fine until you came along."

She never doubted my father would return to her. He was supposed to return when he had finished "wrestling his demons," which I later understood to mean "after he banged enough young women out of his system." Eventually, my father did come back, for a while. As us kids grew up and began to ask more difficult questions, Mother always had a ready answer: a mission we could be read into, another story she told with aplomb. Our eyes would shine at the end of each story, and for a while, we were so proud of her.

"Mom, how can you work if you don't leave the house?" I asked, trying to puzzle through things with the logic of an eight-year-old.

On one occasion, I remember how she huddled close to me, looking to the left and right to make sure no one would overhear. "When you're older, if you're talented enough to work for the organization, I will tell you more, but for now: when this house was built, we had passages installed so I could leave secretly. People have to believe I'm just a housewife, or I can't do my part to keep the United States safe."

I was so excited. "Can you show me just once? I won't tell . . ."

"Classified," was what she'd say, cutting me off. "It's classified, so I can't ever show you. But I can say this . . ." And once again she surveyed the area for anyone who might be listening to us as I ate my cereal. "Remember when I worked at Burroughs?"

"Uh huh." I nodded as I remembered.

"I had them install cables from their biggest, fastest computer to my room in the house, so I could do my work at night through the television. We call it 'teletravel.' I can see my boss and other agents located around the world, and they can see me. We can do almost all our work through the TV, but my project will let us do even more." She paused for a moment and took another deep draw from her cigarette. "Eventually, almost every civilian will be able to work that way, and it will change the world."

"Oh, Mom, I really want to see it, please," I begged.

"Billy, I'm only going to say this once. My room is one of the most special places in all of America. If you go looking around in there, you'll set off the security system, they will cut my line, and if I can't work . . . people will die. This is why it's especially important that you never enter my room without permission."

"Yes, Mom."

"You understand now, right, Billy?"

"Yes, Mom, I promise."

I entered Mother's room without permission only once.

Time was a thief my father never realized he let into our house.

Father was home again, mostly to sleep or during breaks between jobs. He worked at hospitals and mental institutions as a nurse's aide, took college classes, and, on the weekends, between picking up extra shifts and studying, sold bushels of clams he raked from the sandbars between Patchogue and Fire Island. My first job was sorting those clams, by size, into littleneck, topneck, cherrystone, and chowder bushel bags made out of canvas or jute that smelled like the sea. I was five when he started taking me out with him. That was when Father's time spent away from home began to take a toll on Mother. Every day my father was gone, something disappeared from her until what I recognized as my mother was no longer there.

The shift was almost imperceptible.

Every week, her laughter and kindness diminished a little more. One day, it was entirely gone, and we began to avoid her—she was always sad or angry, never wanted to play with us. Eventually, wherever she touched us hurt. We waited for her to come back to us, but what time gnawed away from her never returned. She hid the darkness of what she was becoming beneath a cracked shell of makeup and made-up bliss. But her shell only kept her anger smoldering inside.

For years, she wouldn't leave the house without affixing the mask of sunshine she wore to convince us all that everything was fine. In the end, even that façade grew hard and transparent. We could see her in there, but we couldn't reach her. Mother became little different from the plastic covers she had installed on all our furniture so they would stay beautiful forever. We could see there was something still warm and soft under the hard, cold, clear exterior, but we couldn't feel her presence anymore.

Mother became a caricature of what she had been in the happy pictures spread around her bedroom from the time when she was a bride who believed she was a princess in a story that would have a fairy-tale ending. She believed it with all her heart, and it was her undoing.

One night, Father left again in a retreat of slammed doors, and the muffled crashes of things breaking woke me. When we were still little, my sisters and I shared a room. Isabel and Sophie were somehow still asleep, curled up together under the covers in the lower level of the bunk bed, and I climbed down from the top bunk, careful not to wake them.

It was late, and the floor was cold as I padded up to my mother's room with bare feet. I could hear her crying on the other side of the door. I hesitated, wondering if I should go inside. In little kid logic, I circled back to the kitchen and got out a can of her favorite soda, Tab, because I knew instinctively that an intrusion required an offering. I knocked on the door, but no one answered, so I opened it. The nightstand lamps she'd knocked to the floor illuminated her like spotlights. My mother sat in a clear space on the carpet, surrounded by the debris of women's things. She wore a white bathrobe, her eyes were wet, and mascara ran down her face and stained her sleeves. A green ashtray was on the floor in front of her, a fresh-lit cigarette between her lips.

"Don't cry, Mommy," I said as I advanced into her room with the soda held out to her. "Everything will be OK. Please don't cry."

She took the soda from my hand, looked at me for a long moment, and came to some conclusion. I reached out my arms and took a step forward to hug her, but then she looked away and in a quiet, hard voice said, "I wish I never had you."

I stood there longer than I should have with my arms stretched out to her. Then I felt sad and foolish and quickly backed out of her room, hiding behind the door.

I don't remember much after that. I was six years old. I don't remember crying—though I'm sure I did. I never entered Mother's room again without her permission.

My father had a background in combat and a temper he was afraid of, and my mother didn't know how to stop after she had crossed a line. It was the worst combination for both of them. He would leave in order not to hurt her, and she would push him away even harder when he came back. It was a pattern I wouldn't understand until I was much older. No matter how hard they tried, the good times were always overshadowed by a tension that would build until things blew up again, spectacularly.

Father finished his associate degree and was working on his bachelor's degree with the intent of being a registered nurse. He and Mother continued to grow apart.

We were living in the basement apartment of my grandfather's house, and my father was halfway through his program. He was studying for finals at the picnic table under an awning built off the garage while I played in the rolling field that was my grandfather's lawn. I was busy looking for something. I had a mission, and after a few hours of playing, I was startled to realize my father was standing behind me.

"You've been there for a while, what are you doing?" he asked. He was organizing his notes and textbooks into an old leather shoulder bag.

"I was looking for something, and I finally found it," I said, proud of myself, holding up a four-leaf clover. "Mom said you had to take your tests for college, and since we're part Irish I thought this would work. It's for good luck on your tests."

"I won't make a very good nurse, will I, if I have to rely on luck to pass."

"Oh, yeah," I said, touching my sunburned neck and trying to hide my disappointment. "I guess that's true."

"Hey," he said after a while, "don't worry. Luck is as important as skill sometimes. I'm glad you found this."

"Really?"

"Really." He kneeled on the grass next to me and opened the textbook, then flipped to the beginning and tore out the title page.

I jumped up. "Don't! You'll get in trouble!"

My father just laughed and said, "Don't worry. These books are made to be used. The trick is to get the ideas written here into your head." He tapped his temple. "If these books aren't worn and written in, it means you didn't use them right."

"Is that true?" I asked as he kept folding the page in half until it was the size of his palm. He set the four-leaf clover on top and neatly wrapped the paper around it.

"Yes, and we don't want to ruin the luck you worked so hard to find." He slid the small package into his wallet. "This way I'll have it with me. Always."

His ice-blue eyes sparkled. "See you soon, Billy," he said as he stood up and left for his test. My father still had long auburn hair back then, and the breeze caught it as he walked away.

As soon as his car left, I went to Sarah's.

Sarah was my best friend, and we were in elementary school. We were in every class together except for third grade and sixth grade. She had blue eyes and towhead-blonde hair that fell like ribbons of silver around her shoulders.

As kids, we played together every day in the summer, and we caught fireflies at night. They tried to evade us, but after epic hunts, they wound up in Mason jars with holes punched in the lids. We'd watch the stars and fall asleep on the grass in their glow and bury the fireflies the next morning with elaborate funerals complete with eulogies, Popsicle-stick crosses, and hymns. We called hymns *hums* then because, except for the first verse, we could never remember all the words.

The fights grew worse. I was about eight years old, and after they argued about things I couldn't understand, Father would throw dishes, Mother would yell louder, and he would storm out. Scuffles happened after Father got home from work or school, the shouting got louder, and the first casualties were always our dinner plates. Over the years, we went through a lot of plates, and after Mother finished cleaning up, I always seemed to say or do something that warranted punishment. That night, I was too slow cleaning up my spot at the table, and Mother hit me in the back of my head with her plate while I was walking to the sink. It hit me so hard, it knocked me down. When I dropped the dishes I was carrying, they shattered on the floor, and she went into a frenzy. She picked up a heavy wooden spoon, stood over me, and beat me across the face and hands until she grew tired. She must have been really mad at Father; I could barely open my eyes. Afterward, my sister Isabel helped me.

I spent a lot of evenings with Isabel as she held a washcloth full of ice against my swollen face after a beating. Beatings exhausted Mother. She would grow quiet afterward, shuffle off to the living room or her bedroom, turn on the TV, lie down, and fall asleep.

Isabel was a better survivor than I was. I admired her for that. She could figure out paths around Mother and defuse her anger in ways I couldn't. She was like a magician who could blunt and sometimes even stop our mother's attacks. When that didn't work, all I could do was stand in the way, be her shield, and later have her press another icy washcloth onto my face. Isabel had a talent for stopping nosebleeds with random things from our freezer.

Isabel was always angry with me when she did it. "Why do you have to be so stupid?"

Sometimes she would have tears in her eyes as she mashed a wet, ice-filled cloth hard against my swelling face. At that point, Mother favored bashing me across the face with long wooden cooking spoons or salad servers, one in each hand.

"Don't you know when she does that, all you have to do is . . . to distract her, and you can get away?"

"I know now," I said as I held up one arm, and my sister put first-aid cream where the spoon and tong marks were still bleeding. On the back of my hand, there were already scabs on my knuckles where the thin skin had torn.

I woke up sore. The washcloth on my face was dry and stiff, and my mouth ached. It was time to get ready for school. I rolled off my bed, quickly washed and changed, and ran out the door.

I was in third grade, staring out the window, daydreaming. Eventually I realized the teacher was calling on me. "Mr. Riley. Are you listening?"

I could never figure out why adults asked such stupid questions when it was obvious I wasn't.

That was when I realized she was standing in front of me, and the class was expectantly waiting for something. "No, Ms. Sahara," I answered. "I'm sorry, what was the question?"

Ms. Sahara was a petite teacher barely taller than some of the kids in our school. She had hard blue eyes, and her permed hair was a mass of coiled springs that the tight bun on the back of her head barely subdued. Wild curls and wisps would spring up around her head by the end of class. The angrier she got, the more hair escaped her bun.

She asked me, "What did you do to your face?"

Without even thinking about it, I told her exactly what had happened—the beating Mother had given me—and as soon as the last word was out of my mouth, I knew I'd said something horribly wrong. The entire class was holding its breath.

Then, *kerslap*—Ms. Sahara backhanded me across the cheek.

"How dare you," she said. "How dare you make up such lies about your mother! I won't stand for it."

I felt the hot, stinging heat from her hand spread across the right side of my face, and I looked around wide eyed. I was stunned and embarrassed. I could feel the tears coming, and I didn't want anyone to see me cry in class. Then something happened, and I knew at that moment, I knew without a doubt, there was a God.

At that moment, the principal announced an air-raid drill over the PA system, and we dove under our desks to duck and cover. While the siren went off, I curled up under my desk, put my hands over my mouth and eyes, and wept. When the drill was over, Ms. Sahara sent me to the principal, where I sat outside his office until the end of the day.

When he finally called me in, all he said was, "Now listen, young man, I know things are hard right now, but you have to understand your mother is going through a difficult situation, and making up stories is not helping. You have to listen to her and be a good helper."

"But Mr. Lyons, I didn't lie."

"Mr. Riley," he said, leaning forward on his desk, "lying will not be tolerated in this school."

At that point, I understood. Anything else I said would only make things worse. I was told to wait outside the office as Ms. Sahara and Mr. Lyons discussed what would happen to me next.

They didn't even bother to shut the door. Ms. Sahara wanted me out of her class because I was distracting the other kids who wanted to learn; Mr. Lyons said that while I was troubled, I wasn't retarded, so I was staying in her class. That made her mad. When he told her that he would take care of all my discipline in the future, her words came out in hisses and low growls that I couldn't make out.

Then the principal called me in.

"Yes, Mr. Lyons?"

"Apologize to Ms. Sahara over the disruption you caused in her class."

I gave him an angry look.

"*Now*, Mr. Riley."

I looked hard at the worn carpet on the floor. "Ms. Sahara, I'm sorry I disrupted your class." The words were poison in my mouth. "It won't happen again," I said, and the poison spread.

"Now go home, Mr. Riley. If your mother has any questions about today, tell her to call me."

I left without another word.

Things were different back then. Unless relatives, teachers, or doctors were confronted with undeniable evidence that a child was in jeopardy, they did what they could and turned a blind eye.

That was just the way it was, and life went on. I healed up. Isabel was my leader, I was her shield, and Sarah and I played. We moved out of our grandfather's apartment into a new house built next door, where we finally had our own bedrooms. As soon as we settled in, our parents divorced. Father got an apartment close to work, and Mother spent most of her time making the world safer by teletravel. The rest of the time, she was angry.

CHAPTER 3

Even as a child, I understood on some level that freedom had to be earned. No one was going to give it to us. What I didn't know then was that even little freedoms have a cost.

I didn't have Ms. Sahara as a teacher again until the sixth grade. That was also when my sister Isabel and I began the great sofa liberation operation. Like most military campaigns, casualties occurred en route to our objective.

It was a simple enough plan. We had a huge pair of gray metal scissors big enough for me to hold with the wide bottom ring wrapped around my hand like the guard on a sword. I was left-handed and had trouble using it, but in my sister's right hand, it could easily cut through just about anything. The plan was, Isabel would "slip" while working on a school project spread out over the upstairs sofa, cut through the plastic cover, and after Mother settled down, we would peel the damaged plastic off.

We debated the risk and reward of liberating each plastic-covered chair and sofa in the house and finally settled on the upstairs hall sofa because it was out of the way—company wouldn't see it, and accidents happened.

For years, we were only allowed to use the plastic-covered furniture when company came over. Good children could sit on the furniture, but if you weren't good and got caught, there was a punishment. Usually we sat on the floor and only used the furniture when Mother wasn't around. But the sofas were right there, and we fixated on what was underneath their hard, uncomfortable shells. Being able to see furniture but not touch it ate at us until we couldn't take it anymore.

Isabel thought that, if it were an accident, she could talk us out of a painful ending. I was convinced my mother loved her plastic slipcovers more than us and that beatings would follow regardless, but I thought a beating was a fair price to pay for a sofa we could actually use.

It was an elegant and seemingly victimless crime, if you didn't count the slipcover.

When the day came, we reviewed the plan, checked the scissors, and just before dinner, we carefully laid out the papers for a school project on top of the clear plastic cover.

I took up position at my desk just across the hall from our target.

Just outside my door, Isabel took a deep breath, practiced a few different grips and stabbing motions, then held the scissors close to her chest and waited. Sophie, as usual, would just stay in her room and lock the door at the first sign of trouble.

We could hear Mother's heavy footfalls as she walked to the bottom of the stairs to bellow, "Kids, dinner."

"OK!" we replied in unison. Then we looked at each other, nodded, and Isabel raised the scissors above her head, fell to her knees with a loud thud, and stabbed the hard, crinkly membrane. There was a distinct pop and whoosh of air. It was as though a force field surrounding the sofa was gone.

"What was that?!" Mother roared as she climbed the stairs. "What's all that noise?"

After Isabel pierced the plastic, she paused for a moment at the point of no return. Then, in one quick motion, she gutted the slipcover from edge to edge. With one slice, she freed the sofa from its time capsule and, for the first time in three years, soft, tactile material was exposed to the air.

As Mother reached the top of the stairs, Isabel fell face down in a flurry of homework sheets, the scissors clattered out of her hands across the floor, and she began to wail.

Mother's eyes narrowed, and her face distorted as her mask of civility shattered into a thousand pieces. "What did you do?" she snarled.

"I'm so sorry, Mommy," Isabel said. "I was picking up my project, and I slipped on a paper. The plastic got cut when I fell."

Mother bent down, retrieved the scissors, and held them out point down, the big ring around her fingers as she furiously shook her fist at us and shouted, "What did you do?"

"Mommy, I'm sorry. It was an accident," Isabel cried. Big tears welled up in her eyes.

I pulled Isabel up and pushed her behind me as we backed away from Mother. "Mom, the sofa looks fine," I said. "It just skinned the . . ."

I wanted to say more, but she swung her scissors hand out as she said, "NO," and the force of her scissor-ring-covered fist connected hard with my right temple. I staggered to the side for a moment before I toppled over and crashed to the floor.

I was confused and couldn't get up. I saw white flashes all around me, like snow falling inside the room in fat, lazy flakes that swirled and rang like bells.

Mother grabbed my sister by the throat and slammed her head into the wall.

She shouted at Isabel, but I couldn't make out the words through the ringing in my head. All I could do was watch as she waved her scissors hand around, pulled Isabel back by her neck, and slammed her head back into the wall.

31

Isabel was a slight girl of maybe fifty pounds, a fourth grader with wavy brown hair tangled around her pale face. I had to do something. I kept trying to stand back up to help her, but my arms and legs and head were too heavy to lift. I felt helpless. As hard as I tried, all I could do was inch forward. My vision flickered, but I had to keep moving. I got to my knees. Then the ringing finally stopped, and I could hear Mother again.

"*Fangul.* This is what you think of me. *Fangul. Mannaggia-puttana,* after all I do for you ungrateful kids. *Mannaggia-puttana* . . ."

There was a pattern to it. At "*Fan*," she'd yank Isabel's head back, then slam it into the wall on "*gul.*"

At "*Mannaggia,*" Mother would pull my sister back from the wall by her throat, and at "*puttana,*" she'd bang her head deeper into the wall again. It was Sicilian for "Fuck you, damn whore," and it went on and on.

Isabel's eyes were rolling up in her head. I got up, stepped forward, and grabbed at my mother to pull her off my sister, but my feet were unsteady, and she swung back at me hard.

The tips of the scissors sank deep and cold into my right shoulder.

I screamed and fell back down when she yanked out the blades. Then she turned back and ignored me while she held Isabel up by her hair and shouted into her wide eyes.

I wasn't even worth any more effort.

I was miserable. Blood soaked through my shirt and wouldn't stop. I tore the shirt and stared at my cut shoulder. It was like a small mouth with open white lips that drooled blood.

I hated being small. Inside my head, I screamed, *How could I be so useless?* For a moment, I sat there crying and feeling sorry for myself, not knowing what to do except bleed. I looked at Isabel being shaken and beaten, and I wondered how things had gone so wrong. We just wanted to sit on a couch again. I watched my mother rage and flail my sister around like a doll.

I looked at the couch, and I finally understood. I knew exactly what to do.

I got to my knees, wiped away my tears, and shouted, "Mother!" as I tore at the plastic slipcover as hard as I could. A strip of plastic ripped off with the distinctive sound of seams popping thread by thread.

Mother stopped as though frozen. Her head turned toward me with a slow, jerking motion until her eyes locked on mine.

Then I said it again: "Mother," my voice a low growl, "let her go." I ripped off another ribbon of plastic, and the entire back cushion cover peeled off with it.

I threw the ruined shell across the hall. Her eyes went from me to the strewn plastic.

Mother howled, dropped Isabel, and turned on me.

I was relieved to see Isabel crawling away.

Mother was panting and sweating, shaking with anger. I knew her wrath was all directed at me. She pounced like an animal, and I didn't even try to get out of the way. I only had enough energy left for one last thing. I was going to lose to her anyway. I would finish the job we started.

In the moment before she struck, I did what had to be done. Taking one sharp breath, I ripped the last bit of plastic cover off the sofa, and then she was on me. I was smiling when Mother hit me with the heavy metal scissors, across the same temple, like they were brass knuckles.

My world shook like a snow globe again. She hit me in the face until it knocked the last sound out of my head. Not even a buzz was left. My world was all hurt and silent. The snow blanketed me. My body shuddered, and everything blurred.

I crumpled to the ground, but as hard as I tried, I couldn't move again. Three Mothers shook their scissors at me, their mouths moved, and I closed my eyes, expecting the worst. My heart pounded as I waited for her to finish me. After a few breaths, I opened the one eye I could. But nothing happened. It took some time to focus. Mother was standing over me, staring at the blood seeping through my shirt. Then she noticed the red drops dripping from her scissor tips, and she grew strangely calm. It was as if the sight of my blood had washed her anger away.

Mother dropped the scissors to the floor, walked to her room, and shut the door. I remember Isabel crying and saying something as she pushed a shirt against the wound on my shoulder. She was probably telling me how stupid I was, but I couldn't hear. It hurt. My head was packed with snow, and everything faded to quiet white.

Making a stand has consequences. Like most kids, we were insurgents, and the sofa liberation operation ended with a whimper, a small puddle of blood, and a lot of black and blues. It was my first military operation and my last mission with Isabel.

The first thing to cross my mind when I came to was, *Where's Isabel? Is she OK?* But she was sitting above me, and I relaxed. Then, "Oww." Followed by, *Why am I so pathetic? I couldn't help at all.* But Mother never got around to having the sofa recovered, so it was a victory.

While Isabel patched me up, we rested on the one sofa we had been able to free, hyperaware of the soft, warm velvet cushions that supported us. It would have been luxurious if we weren't completely numb. I couldn't understand how Isabel could still move. There were bruises on her neck and wrists and back where Mother had grabbed her and banged her head into the wall. Patches of her hair were torn out, and her voice was so gravelly she couldn't talk, but the worst part was, as hard as she tried to smile, she cried every time she looked at my face. When I was conscious, Isabel filled the sink with cold water and ice and made me submerge my head for as long as I could hold my breath. Each time, the cold burned like fire, but each time, the water in the sink was a little less red and gray. We thawed and refroze everything in the freezer as makeshift ice over the course of the day.

Even though her head was swollen and it was hard for her to move, Isabel helped me dry off and tended my swollen, broken skin until the right half of my face was painted in iodine and held together with bandages. My bleeding shoulder finally tapered off to an ooze that Isabel was able to contain with tape, gauze, and what looked like staples, but I didn't go to school the next day because my eye wouldn't open, and Isabel, wearing a scarf of frozen peas and carrots, stayed home to rest and take care of both of us.

To this day, I've never met anyone as tough as she was.

The right side of my face was swollen from my hair to my jaw, and if I moved too fast, I could taste blood in my mouth and feel a wet tearing in my shoulder. When I woke up the next day, Isabel had already left for school. My right arm was numb, and I gave up on going to school after finally getting into a clean shirt only to pass out halfway through buttoning my jeans.

I went to school the day after that, and Ms. Sahara sent me straight to the principal before the first bell had rung. I didn't know why I was in trouble, but I didn't care.

I braced myself for the worst, but the principal just frowned, gave me a butterscotch, and brought me to the library to get a book.

"When you find one you like, check it out, and come back to my office."

The few people I encountered looked away as soon as they saw me.

That was how I discovered *A Wrinkle in Time* by Madeleine L'Engle. Even though the main character, Meg, was hard on herself and a little mouthy, I liked her immediately. She introduced me to a strange new world and her crazy family as they searched for their missing father.

After I settled in to read, the school nurse brought me an ice pack. If I balanced it just right on my head, tiny drops of ice-cold water would slowly creep down my face as I read. It felt good, and the few droplets that made it all the way down my face collected in a salty pool at the corner of my mouth.

I was sitting in the least hard chair in front of the principal's office, deep into a story I wouldn't have been able to read a few years earlier. When I looked up from my book, I was startled to see my father and mother coming through the door. My father was angry, and my mother looked . . . inconvenienced.

I read until I had an awful headache, and I closed the book just as Meg was trying to crash through an invisible wall. It reminded me too much of Isabel.

We left when my parents came out. Father didn't say what happened with the principal, and I fell asleep on the way home, but he must have noticed the book I was reading.

I awoke in my room, and the house was quiet. The only light came from the lamp across the street, and all the books in *A Wrinkle in Time*'s series were stacked neatly on my nightstand. I was propped up on pillows; there were black stitches in my shoulder and bandages wrapped around my head and face. They felt cool against my skin, and my lips and fingers tingled pleasantly with every heartbeat.

The next time I woke, a policeman was in the chair across from me. I almost jumped out of bed when I realized he was there. He asked about what had happened, but I was still groggy from the medicine. When we were done, he pinned a plastic badge to my PJs and left his card on my desk.

Mother didn't talk to me for a while after that, but she never hit me in the face again.

A few days later, we left her at the house, and Father took us camping.

Isabel's bruises worsened, then slowly faded, and her voice returned. I answered Father's questions as best as I could, but I didn't really know what to say.

Our days together were filled with the sound of moving water, hikes to views past fields of flowers, and drinking hot chocolate while we watched Sophie splash in puddles when it rained. I saw more stars on that trip than I'd ever seen in my life, and Father pointed out all the constellations. We impaled hot dogs, chunks of meat, and marshmallows on sharp sticks and cooked them over the fire, and I fell asleep watching pine logs crack and spit as they burned.

When Isabel's voice came back, we talked about it. Isabel was hurting worse than I knew. She sat on a rock at the edge of a sunny glen. I was just across from her in the shade of an epic fir.

"Billy, I can't do it anymore," she said.

"Do what? It's OK now."

"No. It's not. It's not OK. I can't stand it," Isabel said, tears streaming down her cheeks.

I reached out to her, and she grabbed on to me and buried her face in my chest and sobbed.

"I hate it, hate it. I hate it. The blood. The purple, swollen skin. It hurts, and I hate it."

I just held on to her, and she wailed. "I hate it, and I hate her, and I can't stand having to . . . I had to use tape, and you were still bleeding, and all I could find was a stapler . . . so I stapled your arm to close the skin together, and you still wouldn't wake up. I tried to use the phone to call Dad or 911 but she unplugged it and took it off the wall so . . . I stapled your shoulder to keep the skin closed . . ." She cried until she was gasping for air. "Because that was the only way I could get the bleeding to stop."

"Shush, I know it was scary," I said. "You were so brave, you did great." I sat down with her on that rock, in the sun, with my arms wrapped around her as she wailed and sobbed, and the shadows grew.

"You know," she said, "at night, while the other girls in my class are doing their homework or watching TV or thinking about boys, I do surgery with office supplies and stop bleeding with mixed vegetables, and I can't stand it anymore. I love you, but I can't do it anymore. And, and—I'm so sorry."

Isabel cried for a while after that, and we just stayed there until the shadows finally covered the rock we were sitting on.

"It's OK," I said. "You did great. I know what to do now. I'll be fine."

"No, you won't," Isabel sobbed. But I reassured her as best I could. That was how my first mission ended. With one exposed sofa, a new scar, and an understanding that things would never be the same. Like all first missions, it was a graduation of sorts.

We held each other, she cried until she ran out of tears, and Isabel became Sophie's shield.

When we returned from the Adirondacks, Mother was seeing a doctor for what she called her occasional fixations and outbursts. The treatment was called Thorazine. Pharmacologically speaking, it was an antipsychotic drug and the prescribed M&M's of the seventies and early eighties.

She took her medicine, and it was a golden time for us. She was kinder and seemed happier.

Mother also rediscovered religion while we were gone. When I went to my room after putting up the camping gear, I found a statue of the Virgin Mary on my desk. It was an oversized, mostly blue-and-white-painted, cast-stone Madonna molded with a kind face, probably more accustomed to looking out over a yard than a boy's room. It must have weighed ten pounds, but it always seemed bigger and heavier. There was no note, and Mother would never answer my questions about why she put it there, but I held on to it as a peace offering, a first step forward, a symbol of contrition if not quite an apology. For me, it represented hope. That, maybe, my mother loved me.

But that effigy of Holy Mary, Mother of God, proved to be something else entirely.

After we settled back in at home, Mother started taking me to Boy Scout meetings again, and, around that time, I learned tap dance and ballet. Not that I wanted to—I wanted martial arts lessons, but my sisters wanted to dance and, with the exception of Boy Scouts, all our activities had to be together. So, I tried my best and learned to shuffle-ball-change and master the five basic positions of ballet. I also learned confidence—which for a young teenage boy in dance class is defined as participating in recitals. They were grand events. I'd skip left and right and then hoist mostly skinny girls, wearing little more than spandex and sparkles, up into the air by their pelvic bone, hips, or the curve of their back, often using only one hand to hold them aloft without dropping them. Their legs gracefully flexed and extended with pointed toes, and their arms reached out until I swung them around, returned them safely to the ground, and began the next move in our sequence. Each lift was done in one swift motion. They'd leap, and I'd catch and hold them aloft. All while I wore a spandex unitard in front of a hundred strangers who could see, at a glance, not only that I was circumcised but also exactly how excited I was by each girl I held aloft by her hips or crotch.

After recitals were the only time in my life I've ever been besieged by excited parents dragging their girls over to ask me if I could "do that thing" to their daughter again. So they could take pictures. We did the best we could to stage the photos. We were already exhausted from dancing, and our muscles were twitchy, but in most of the pictures, even though we smiled, our faces were bright red. I didn't like dance, but my upper-body strength, confidence, and smile improved with every lesson, even though my sisters teased me without mercy. We didn't know it at the time, but after our last recital, Mother stopped taking her meds.

Seventh grade started, and Sarah was in two of my classes. We walked to and from the bus together, and whether it was rain or sunshine, crunching through fallen leaves or shattering layers of ice on puddles, I tried to avoid certain topics. We laughed a lot together, and despite having other friends, anytime something good or bad occurred, the other was always the first to know. She was the only person in my whole life I ever ran to when something happened.

Sarah was a great student who took advanced classes at the high school during lunch. Me? Not so much. As we walked to the bus stop, she would inevitably take a deep breath, put her hands on her hips, and grill me on where I was on assignments. Sarah was a finger shaker. From first grade on, she would listen to my lame excuses until her fingers pinched the bridge of her nose and she squinted her eyes like an adult with a migraine. Then she'd put one hand on her hip and shake the index finger of her other hand in my face as she made point after point. It didn't matter if she was taller or shorter than me at the time.

My best tactic was avoidance.

I was imitating one of our teachers, and Sarah was laughing so hard at a face I was making that she had tears in her eyes. I could see the bus stop and figured I'd avoided the finger shake. Then I saw a movement and tensed up.

When she pulled a handkerchief out of her pocket, wiped away her tears, blew her nose, and folded it back up again, I smiled and started to relax.

Then she put it away in her pocket, cleared her throat, took a deep breath, and put her hands on her hips. "What did you think about the history homework last night?"

"We had homework?"

"I don't know why I ask," she said.

"Me either. I'm—"

"You *do* know you're not stupid, right?"

"Yeah, yeah," I said as I walked with my hands in my pockets.

"Then why do you keep acting like it?"

"That's a good question. Why do you keep asking questions you already know the answer to?"

"I'm optimistic and contrarian," she said with a smile and with clear emphasis on each syllable.

"What the hell does that even mean?"

"It means," she started, standing in front of me and wagging her finger under my nose, "that you can do a lot more than what you let everyone else believe you can do."

"Really?"

"At least, that's what I think."

"Does that mean I can copy your homework?"

"No," she said, turning red. "It means that even though you're a moron now, I didn't think it would stick."

"Didn't think? Don't you mean you *don't* think it'll stick?"

"I did," she said. "But then you kept talking."

Due in part to Sarah's prodding and the miracle of no teacher ever wanting to teach me again, I passed seventh grade. Sarah made me promise I would try harder in the eighth grade. She even made me pinky swear because, smart as she was, she still acted like a little kid sometimes.

Sarah spent that summer in Switzerland and she promised to bring back chocolate. Every week or so, I'd get a postcard with a picture of a mountain town, a huge lake, or people wearing strange, medieval clothes and a note on what she was eating or how she was learning to ride horses. Her last note said her dad was meeting with people about a new particle accelerator they were building that would eventually be one of the biggest in the world. She signed it, *Wish you were here, Sarah.* And it arrived the day before she was due back home.

Mother wanted cigarettes, and we needed groceries, so I was hurrying home from the store. Father was picking us up for lunch, and I didn't want to be late. To save time, I cut through a pulled-down section of chain-link fence between our old elementary school playground and the supermarket that used to be an A&P. That store changed owners so often that we were always a store name or two behind. It didn't help that the new owners used the previous store's grocery bags until they were all gone.

There had been a grass fire at the playground. The grass was starting to grow back, but there were still bare spots with scorched edges. Ash grayed the sand around the swings and slides, but the playground equipment was fine, and kids played there regularly.

I saw a bunch of kids clustered around a girl on the swings, yelling at each other.

I was skirting the drama when I realized the girl on the swing was my little sister Sophie. There were about a dozen kids on the playground, and it looked like she'd managed to piss them all off. Some were a lot smaller than me, but most were bigger. I set down the groceries under a tree, took a few deep breaths, and waded into the crowd of kids.

Sophie was at the tender age little sisters pass through where they look cute and innocent in their pastel-colored jumpers with their hair tied up in pretty ribbons. But when the adults leave, their perfect smiles bare fangs. She was more like a little brother than a sister, going through that annoying stage where she'd pick a fight with me by walking up and smacking me with no explanation whatsoever. It was how she expressed both her love and unhappiness. Then, if I pushed her or smacked her back, she'd smile and screech at the top of her lungs, "Billy's hitting me!"

The problem with sisters is you're not allowed to hit them.

Isabel kept telling me it was something that would pass and that Sophie was really a good girl, but at the time, I didn't believe her.

"Sophie, there you are," I said. "We were looking all over for you. It's time to come home, you have to get ready for lunch with Dad."

"Hey, is this your sister?" the biggest kid in the crowd asked. "She's got some mouth on her. Do you have any idea what she said to Tony?"

The angry crowd pressed in around us.

"Look guys, she's just a little girl. You don't really want to beat her up, right?"

The kids looked around at each other, and the mood eased a bit. "OK, but she needs to apologize."

"That shouldn't be a problem. I don't know what this was about, Sophie, but we need to go. Can you say you're sorry, so no one has to fight?"

Sophie hesitated a moment, and I thought I was going to have to say something to her. Then she hopped off the swing, walked over to the largest kid, looked up at him, and gave him a big, beautiful smile. For a moment, I could see him melt a little. It looked like she was sparkling in the sunlight, and a few kids in the crowd actually said, "Aw."

Then she said, "I don't know why I have to apologize. You need to just put him and his jerk friends in their place and kick his ass."

Needless to say, the mood changed again.

"Well if that's how it is," the big kid said as he reached back and hit me. I was able to barely block that punch, but it knocked me back into the crowd, and someone else hit me from behind. After that, it was a free-for-all.

Sophie watched from the sidelines for a while before she turned and walked toward home. I swear at one point she was skipping. I gave it my best, but I was a better wrestler than fighter, and there were just too many kids grabbing and punching me. It was over quick. I was beat down to my knees, and the boy about my age called Tony was pushed into the middle of the group for the finishing blow. I looked up at him while two other kids held my arms back.

Tony was smug as he swaggered over to me. "Any last words?"

I spit the blood in my mouth on the ground. "Too late to give peace a chance?"

He flicked me in the forehead, and the other kids laughed. "You're a funny guy. Yeah, way too late for that."

"I don't know what she said, but it must have hit a nerve."

"Yeah, that little skank has a real mouth. Sucks to be you. Want to beg for mercy?"

He made a fist with his right hand and held it in the air. The kids went crazy and started chanting, "Do it, Do It, DO IT."

"I'm pretty sure there won't be any mercy."

"You're right," said Tony, leaning into my face with a sneer. "This is fuck you and good night."

I was able to turn my head a little, but his fist hit me in the eye like an axe, and my lights went out. I would have called the punch a widow-maker. Sarah would have called it the *coup de grâce*. I'm sure there was some kicking and spitting before the group moved on. When I could pick myself up, they'd drifted down to another part of the playground, and I crept away.

The groceries and cigarettes were still where I left them, so I retrieved them and went home.

Summer break was almost halfway over. There was still one more year of junior high, but I was looking forward to high school. It was the beginning of freedom, and I could reinvent myself into a new me. After high school, I could get away. Those were my thoughts as I limped home.

I hurt everywhere.

I walked into the house and leaned against the wall in the entry. It was sweltering out, and the air conditioning felt good. I ran into Sophie in the kitchen when I put up the milk, eggs, and cigarettes.

"So how did it go?" She was in good spirits.

"You know, you can be a real bitch sometimes. Take a good look. All you had to do was apologize." I rested my face against the window air conditioner. The ice-cold breeze blowing on my face in the coolness of our avocado-green kitchen was the best part of my day.

"They were mean, and they were wrong," she said, still angry and defiant. "It's not my fault you're a bad fighter. There weren't that many of them. You should have been able to—"

"Sophie, apologize," said Isabel, walking into the kitchen.

"But sis."

"Just look at him. Apologize now."

Sophie made a moaning noise like the words wouldn't come out without tearing open her throat.

"Sophie . . ."

"*Fine*. I'm sorry."

I pulled one of our old metal trays out of the freezer and had begun cracking ice over a plate when Isabel said, "You look awful." Then, "Stop. Let me help," after I failed to get any of the cubes wrapped into a washcloth. With a few quick motions, she had everything assembled and pressed it over my eye.

"She really is a good girl."

"I'm sure, eventually, I'll see that." I took the compress into my hand and sat in a chair. "Thanks. This feels so good."

That was when Father walked in. "Where is everyone? What the hell is going on in here?"

He stopped cold when he saw me. His eyes went from my face to my torn clothes. "What the hell happened to you? Wait." He paused for a moment. "Who won?"

My little sister Sophie, whom I tried to protect, was quick to answer to his question. "Billy got his ass kicked."

I rolled my eyes at Isabel, and she looked away. Then she took Sophie's hand and led her out of the kitchen.

"Are they still there?" he asked.

I couldn't answer the question. I couldn't *understand* the question.

I didn't know. I wasn't quick enough to answer, and I definitely didn't see his hand come up and slap the icy compress from my face.

The bloody washcloth came open, and ice cubes bounced across the floor. They formed an archipelago of pink islands in a linoleum sea, and my father dragged me from the house by my hair and back to the playground. Most of the kids were still there. Before he talked to them, he said to me, "I told you before. You need to toughen up."

I fantasized that he was there to beat the snot out of them, but even though he could, it wasn't something he would ever do. He was an actual Golden Gloves series boxer. A well-regarded marine pugilist. A prince of the ring. He could have at least taught me how to fight. Instead, he promoted my rematch against the reigning champ, that other kid. Tony. It seemed like a fun idea to everyone but me. I could barely stand.

I already had a black eye, an easy-read Rorschach test worth of bruises, and two legs that wouldn't bend all the way, but my father dragged me back to fight again. He often reminded us that we had to be strong and determined to survive. Strong enough to reach out, grab the world by the ass, and shake it for all it was worth. His world, our world, was a stark, stocked laboratory of opportunities. That day, the lesson was about toughness. Toughness would be measured in pain. Pain would be given and received. The winner would be the last one standing. One on one. Mano a mano. Fight.

I was pushed back into the middle again. Tony and I circled around, fists up. "So you didn't get enough the first time. That's just great."

He darted in and out. He was fast, and I wobbled around.

I stood there barely moving, just turning to face him, swatting away his attacks. I didn't have much left, but he kept taunting me and dropping his arms and playing to the crowd. So, I kept facing him and protecting myself, until finally he dropped his arms again and stepped right up to my face. "You got nothing. Are we here to fight or dance, motherfucker?"

I hit him with everything I had, connecting hard to his chest and neck. Then I stepped in and nailed him in the chin.

It wiped the smile off his face, and he fell to his knees. He stayed down for a few seconds.

The crowd got quiet for a moment, and then they started chanting, "Just get up."

He looked up. His mouth was bleeding. Then he picked himself up and said, "So you *do* want to fight. That's good, really good, because I'm going to fucking destroy you."

The fight turned after that. He would lunge in from the side, hit me in the ribs, and dart away before I could land a hit. It was obvious to everyone there. I couldn't go the distance.

After a few minutes of whittling me down, he hammered me in the gut, and I landed on the ground. A throng of kids shouted at me, but only one voice was familiar, screaming, "JUST GET UP." Over and over went the chant. "JUST GET UP."

The roar in my ears faded into a dull drone, and I picked myself up.

He was back on me immediately. I was too slow, and slow almost always equals pain.

The fight was already over, and the rest of the brawl was about punishment.

I missed a block, took it in the face, fell straight back down, and hit the ground hard.

"Get up, God damn it." That was my old man. That was him cheering me on. "What are you, a fuckin' pussy?" That was the motivational speech and sum of the advice he had for me. "Get the fuck up."

My head throbbed. I made it to my knees, but I was still moving too slow.

"When I say move, I mean *now*!" Father shouted. Then he encouraged me with a few swift kicks in the ribs. I thought the other kids would be shocked, but they ate it up and cheered.

I clawed my way back to my feet again. I was unsteady, but I was up and moving.

Tony was showing off again now that he was sure it was over. "Thank your dad for me, kid," he said. "I thought this was gonna be another boring day."

Tony was stretching it out. Circling around me, laughing, playing to the crowd.

I could barely keep my arms up anymore. When he lunged back in, instead of even trying to punch him, I grabbed his arm, held it tight, and twisted it hard. For the first time in a while, he didn't look so cocky anymore. He looked scared. So I twisted harder until it was behind his back and all my weight was on him. Tony's face was wracked with pain, and he dropped down to his knees.

He was about to cry uncle when I was picked up from behind and thrown to the ground.

"This is going to be a clean fight."

Tony started to laugh again. He picked himself up off the ground and shook out his arm. He had the edge again. "Yeah, a clean fight."

"Clean fight, clean fight!" the crowd cried responsively.

I rolled around on the ground trying to see who hit me.

Wrestling violated the rules? What rules? Through the blood, sweat, and nausea, I wondered who the hell made up "the rules"?

The referee that had broken us up and thrown me to the ground was my dad. It broke my heart when I saw him. All the pain of that fight put together was nothing compared to that one betrayal. He was stacking the deck for some kid he never met before just so I could learn some lesson.

"What do I do?" I mumbled at him.

"Don't be a pussy," he replied. "You're embarrassing me."

Well, I got it. I got my feet under me, lunged in, and connected two hard blows to Tony's face. I split his lip in another place, but by then, I had nothing left to give, and the rest of the fight settled into a sad, predictable rhythm until I was knocked out.

I woke up alone. The playground was empty. The sun was nearly gone. It was still hot. I laughed, but it hurt so bad.

I was thirsty, and my body felt stitched together and limp, like I was filled with sawdust.

I was sprawled out there for a while, wheezing through a bloody mouth and nose. The air smelled like burnt schoolyard chalk. It was a smell I hadn't known, and it tasted thick and bitter in the back of my throat.

Then the hacking started. After I coughed up enough clots of mud and blood, I rolled back, enjoyed breathing, and woke up again later.

I got up in the dark, and like some raggedy man, I lumbered home.

It took me a long time to get back to my house. We only lived a few blocks away from the schoolyard, but I kept stopping. Field to the monkey bars. Rest. Then to the slides. From there to the curb by the basketball court. No one was there but me. By the time I got past the school fence, my breathing was strained, but I didn't have to stop the rest of the way home.

Mother met me at the front door. I was surprised, but then she blocked my way into the house and made me change in the mudroom, so I wouldn't track dirt and blood through her house.

When I was finally stripped down to my underwear and clean enough, I went to the kitchen for dinner, but Mother blocked my way again.

She didn't say a word to me. She only pointed toward a series of sticky pink stains I could barely make out. The dried remains of the puddles I'd made with my compress ice on her immaculate linoleum floor. I sighed and filled a bucket with water and ammonia and took a rag from under the kitchen sink. After I finished scrubbing my blood off the floor, Mother let me eat the dried remains of my dinner, still in the oven.

Isabel helped me up the stairs, to the shower, and into bed. I could hear Mother playing "Ave Maria" in the next room. It was one of the few songs in her collection I really liked. I looked at the statue of the Virgin Mary Mother had left on my desk, and I still wondered why it was there.

I awoke at one point to find Isabel covering me with bags of frozen vegetables.

Daylight streamed through my window. I tried to move, but it felt like I had polio. The bags of vegetables were gone, and I had proper bandages all over my body, so I figured that Father had come by. I heard a rustle and turned to see Sarah in the chair by my bed.

"Hair is different. Braids look nice. Welcome back," I croaked out the words. Sarah helped me with a glass of water, and I tried to turn the worst of my face away from her.

"Thanks," Sarah said. "I brought you back a present. Here." She put a box in my bandaged hands. Then took it away again. "Wait, let me open it."

She handed me a snow globe that had a chalet flying the Swiss flag halfway up the side of a mountain. The base was decorated with mountains and trees, and a girl with yellow pigtails held hands with a boy with brown hair as they walked through a field of flowers. I smiled. It was kind of ironic. When I shook it, the snow was white and silver.

"Cool," I said. "The kids look like we did when we were little."

"I thought so too."

"Tell me about Switzerland."

"Tell me about what happened," she said.

"Sophie picked a fight. I lost bad. I got a few good hits in, though."

"Is that all?"

"You know it isn't, but I know a lot about fights, and I don't know anything about Switzerland. I promise I'll tell you anything you want to know. Just not today. OK?"

"Promise?"

"Promise." I shook up the snow globe and set it down on my nightstand, then held out my hand so she could get to my pinky. But instead of taking it she took my hand in both of hers.

"You look terrible."

"I've never been pretty."

"That's true."

"Don't agree so fast," I said.

Sarah smiled and unwrapped a chocolate for me. "Say *ah*."

"You know I can feed myself."

"Yeah, but these are expensive chocolates."

We stayed that way for a while. Eating chocolates while Sarah told stories about sailing across lakes, climbing mountains, and navigating old museums. We talked until it was late and she had to go.

Neither Mother nor Father talked to me again until just before school started. At least they finally agreed on something. I was angry every time I thought about it. Angry every time I moved and it hurt. It even hurt to piss. But then I'd shake that snow globe and watch its little storm cover the chalet, and I'd eat another chocolate Sarah had left, and I'd feel a little better. The chocolates were delicious, but it felt really good to have a friend.

I needed to hear Father say why he did it. Why force me into a fight I couldn't win? He could, at the very least, tell me what I could have done differently? But he wouldn't, and I got the message. Life owed me nothing. The strong survive. Fighters win. People like winners. The weak are irrelevant. I didn't have to like it, but I would have to decide soon if I was going to toughen up and get strong or stay weak before I left to make my own way in the world. In the end, I overthought it, but it was the first time I can ever remember trying to figure out who and what I wanted to be.

The moral of the story was simple: don't be a pussy.

For weeks, everywhere I went smelled like blood and sweat and the burnt chalk dust of that schoolyard beating. When the heat finally broke, my nose stopped bleeding, and I could finally taste food again. That was when I promised myself I was going to figure out how to not be a pussy. I wasn't exactly sure how to get there or what it entailed, but I was going to get stronger. When I did, I was going to protect the people who weren't, and when that day came, I would make the rules.

CHAPTER 4

1978–1983—Long Island, New York

I had a strange dream. Mother and I were sharing a glass of Tab, and we were both laughing. I couldn't figure out why she wouldn't let me hold the drink by myself, but it was weird that we were drinking Tab in the small bathroom off our mudroom. Then our family doctor came and gave me a shot while my father and grandfather argued.

Other adults came into the room and talked in hushed voices. They seemed sad. As for me, elastic drool hung from my mouth, and I couldn't wipe it away. It either stuck to everything I touched or stretched in bounces from my fingers nearly to the floor. It was like I was controlling the strings of an invisible marionette that didn't dance well. It was funny until rope burns and welts began to appear on my wrists and arms, one after the other.

I screamed, Father held me down, the doctor gave me another shot, and everything was better again. Before I passed out, I realized I wasn't in our small bathroom. I was on an exam table. I know now that the burns and welts had been there all along, but at the time, I wasn't right, and it felt like they were growing on me while I watched.

— ★★★ —

I woke up in my pajamas in the spare bed at my father's apartment. Father was talking to a man and woman I didn't recognize. They seemed nice, but they asked a lot of confusing questions. Mostly they wanted to know what happened, but I wasn't sure, and they didn't seem to like it when I said, "You'll have to ask Mother about that. I don't know."

They left their cards on the nightstand. The man said, "Call us if you remember anything else." But I never saw either of them again, and Father seemed relieved when they left.

Summer was nearly over, and it took me a while to figure out where it had gone.

"Dad. What's going on?"

"OK," he said, after pausing to think. "You still have a lot of medicine working its way out of your system, but you're all right now. You're going to stay with me for a while, and your sisters are staying with your grandparents."

"Dad, it doesn't make sense."

"I know. Just rest. We'll go over things in more detail once your head clears. I knew something was wrong when I asked to talk to you on the phone and your mother got evasive, but I didn't know what. When I got to the house, no one answered the door. When I let myself in, I looked around, and there was a new lock on the bathroom door off the mudroom that I couldn't open."

"I don't understand."

"I know," my father said. "You will, but it may take a little time."

"Your mother locked herself in her room. She screamed and fought me the whole time, but I finally got the key and opened the door. You were naked. Drugged. She tied you to the toilet with clothesline."

"Why don't I remember it?"

"She mixed the medicine she was supposed to take into Tab and made you drink it." He paused, and I could hear his teeth grind. "She said it was my fault. I was the devil. That I made her do it."

I felt sick again.

"I cut you free and took you to the doctor. Your grandmother got the girls, and after the doc said you would be OK, I cleaned you up, put you to bed, and checked *her* into the hospital."

"How long was I like that?"

"It's hard to say exactly. She probably started before she moved you to the bathroom. Judging by your sores and bruises, it was more than a few days."

"What did she give me?"

"Thorazine. Medicine to help regulate her mood swings and extreme outbursts. She was doing well, then she stopped taking it. Giving it to you was bad, but you're going to be all right. You'll be sick off and on. But that will pass, your head will clear, and you may remember more."

"Why does she hate me so much?" I asked, but my father just looked away.

I knew without asking. It was my birthday.

"She does love you in her own way," Father eventually offered. "She's sick, but we're getting her help, and nothing like this will ever happen again."

"I know you believe that, Dad, but I don't know."

"You've been through a lot," he said. "Give it some time."

The bits and pieces I started to remember turned out to be days, but I was still missing weeks. I knew why I had rope burns and welts, but there were big gaps. I did remember drinking "Tabizine," but my memory was random and fragmented. It took a while to come down from the high. For a kid, it was a rough ride. After Tabizine was confusion, cold sweats, hot shivers, and throwing up a lot more than I remembered ever eating.

Wash. Rinse. Unabashedly sleep in the toilet's cool embrace. Repeat.

Mother was released from the hospital, and I was getting better at separating my dreams from reality. I'd recovered enough to realize that the noises I heard late at night weren't in my head. It was Father and his girlfriend arguing because I was there.

The next morning, while Father cooked us his favorite breakfast of sunny-side-up eggs and fried bologna, I finally asked, "Now that Mother's back from the hospital, don't you think it's time I go back home?" I don't know why I asked. I didn't want to go, but I didn't want to stay either.

I didn't want to see Mother again except to ask, "Why?" And I wanted to hear a different answer than what I already knew in my heart. I wanted to run away and hide. I hated her, but I still believed that, somehow, my relationship with Mother could be fixed. She was sick, the hospital had treated her, and she was better now. I was afraid it was just another lie, but I desperately wanted to believe that it was true. It was childish of me, but in a lot of ways, I still was a child. Looking back, I was naïve. I was a hand that refused to learn from being burned.

Father shut off the stove and sat down with me at the table. He paused for a long time, collecting his thoughts, then began. "If you want, this can be your home. You can stay with me and—" He was interrupted by a crash. We looked to see the frying pan settling to a stop on the tile floor.

"Sorry about that," his girlfriend said. "At least I was able to save breakfast." She smiled as she put our plates down in front of us, but tears streamed down her cheeks. "I'm running late for my shift and I can't stay, but you boys eat up, OK?" She smiled again, gathered her things, and left. The door closed with a *snick*, her car drove away, and I watched my father's scarred fists tremble on the table in fury or frustration as he looked from the third plate of food sitting on the counter, to the door, to me. We sat in silence at that table in his small, clean, sunlit apartment. I wasn't sure what to say. I was about to cry, but I wasn't sure why.

Father banged his fist down on the table and said, "I want you to stay here. It's your choice. I know I'm not easy to live with. But think about it. Now, eat your eggs before they get cold."

"Dad, thank you for everything. But it's time for me to go."

"Why?"

"I don't know. Going back won't be great. I know that much, but if I don't try . . . If it ends like this, I'll feel miserable about it forever."

"Are you sure that's what you really want to do?"

"Yes. And my friends are there."

"You're *sure*?"

"Yes."

Father let out a heavy sigh. "All right. If that's your decision, so be it. But you always have a place here."

"Thanks, Dad," I said, then I ate with him in silence for a while before I asked, "Do you think she'll hurt me again?"

He sighed again. "Honestly, once she gets caught, she never does the same thing. I think the worst is over, but if you're not careful, she *will* hurt you again, if you give her an opening."

"That's what I think, too."

"You still want to go? You've done all you can. The girls will be all right."

"It's not that I want to. I have to."

Father needed to coordinate with my doctor, the people who'd left their cards, and Mother before I could move back. A week later, everything was done except my last doctor visit. I woke up with a bad sore throat and fever. When the doctor looked in my mouth, he checked me into the hospital. One of my adenoids had ruptured, and my tonsils and everything else infected had to be removed. I stayed at the hospital after the surgery. It took a while to get the infection under control.

After I felt better, the hospital staff gave me free ice cream and my first cover story.

I finally moved back home. Mother barely acknowledged my existence, but that was OK. It was good to see my sisters, but they were wary, and it didn't take long for me to understand that things hadn't been easy for them either.

My friends asked where I'd disappeared to, but I had my cover story. I was sick over the summer and had my tonsils out. There were some complications, and I stayed with my father until I was better. That was the story, and that last part was true. I couldn't tell my friends that Mother had drugged me and kept me tied up. I'd learned the lesson of telling too much truth in Ms. Sahara's third-grade class. Then Mother taught me that a little truth can cover up a whole lot of lies.

Everyone believed me except one person.

Sarah found me as soon as she heard I was back.

"So, tell me again what happened?" she said with a scowl.

"I had my tonsils removed, but there was a problem, and I stayed with my father until I was better." We had a secret base hidden inside the big lilac tree by my grandfather's garden. There was a wide, open space between the trunk and branches that reached the ground like a weeping willow. We talked on a broken lounge chair we had rescued, and on an old table, Sarah lit a Coleman lantern that hissed as it burned a yellow circle into the darkness.

"And what else?" she said. "I was really worried about you. Every time I went over to your house, all your mother would say was you couldn't come out to play."

"Ah, well, that was really about it."

"Really?" Sarah said, her eyes narrowing as she crawled up the lounge chair and got in my face.

"Ah, yeah, really."

"Really? You realize every time you lie, you say, 'Ah, something.'"

Her face was right in mine, and I looked away. "Ah, that's . . . not true."

"Ha," she said, sitting back on her knees. "I win. So, spill."

I took a deep breath and totally spilled. I told Sarah everything.

Sarah and I were both crying when I finished. She had her fingers balled up like fists and was wiping the tears away with both hands. "That's just too sad."

She hugged me, then we talked about other things until the Coleman lantern began to sputter.

All I ever wanted to be was invisible enough to make it through the day. I was the kid stuck out in left field during the baseball game, watching bees buzz in the clover, who prayed each and every time I heard the crack of a bat connect that the ball wouldn't come anywhere close to me.

It was my first day of high school. I got up a little late, showered a bit too long, and, with almost no time left to get to the bus stop, found the clothes and sneakers I'd laid out for school the night before—gone. Instead, draped over my chair were a tan cowboy hat, an embroidered white shirt with a blue chest, a string tie, tooled leather boots, and a thick belt with a heavy buckle that I had never seen before.

I'm sure the neighbors heard me scream when I pulled open that last drawer after circling my room, surrounded by an empty dresser, a vacant closet, and an unmade bed. The only clothes I had were what I'd brought into the shower—a pair of white cotton briefs and over-the-calf tube socks with two green bands. My discarded *Star Wars* pajamas were still on the floor, but they didn't improve my situation.

Staring at the urban cowboy garb . . . I screamed again.

"Where are MY clothes?!" I shouted, running down the stairs.

I found my mother smoking at the kitchen table.

"Mom, where are my clothes?"

"I left them on your chair."

"Not those, my real clothes."

"Oh, your old clothes. They're gone, dear, you have new clothes now."

"*Mom.*"

"There really is nothing else to wear, so you need to get going, or you're going to be late."

"MOM. I can't go out dressed like that."

"You'll make a memorable first impression this way. Now get moving, you don't want to miss your first day of school, do you?"

"Ahhh!" came out first, then, "I can't believe you!" as I stomped back upstairs. "I hate you!" I slammed my door.

In my room, I yelled once more for no other reason than that I could. I couldn't find anything else, and what was laid out was all I had to wear. Even the dirty laundry was gone from the hamper. In the end, looking at the clock, I snapped closed the last chrome-rimmed, plastic mother-of-pearl button, tucked my shirt into tight jeans, and wrapped my waist in an extravagance of cow and pewter.

Luke, Leia, and Han looked down at me from the *Star Wars* wallpaper adjacent to my bed. Luke mumbled some crap about the Force and told me it would all be all right, but he didn't seem to mean it. Leia looked away and whispered, "Lame." Han Solo just shook his head and said what everyone was really thinking: "Kid, it sucks to be you."

I'm sure I screamed again.

As I struggled to get out the door, Mother made a point of adjusting the string tie around my neck and firmly planting the wide-brimmed hat on my head. For a moment, she looked like she might relent and apologize, or maybe abandon her Western doll experiment and return my real clothes. Instead, she kissed me on the cheek to leave a lipstick mark, shook me by the shoulders, stared deeply into my eyes, and said, "Make sure to address all the ladies as *darlin'*."

If I'd had a six-gun on my belt, I would have put the barrel in my mouth and pulled the trigger.

I left the house as something new, a sight theretofore unseen on Long Island in 1980: a suburban cowboy with all the home-on-the-range experience of a kid who went away two weeks a year to a summer camp. I ran to the bus stop as fast as I could and made it just in time. Feeling awkward and stiff-legged, I joined the line and climbed into the bus. By the time I found a seat, my feet were already blistered. It was the first time I could remember sitting by myself on the bus.

My first day of high school, and class hadn't even started yet, yippee-o-ki-yay.

I was excited. I was going to a big school where each grade had nearly a thousand students. It was a new beginning.

The words "Make sure to call all the ladies *darlin*'" still echoed in my head. I was already a new me—just not one I would have picked. I took a few deep breaths and joined the mass of freshmen searching for lockers.

My homeroom was a big room full of neat rows of old-fashioned right-hand desks. Our teacher was in front of the class, telling us to find a seat before the first bell rang. She had short blonde hair and blue eyes behind steel-rimmed glasses. She didn't look much older than us.

I took a desk in the second-to-last row by the windows in front of a kid that looked familiar. Moments after I settled in, the bell rang, and the teacher began calling attendance. We were in a homeroom for students with last names beginning with Q, R, and S. We didn't have a lot of Q students, so my name was quickly called.

"Riley."

"Here."

A minute later, the kid behind me was called, and right after that, he took one of his feet and jammed his heel into my back and started twisting.

I smacked it away and turned around. "What's your problem?"

"Nothing, Tex."

I looked at him. He smiled. The moment I faced forward, he jammed another heel into me through the space between the seat and backrest. His biker boot dug into my back even harder, twisting from my kidney to my spine. The teacher was midway through the *R*'s in her attendance book.

"Here," said another student.

I moved my desk forward and then turned back. "I'm not going to say it again. *Stop.*"

His foot fell back to the floor.

He smiled again and said, "You really shouldn't have done that, cowboy." I couldn't figure out why the kid was screwing with me. He looked like a standard-issue punk with a big mouth, a short fuse, and a résumé that included being smacked around enough to figure out how to inflict his own brand of pain on soft targets. I didn't get his beef with me.

The teacher was almost done with the *R*'s, and the kid behind me was still grinning ear to ear. I turned back to the front of the class.

I heard his desk shift, then I turned back and saw him walk up to me on my right.

He stopped and smiled, the teacher stopped calling attendance, and he belted me in the face. My head snapped back like a punching bag. I felt the wet, indignant flush of blood rushing to my face, and I barely held myself from being knocked out of my seat.

The class looked from me to the teacher. I looked at the teacher, expecting her to send him to the principal's office or call someone to restrain him. It looked like the kid was expecting it, too, but then she looked at me like it was my fault, looked back down at her book, and started calling roll again. She was up to names starting with *S*.

Mother always told me to turn the other cheek, but when I did, I always got beat some more. When a kid punches you in the face in the middle of class and you look at the teacher and she ignores it, you're at a crossroads. Take it, or don't. I knew whatever happened next would define me for more than just the next four years. Take it, or don't.

I decided not to take it.

He laughed and said, "What are you going to do? It looks like no one cares."

Before I could get out of my desk, he took two more swings at me. The first one hit me in the eye hard. The second I was able to block.

Then I punched him in the only place I could reach.

I socked him in the crotch with every bit of anger and animal rage I could muster. I hit him so hard he folded over, hit his head on the side of my desk, and crashed to the floor. Anger flooded through me. I picked up my desk and hit him with it until he stopped trying to get back up again.

Then I set the desk down and leaned on it to catch my breath. The teacher just looked at me, but she still didn't say anything.

He stayed down.

When I finally caught my breath, I asked the teacher, "I guess I need to find the principal now?"

She nodded yes. I wiped my face and a handful of blood came away. I wiped most of it on my sleeve. I hated that shirt anyway. No one said a word as I walked to the door; everyone stared.

"He's going to need the nurse," I said to the teacher before I left. I looked down at the kid one last time, and then I realized why he looked familiar. His name was Tony. He was the kid who'd beaten the hell out of me when my father dragged me back to that playground.

I guess he didn't want to be someone different in high school.

The school nurse checked my eye and mouth, wiped on some iodine, and gave me an ice pack. I waited outside the principal's office. When I was called in, I told the principal what had happened.

"Mr. Riley, it's highly unlikely a teacher would ignore a student assaulting another student in her class."

I pointed to my swollen eye and split lip. "It's a big class. I'm sure all of them saw what happened."

The principal stared at me for a while, not saying anything. He was appraising me. I got it. Day one, and already I was a troublemaker. Then he asked something I didn't expect.

"Well, are you sorry?"

I knew it was a loaded question. I knew what I was supposed to say, but I told him the truth. "I'm sorry I got into a fight, and I'm sorry I disrupted class. I really am. I didn't do anything to that kid, and I hate fighting." I sat up and looked him in the eye because the next part was important. "But if anyone ever tries to hurt me like that again," I said, "I'll do it again. I'll do whatever I have to do, and I won't stop. Until either they can't hurt me anymore, or I'm dead." The last part came out more like a shriek than anything cool or calm. It wasn't the charge of the light brigade. I was out of breath and worried about what would come next. I felt like I'd just delivered my final confession. Then I added, "Sir," and looked at everything in the room but the principal. He told me to wait outside.

As I waited for my father to come pick me up, secretaries at the front desk whispered about me and Tony. All I could make out was, "That's how it is. That's what happens to boys from broken homes."

It sounded like Tony and I had some similarities. The difference was he'd beaten me to the ground a lot of times in a dusty field, for fun. I didn't recognize him at first, but he sure thought he knew me. And he did, until I found my resolve and made my choice.

Tony was retrieved from the nurse's office and parked two seats down from me. After an initial look at each other, we worked hard to ignore each other. He had a lot more bandages than I did. Seeing that made me happy. The swelling seemed to shut his mouth, and his silence felt good.

When my father came in, I had a fat lip and a black eye.

"Who won?" Father said as he looked back and forth between us. I looked at Tony. He looked away, and I smiled despite the tearing sensation. It was my happiest smile in a long time. It didn't matter that my teeth were grouted with blood.

"I'm no pussy. I told him I wasn't going to take it."

Father shook his head and almost smiled. "Good. You finally get it. Life doesn't owe you anything."

Then my father glared at both of us and went in to talk to the principal. It was the first time he'd come to see me at school since the sixth grade.

I got two weeks of suspension plus another two weeks of detention, and by the time I was allowed to return to class, Tony had already transferred to a different school. Apparently, he had a history, and our fight was his third major strike.

I had to meet with the school psychologist every Thursday during lunch for the rest of the year. Mostly, we talked while we played chess, and even though I wouldn't admit it, I looked forward to our sessions. He was the most ridiculously optimistic person I ever met.

Over time, the story of my fight grew and took on a life of its own. By the end of my first year, a kid told me the story like this: "I heard this freshman went crazy and put three teachers in the hospital on his first day of school, and the police had to come and drag him away in handcuffs. He went to jail, but he may be back." As violent and stupid as my first day of school was, I stood up for myself. My story grew into an urban legend, and fortunately, no one seemed to remember it was me.

Sophomore year, my friend Eric came up to me and said, "We should join the swim team."

He convinced me and a few friends to go with him to tryouts. Tryouts were easy: swim the pool from end to end and hold your breath underwater for a minute. The hardest part was walking around wearing a Speedo swimsuit not much bigger than my hand. Training was relentless. I was so tired by the time I made it home that my muscles quivered as I ate what I could. Most nights, I fell asleep at my desk. The first month was miserable, the second painful, but by the third month, I was competing in events. Being part of a team was tough, and I wasn't a great athlete, but I never gave up. I competed in relays and the one-hundred- and then the two-hundred-meter butterfly, and swimming made me stronger and more resilient. It even helped clear up my skin. Occasionally, I'd win an event, my name would get announced over the loudspeaker, and people would treat me differently—better. After the swimming season was over, I joined track and field to stay in shape. I was a tragic pole vaulter, but I did get good at throwing the discus.

Then a couple of teachers recommended me for honors and advanced-placement classes. It surprised the hell out of me. I wasn't sure I wanted to work that hard, but I sat in on a couple of those honors classes with my friends Adriana and Patty. The classes were small, and the material was interesting. Teachers held their students accountable, then made them argue their points to prove they knew what they were talking about. I imagined it was what college was like. Sarah would have called it the Socratic method; all I knew was I wanted in.

It took a terrible effort, like swimming did, and I wondered why I bothered. I was the only kid in honors-program history who ever danced in the middle of class when, after months of banging my head into the academic wall, I finally got a passing score. My English teacher commented that my work was "prosaic, provincial, and vulgar, but my argument was well made and insightful." When I proudly presented my paper to Adriana, she tossed back her dark mane of hair, set her elbows on the desk, interlaced her fingers, and explained to me what "prosaic" and "provincial" really meant.

"I passed, and I made an insightful argument. That's all that matters," I said, undefeated. I already knew "vulgar" wasn't good. "I'm a work in progress."

"Well, you did more than double your last score," she said, smiling.

"See?" I said. "Big progress."

It was the review week before senior finals and AP tests. I was pouring a glass of milk to take up to my room along with a few snacks to munch on while I studied. Mother was in the kitchen. She was getting ready to cook something for herself and had a frying pan on the stove. We'd argued all week about nearly everything I did, and the silence in the kitchen was angry and heavy. Her lashing out got worse the closer I got to finals, so I was working hard to get in and out without giving her cause to yell again. I tossed the empty milk carton into the trash.

"What do you think you're doing?" Mother said. She took a deep draw off her cigarette before carefully setting it in the ashtray like it was a precious thing. The kitchen was thick with her smoke, and I hated it. It was hot outside and the air conditioning just circulated the smoke through the house.

"Throwing out the empty carton," I said, "then going upstairs to study."

"That was the last of the milk. You need to buy more now."

"No. That's your job!" I yelled back at Mother. "Like cooking dinner and feeding the girls. That's your job. Normally, I don't mind doing it, but these are my finals, and for the next couple of weeks, I really need you to be their mother." I was rude, and I wasn't proud of it. Lately, I was furious with her all the time. "I'm going upstairs to study. If you can ask nicely, I'm happy to run to the store after I finish this section."

"*Vafangule!*" Mother screamed, then repeated it in English—"Go fuck yourself"—for good measure. "You think you're so smart now, *sfaccimma*, devil spawn. I'll show you how smart that mouth really is."

I set down my glass of milk when I saw her reach toward the stove. I put it down just before she was on me, swinging the hot pan like a cleaver.

I grabbed the handle before it connected. I could hear the metal sizzling inches away from my ear, and I could feel my forearm burn as I twisted the frying pan out of her hands and twisted her arm until it locked.

"Stop," I growled. "This ends now."

The frying pan felt good in my hand. I wanted to hit her with it, the way she'd beaten me for years. Because I was small. Because she could. I wanted her to know what it was like.

"Understand?" I said, tightening my grip on her. I wanted to hurt her so badly, it was exhilarating. I swung the big pan back, enjoying its weight, and she closed her eyes and whimpered.

I could stop her from hurting me and my sisters. All I had to do was follow her lead. I just had to swing and swing and swing. It would be simpler than throwing a discus and easier than swimming the two-hundred-meter fly. That was how the world worked. I was the strong one; I could do whatever I wanted for a change. She realized it, and there was nothing she could do to stop me.

She was finally afraid.

I held her like that for a long moment, and only one thing stopped me from hurting her. It wasn't that it was wrong, or that there would be consequences, or that the police would come. What scared the hell out of me was that hitting her because I could would make me *just like her*.

I set the pan down. It took everything I had to let that handle go. I was shaking with rage.

"Mother. This has to change. We have to change. We can't do this anymore. We're a family. It's time we start acting like one."

She looked back at me with pure hatred in her eyes, but she nodded her head, and I let her arm go and shut off the burner.

"I'm a man now, and I'm not going to let you hurt me or the girls anymore."

"You've hated me since the day I gave birth to you," she whimpered. "This is how you treat your own mother."

I was fit. My head was clear, and I took a big step from boy to man. I told her again in the calmest voice I could muster, mostly to convince myself, "Mother. You will never, ever, hit me or the girls again. Do you understand?"

"You're just God's way of punishing me."

"You told me once that God doesn't allow anyone to suffer more than they can bear. All I'm asking is we try something different."

I picked up my milk and left her in the kitchen. I felt good, and somehow different, like I'd done something right and things would change. My arm ached. The burn left a thick red welt.

I put burn cream on it and studied until after midnight before I finally showered and stretched out in my bed. It was hard to relax; my head was full of physiology and physics and English concepts. I was wired, but I finally came down. I felt I could take charge of my own destiny. I'd stood up for myself, stopped a beating, and acted like an adult. I was happy. It could have gone so wrong. I fell asleep believing my life had just gotten a little better.

A few weeks before finals, Mother had repainted the statue of the Virgin Mary she'd bought me years earlier. She painted it with great skill, and when I looked closely, I could see the intricate details of the belt on her robe and the variations in the golden halo that radiated around the Madonna's head. It was the most thoughtful thing Mother ever gave me. I always saw it as a peace offering, an olive branch, physical proof there was still a chance we could reconcile.

I woke up convulsing. My head ached. My back was on fire, and my legs were twisted with cramps like growing pains, only it hurt so much worse. There was a sound like chopping wood, and someone was screaming.

I was dazed and couldn't understand until I rolled over. Mother was standing over me, out of breath, holding the statue of the Virgin Mary by the head and swinging it back like a sledgehammer to hit me again. I tried to get my arm up, but something was wrong, and I was too slow.

Mother stood in a rectangle of mixed moon and street light that made everything look harsh and unreal. I thought it was a nightmare, but the person screaming was me. I couldn't even move anymore. I watched the Virgin Mary's painted blue-and-white robes flash as Mother raised the statue over her head and hit me with it again and again, and there was nothing I could do.

There was a cracking sound every time she hit me. The plaster cracked, and Mary came apart blow by blow. Mother didn't stop until all that was left of the statue was a cracked head and a metal cage with a rebar spine. When Mother was spent, she finally let go of the shattered Madonna, and it crashed to the floor.

Mother leaned over the bed and pulled my head back by the hair until my eyes were inches away from hers and I thought I was going to die. Before I passed out, Mother said, "Do you feel like a man now?"

My sister Isabel found me the next morning, swollen, bleeding, and covered in bits of plaster. I couldn't move by myself, and she helped me to the bathroom. We didn't talk about it, but Isabel cleaned me up, made me bologna-and-grilled-cheese sandwiches, and then made me eat them.

I was a swollen, purple mess. I thought my legs and arms were broken, but the swelling went down after a couple of days, and I was able to walk. The back of my head was covered in lumps.

Mother wasn't home. That wasn't a surprise. I didn't want to talk to her or anyone else anyway.

I thought I finally had everything figured out. I assumed I was strong enough to change things. I believed I had gotten through to Mother, but I was wrong about everything. All I did was back a monster into a corner. I was done. I couldn't take any more. It hurt to breathe.

It was the morning of finals. The alarm went off, but I decided I wasn't going in. I didn't care anymore. I had enough credits to graduate ... probably, and I was finally at the point where the pain of moving in my sleep didn't instantly wake me up. I'd made up my mind. I was going to heal up a little more and then I was leaving. I still had to work out the details.

I was almost back to sleep when I heard a commotion downstairs.

Then came a knock at my door.

"It's time to go," said Adriana. "I can't believe you're still in bed."

"Get moving, or we're going to be late," said Patty.

"I'm not going. Sorry. Good luck."

"Get up now, or you'll be sorry." I don't know who said it, and I don't remember my exact response, but I know it was less articulate than, "Leave me alone, and piss off."

There was silence, so I embraced it. I was warm and snug under my covers, and I started to drift back off.

Then the bucket came. They dumped it over me from toe to head. Cold water and ice cubes. I was shocked, then angry and cold. I was soaked through. My nest was ruined.

I jumped up out of bed, yelling, but Patty and Adriana began pelting me with whatever they could find. I couldn't even get a word in as they admonished me.

"Let me just—"

"No. Get up now, or we'll get the hose."

"But I'm—"

"Where are your clothes? Never mind, wear this."

"I'm not—"

"Yes, you are."

I agreed to get dressed and go if they would just stop. They gave me less than a minute before hauling me away down the stairs, still trying to get into my clothes, and into Patty's car.

I made the trip in sputtering fury.

They walked me to my finals just to make sure I wouldn't cut the exams out of spite. If they had left me, I would have. I was still more emotion than reason back then.

I was pissed off they had the audacity to drag me out of my room, but I was also impressed, and touched that they cared enough to do it.

After finals ended, Patty, Adriana, and I were sitting on a bench outside the school, drinking Cokes. I was thinking Patty had the prettiest reddish-brown hair with big natural curls, yet she worked tirelessly to keep it ironed flat. Why do girls do that?

"Why did you just give up at the end?" Patty asked me. "The hard parts were already over."

I couldn't figure out what to say. I wasn't ready to talk about my week with Mother.

"Because I didn't think anyone would care." It was what got past all the anger, hurt, and confusion churning within me. At that moment, I believed it.

Patty put her arms around me and said softly, "How could you ever think that?"

I wanted to stay like that, but it hurt too much.

I passed all my courses, even posted a few high marks, then got hold of my father. Our old doctor had retired, and I saw a young, new doctor. I had a couple of cracked ribs, a concussion, and a lot of bone bruises, and I had to splint my leg and wear my arm in a sling for a little while. When the doc asked me what happened, I told him I fell down the stairs. It was easier that way.

For years, I believed that the Virgin Mary statue meant there was hope for us. It was a gift Mother tended and repainted over the years to watch over me; it was the possibility of a mother's love.

Later that summer, I told Patty and Adriana everything. I totally spilled; I thanked them; I'd gotten lost in despair, and I'll never forget what they did. When I needed it the most, they cared.

Everyone breaks at some point. I did, and I didn't know how to get back up. But my friends helped me find my way again. In the end, I understood what was right in front of me. I couldn't change someone who didn't want to change. I was a burned hand that finally learned.

I left home. Father took me to a military recruitment office, and I enlisted in the air force.

PART II: COMING OF AGE

A dog starvd at his Masters Gate
Predicts the ruin of the State
A Horse misusd upon the Road
Calls to Heaven for Human blood
Each outcry of the hunted Hare
A fibre from the Brain does tear
A Skylark wounded in the wing
A Cherubim does cease to sing.

—William Blake, "Auguries of Innocence"[6]

---

6   Blake, "Auguries of Innocence," lines 9–16.

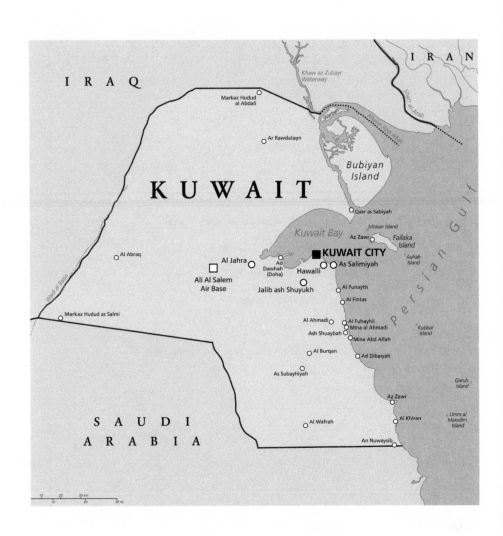

CHAPTER 5

June 1996—Colville/Kaniksu Training Area,
eighty-three miles from Fairchild AFB, Washington

I was leading a small team of airmen as quietly as possible through the middle of a swamp. We were paused chin deep in fetid muck, waiting for the patrol of aggressors searching for us to finish their sweep. Voices carry in the wilderness, and from the red-force instructor's radio conversation with the search helicopter, we were one of the last units still managing to evade capture. The mosquito-caked nylon mesh over our faces barely kept the swarm of bugs from blinding us.

Aggressors blocked the path ahead and searched from the high ground for any sign of us in the sector. We were one of two dozen teams they tracked that day. Our orders were to cross a wide area, evade capture, and make it to a series of checkpoints, miles apart, at exact times. The direct paths would make us easy targets, and the use of exact checkpoint times meant the aggressors were likely lying in wait to capture us. It made contact and egress tricky.

The longer the day went on, the more physically exhausted we were, the more worn out we were, the more likely we were to screw up. Time and our physical limits were the real enemies. Their advantages were baked into the game, but the aggressors were human, just like the rest of us. They made their own mistakes, and they couldn't be everywhere at once. We had to pick our fights and use the terrain and their expected tactics to our advantage. The deck was stacked against us, but that's life. There's nothing that can't be made harder.

We waited an eternity for them to finish scouting the area.

The buzz of a single mosquito circling just out of reach is infuriating, and a million of them pressed against us thick as fog. We were soaked through, the swamp reeked of decay, and we had to suppress the discomfort, focus on the mission, and stay hidden despite the stench, the things moving through the water, and the insects trying to eat us.

We held our position for ten minutes. We needed to wait long enough for the aggressors to move on and longer still for anyone watching from the ridge to lose interest.

It felt like forever.

Survival school isn't like other schools. If they send you home for any reason, you start over at the last block of instruction you successfully finished. No one wanted to go back if they didn't absolutely need to. Getting another class depended on when there were openings in the training pipeline, and if the delay was too long, the air force would find another job for you in whatever field was currently hardest to fill. You didn't get to go to SERE (Survival, Evasion, Resistance, and Escape) training in the air force unless you were in operations, which was where military power was projected to directly fight our enemies. Ops included flight, special, space, and intelligence, plus a few other fields of operation. They were tough careers to get into, and if you didn't pass SERE, no matter how good you were, you couldn't be in operations anymore.

Every aspect of that second phase of training was designed to reinforce "Don't get caught." You never, ever want to destroy your enemy's last position and then get caught by the survivors. It's guaranteed to be awkward and unpleasant. Surviving and evading capture is hard, sure. But every hour you *do* survive and evade, you increase your chances of getting home. For every hour you avoid the enemy, you stay a little free. Little freedoms go unnoticed and seem unimportant until the enemy—or instructor—puts you in a cage. When they put you in a cage, the only real freedom you have is what you keep with you inside your head. I learned that lesson long ago.

"In the cage" is a different game than "Don't get caught." There are myriad negative reinforcements available to hammer home the "Don't get caught" lesson. In training, the "enemy" could do uncomfortable things. They couldn't kill us, but our instructors were creative, and they could make discomfort hurt. The worst I ever saw happen was when a guy got a few of his teeth knocked out. It was an accident. The student and instructors zigged when they should have zagged.

Bob was the student who zigged. He had two days left in survival school before he could fly a fighter jet across unfriendly skies with his unit. Bob became the lieutenant with a swollen jaw, a split fat lip, and blood trickling out of a gash in his face. As he was receiving medical treatment prior to being sent home, he tried his best to reason with the senior instructor so he could stay.

The senior survival-school field instructor was a corn-fed Montana boy whose call sign was Mongo. There was no real proof he was a genetic experiment that had combined a professional wrestler with a Spanish fighting bull, but he did look the part. He pulled the call sign Mongo because if you took the human and the rest of us out of huMONGOus, what you got was Mongo.

While a medic worked on LT Bob, Mongo cut to the chase. "You're missing one tooth, a couple of others are broken, your lower lip has a hole in it, and we can't treat you here."

"This is nothing," said Lieutenant Bob with a shrug. It came out as, "Wit hit not hig."

"If your injury is serious enough, for your own good, we need to pull you out."

"Hell no—I'm good to go," sounded like, "Hew oh . . . goo to oh."

"All we can give you is Motrin."

"Love Motrin," for some reason, came out fine.

"What can you do now, little airman?" asked Mongo, towering over LT Bob. "You're sad and broken and useless."

The gist of Bob's slurred reply was, "Anything you need me to. Survivors and POWs don't get pulled out when they get hurt. They do what they have to do." Bob's words weren't well articulated, but he latched on to Mongo's uniform and pulled himself up from the floor until they were face to face. Bob had heart—that much was crystal clear to anyone close enough to hear. He said, "I can do this. Let me do this. Please."

It was the first time we ever saw Mongo smile. It didn't light up the room as much as resemble a predator baring his fangs. Mongo gently eased Lieutenant Bob back down to the floor. "Well then, it's your lucky day, L-T. The next available dental appointment isn't until ENDEX."[7]

That was how Lieutenant Bob came to be propped up by sandbags in his cell with a safety-orange Kevlar helmet strapped to his gourd to identify him as injured.

Bob spent the next two days with a stupid, drooly jack-o'-lantern grin on his face, but he never checked out of the game. He fed us intel from the medics and senior camp staff that helped us identify guard movements and weak points in the detainment compound.

We used that information to aid our escape. That was his job.

---

7 End of exercise.

That was cage training. Stay strong, help each other where you can, resist by all means possible, and survive to return with honor. We did our best to prepare for a day in the life at Andersonville, the Gulag, or the Hanoi Hilton. Torture rooms, structured abuse, and interrogation. If we failed out in the real world, where war was not an exercise or a game, that would be our reality.

But at that moment, we were still a soundless phalanx of unmoving statues sinking in the mire, holding our position in a swamp until the last patrol was gone. Still stuck in the middle of our "Don't get caught" training. Waiting. Skin crawling, enveloped in a primal buzz, fighting the smell.

Finally, the aggressors moved on.

While they scrambled over the stone ridge that walled in the mountain drainage and formed our cesspit, I asked our instructor why he did this. I was already impressed that he stuck with us. He couldn't interfere or advise us, but he did stay to make sure our decisions didn't get us killed.

"Aside from the draw of being the only enlisted career field in the air force that exists to beat the snot out of officers," I whispered inches from his ear, "how do you keep this up every day?"

He turned his head and said into my ear, "Sir, smacking you around is really more of a perk." I imagined him smiling under his face wrap. "Some lessons have to be hard. We do this so that others may live. What you learn here could save your life someday or the lives of your men. What you learn today will help you return with honor."

We waited a few minutes after the last aggressor crossed the ridgeline. When all was clear, I gave the signal, and, slowly, we moved out.

We were the first team to make the final checkpoint that day and the only group not detained. As a reward, we were allowed to wash our clothes and bathe at the sandy bend of a river. It was for the morale of the people downwind from us as much as it was for us, but cold water and a half hour by a roaring fire never felt so good. It was an amazing reward. Proof that, if we had to, the instructors believed we could evade and survive. We were six weary students, four men and two women, with our backs to each other in the slow-moving water, laughing and joking about how disgusting we were as the gentle current washed the worst of the filth away.

That night, the air in the mountains was cold, and clouds reached across the sky and hid the stars. We looked like students camping on a school break as we sat before the fire and steam rose off our very gray, very utilitarian underwear. We were content for the first time in a while, but a storm was coming, and as we headed back to our bivouac, the first raindrops began to fall.

CHAPTER 6

June 1996—Colville/Kaniksu Training Area, Washington, and Florida

My father died while I was in survival school. We were settling into our shelters for the night when bad weather rolled in. Mother Nature was pissed, and all we could do was hunker down.

Instructors found me in the middle of the night and escorted me to the old modular building under drenched camouflage netting that served as the field command post. The school commandant let me know about my father's death over the radio, his disembodied voice breaking up and dropping out as the storm played havoc with the signal. It was like having a conversation in German, where you don't really know what's going on until the last verb clicks into place at the end of the sentence.

Sorry.

Father.

Dead.

It took almost five minutes to piece it all together—an eternity over the radio, where brevity is the rule. He said it happened suddenly, my father didn't suffer, and I was needed at home. The weather had washed out the road back to base. Nothing could fly. They'd get me out as soon as they could.

I returned to the tent I'd made by fastening my poncho over the hollow left by the roots of an overturned tree. It wasn't much, but it kept me dry and diverted the wind.

I could feel my ribs.

I was fifteen pounds lighter and exhausted by a week of fieldwork.

My father was dead, the rain pounded, and streams of water rushed around my shelter and gurgled down the mountain. I listened to the wind wail, and I tried to remember all the times my father and I had together. The bad ones came first, but there were good ones, too.

I moved a lot and had been gone for a long time. After basic, there had been intelligence schools, increasing responsibilities, analyzing Soviet operations, and side jobs. I'd seen the start of Yugoslavia coming apart and the Berlin Wall fall. Then I'd gone back to school, worked odd jobs, gotten my commission in the air force, and married a woman I loved. Now, I was learning how to direct weapons and to command, control, and communicate in combat. In between, there'd been a lot of drama. Father and I hadn't talked much. We'd both meant to, but we had unfinished business.

I replayed all the could-haves and should-haves in the comfort of a turned-earth hole that would have smelled like a spring garden if it didn't feel like a grave.

They were waiting for me with a staff car when we got back to Fairchild AFB. One shower, one bag, one ride to the airport, one flight, one funeral. Just a blur of scenes, one after another. One moment, I was disgusted at the thick brown mud ring I'd left at the bottom of the survival-school shower; the next, I was saying heartfelt words to a small group of people I didn't know about a man I still didn't really understand.

What do you say when God dies, and he didn't answer many of your prayers? Parents are like that when you're little. They're the gods of our world, and the old gods weren't always kind to the people who worshipped them. They were capricious and cruel and arrogant, but there were also times when they could be generous and spectacular. Like parents to a child, they were larger than life, and at the end, I was left with the enormity of it, stuck in the middle, standing before the quiet dead and the tear-stained living. His funeral was in a cold, bland room. Rife with the scent of death-flower orchids. And it fell to me to say the words.

I didn't know these people. The truth was, I didn't know what to say. Would anything I had to say to grieving friends and family really make any difference at all?

I understood my role. I was a Band-Aid. A salve for a wound. A time slot someone was required to fill. Just a sad, jet-lagged boy in a shiny uniform who was expected to put things in perspective, say goodbye, and then get off the stage.

I realized I was standing at attention in my service dress uniform, and it was time to begin. I was remembering things I thought I'd forgotten, but you remember whether you want to or not.

"My father, Harland W. Riley—'Skip' to his friends—taught me things I'll never forget. He was a marine, a boxer, a nurse, and a fighter all his life. He was a husband, a father, and a manager of mental institutions. It took him a while, but he finally found the life he was looking for. He loved solitude and quiet time to read and paint. He loved my stepmother and half brothers very much. They were his world, and he would be the first to say they made him a better man."

I took a deep breath.

"He's gone now, but his stories live on. He often said, 'Make your own way in the world, because life doesn't owe you anything.' He had a binary view: things were always black or white, good or bad, right or wrong. He believed the burned hand teaches best, and you either take what you can in life, or you settle for the crumbs you're given.

"He was quick to anger, then quick to laugh, and brutally honest to a fault. But he was also generous to anyone in need. He was a good father to my half brothers and a good husband to my stepmother, and he left us well prepared for life. Because of him, despite hard times, we always had a roof over our heads, and we never missed a meal. He grew up poor. For him, success was a full refrigerator and stocked pantry. He believed if you could eat whatever you wanted, anything else would work out. He was an amazing cook; ask anyone who ever ate at his table.

"Father believed that actions, not words, made you a man, and if you wanted his respect, your actions had to earn it. He was a tough grader, but the code he passed on to me is something I've come to believe in with all my heart.

"My father once dragged me back to a fight and then stacked the deck against me to prove that I had to be prepared for anything, that I couldn't expect help from anyone, that life didn't owe me anything, and that if I wanted something, I had to fight for it with everything I had.

"I hated him for a long time for how he taught me life lessons like that, but I never forgot them.

"We live in a hard world, and even though our success makes it so we don't have to see the harshest realities every day or miss any meals, it's always out there. I've traveled to brutal places, and I'm grateful to him for what he taught me. I can say with certainty that I wouldn't be here today if I hadn't learned what I did from him.

"Not all his lessons were hard. I remember one when I was five or six. It was the middle of a terrible thunderstorm, and my father found me hiding under my bed. The storm was on top of us. The sky went from blue to green to black. Lightning flashed, thunder shook the house, hail hit the roof, and it terrified me.

"He coaxed me from under the bed, and he told me that storms move and that lightning could only hurt us when it was close by. But if it was more than a mile away, there was nothing to worry about—it was just wind and noise. I was skeptical, but then he tucked me back into bed and asked if I wanted to learn a trick to know how far away the lightning was.

"'Wait for the lightning flash, and as soon as you see it, slowly count Mississippis until you hear the thunder. For every Mississippi you count, the storm's about a mile away,'[8] he said. 'If the number of Mississippis keeps getting smaller, the storm is getting closer. If the number of Mississippis gets bigger, the storm's moving away. If you can't finish a Mississippi before the thunder comes, the storm's right on top of you.'

"He was patient as I tried it out. *Flash.* One Mississippi, two Mississippi, three Mississippi. *Boom.* That meant the storm was almost three miles away. As more lightning struck, we counted together. Storms getting closer, storms right on top of us, storms receding away.

"I felt like I was in control of something terrifying. I knew it was a trick, and thunderstorms were still scary, but I wasn't afraid of them anymore.

"I think I'm finally starting to understand my father. I didn't think I ever would. I loved him and hated him. We had good times and bad times, and he taught me things to prepare me for life that I'll never forget."

I'd like to say my Father regretted a lot—that pride had gotten in our way but we finally had everything worked out. It would have been an easy, feel-good lie that no one would ever call me on, but our happily-ever-after was always going to be more complicated than that.

---

8   This is how it was taught to me—one mile for every Mississippi counted. Fact is, the lightning is about one mile away for every five seconds counted, which is really four to five Mississippis, depending on how fast you count.

Despite how we reached that last day, a baton was passed. Thinking back, he actually passed it to me a year before his death, when I took my wife to meet him. It happened after breakfast.

I was doing odd jobs on a thoroughbred stud farm for a former CIA deputy director when I accepted a commission in the air force. I spent the night at my father's place in Florida. Early the next morning, we said goodbye in his driveway, and I left for officer training school (OTS). Father gave me one piece of advice before I drove off. "Don't fuck up."

OTS wasn't as hard as I expected. Parts were challenging, but it was mostly an exercise in decision-making under artificial time constraints in a game with capricious rules and a lot to memorize. To be fair, we didn't get the A-team of instructors, but that wasn't even their fault. The air force moved OTS from Texas to Maxwell AFB, Alabama, that year. I was in the third class to graduate in Alabama.

OTS was divided into two parts, a lower class of new students and an upper class of senior students. Upper-class students were responsible for training lower-class students, and the cadre/faculty guided the upper class, taught specialized courses, ruled over discipline, and decided who graduates. The OTS format gave new students a chance to adapt to the military and learn the rules, and then it gave senior students opportunities to manage and lead in a controlled, observed environment. That was the theory, anyway.

The air force moved OTS in the worst possible way. The first new class to graduate started their training in Texas; then, halfway through, they loaded all the OTS materials, cadre, and students into a transport aircraft and flew to Alabama, where, in addition to completing their OTS training, they also stood up the new school. Of course, there were problems. The buildings and infrastructure they were given for the school were falling apart, the rules and prohibitions for OTS had been written for locations in Texas, and not everything made the trip, so there were big holes in all the instructions. I spoke to a lieutenant assigned to Maxwell after graduating OTS, and she summed up the whole experience with one story. "I asked the cadre commander, during the town hall meeting after we arrived, what the plan was to get our cars from Texas, because they were all still there. He told us if we weren't smart enough to figure that out, we weren't fit to be officers. Things went downhill from there."

So, her class took their frustrations out on my upper class, and the children of abusive parents tend to grow up and do what they know. My plan was to keep a low profile, keep my mouth shut, and not fuck up. I managed to do two out of those three things.

When we became the upper class, each of us was required to take a job that would define our role in training and in taking care of the new batch of officer trainees (OTs) who'd just shipped in. Jobs came with ranks; the higher the rank, the more responsibilities and privileges. I was picked to be a deputy for a member of our student leadership staff. It was a plum job that came with the rank of OT major, and I would have been good at it. Problem was, the night I was on security patrol, I walked into the conference room and found my would-be boss banging one of his new subordinates on the table. I said, "Carry on," shut the lights, and closed the door behind me. He found me shortly after that to ensure I wasn't going to rat him out, as fraternization was an expellable offense. I told him I didn't care about that, or that they were married to other people, but if he was too stupid to lock the door, I really didn't want to work for him. The next day, our cadre flight commander called me in. He told me he didn't think I could handle a major's job, and I was given the last job left—OT lieutenant in charge of building maintenance. It was a shit job, but it made my life easy for a while.

My job was simple: set out discrepancy cards so the OTs could let us know if anything was broken in the three buildings that made up the OTS barracks. Every day, I'd collect the cards from a box, fix what I could, and then turn in a report of what had been fixed, what hadn't, and why to a sergeant from the cadre so he could get the right organizations on base to schedule repairs. The problem was that the cadre just threw those cards out. It didn't matter until winter, when the steam plant for our buildings broke, and the heat and hot water went out. Cadre said they'd take care of it, but after three days of being able to see our breath at night and washing with ice water, I went to base civil engineering to see where they were on our job. Turns out it was never reported, so I worked with one of the CE captains, who cobbled together what we needed from soon-to-be-demolished buildings and nine hundred dollars to buy additional parts, and all the heat and hot water was back on. I was a hero, and I felt pretty good about myself. Until I got called into the wing commander's office and got my ass chewed.

His guys said the heat and hot water had never been out and that I'd somehow spent cadre money without authorization. I got yelled at for a while. Mostly it was how dare I commit funds that weren't mine; his staff was right, I was a liar, there was never any problem. Fortunately, I keep good records and had copies of everything I submitted. After he looked though them and the project report from CE, the wing commander told me I was done. We went a few rounds over what "done" meant, and I was stripped of my OT rank. He told me that if he ever saw me again, I wouldn't graduate, and I was dismissed from his presence.

I left his office more relieved than angry. I was going to graduate OTS, and the heat still worked, so I took a hot shower and wondered how I was going to use my newfound free time.

I met Jodi at OTS. She was in my upper class, and it was love at first sight, at least for me. I saw her, and I knew I was going to marry her. She looked at me, smiled, and gave me enough demerits to ban me from going off base for two weeks. That was enough to pop my warm, fuzzy love bubble. I thought, What a bitch. *And I didn't think about her again until we got stuck together on a work detail the cadre put together to keep trainees gainfully employed when OTS closed over winter break. That was when she finally fell in love with me. Jodi was a lot nicer when no one was around. She loved airplanes and flying even more than I did, and I found it attractive that she didn't have a complicated backstory. She was an honest girl who actually believed in the rules and followed them. That made her different from almost every woman I knew.*

Less than six weeks later, I was commissioned a second lieutenant on the morning of March 15, 1994, at Maxwell AFB. We were married that same afternoon by the Montgomery, Alabama, justice of the peace, and we left, almost immediately, for our first assignment at Langley AFB. After our respective promotions to first lieutenant, we got orders for Tinker AFB, and we took the long way from Virginia to Oklahoma so I could finally introduce Jodi to my father in Florida.

The first argument started on the phone over why Jo and I were wasting money on a hotel when there was room at the house and why we'd only be there for a couple of days. It got worse, my father hung up, and I was sure we'd wasted a trip and our time. But my stepmother called later and said they'd meet us the next day for breakfast. I was angry, but Jodi calmed me down—we were in a nice hotel near beautiful spring-fed rivers and pools, and Jo wanted to see it all.

Sunday brunch was served in an airy room with crisp white linens and deep-green leather chairs. Paintings of racehorses raised and trained on local farms, thoroughbreds that had left Ocala, Florida, and made names for themselves at tracks around the world, covered the walls. The restaurant owner was a horse breeder, and the paintings were displayed like portraits of his children—proud images of local stallions and mares that had left the small town and done good.

When my father and stepmom arrived, we exchanged awkward greetings and were quickly seated. The girls talked over pretty brunch drinks while my father and I left to conquer the buffet. It was our common ground. We caught up as we filled our plates. He picked everything I said apart, and I got angry. When we got back to our seats, I asked, "Why are you always like this?"

"Like what?"

"It's like when I was a kid. Everything's gotta be so negative."

"What are you complaining about?" he said. "I was a great father."

"Really? Don't you think you always took things too far?"

"You turned out OK."

"Was that because of you or in spite of you?"

"Doesn't matter," he said.

"How can you say that? Of course it matters."

"How's your life right now?"

"It's fine, Dad."

"It's better than fine. You've got a career, a wife with a career, a house, money in the bank. You've got the world by the ass. So, why keep complaining? If it was me, I'd brag."

"So, you were a great father?"

He scoffed. "I can't believe you're a grown man and still going on about this. OK. I wasn't perfect. That's what you want to hear, but I was a good father. Things didn't go the way I wanted with your mother. If I'd gone easy on you, do you think you'd still have the same drive and be the same person you are now?"

"I don't know."

"There you go," he said, opening up his hands and holding them out, palms up to the sky, like some retired-in-Florida Happy Buddha with a bald

head, copper complexion, and wide smile over a big belly. "No one knows, but I'll say this: let's table this topic for now. In a few years, after you have a few kids of your own, let me know how your image of a perfect father holds up. If you can honestly say you were able to be that guy and have no regrets, I'll apologize all day for anything you want. I'll even get down on my hands and knees and beg, but not until you walk a mile or two in those shoes and put all that theory about being a father into practice. I can guarantee you one thing: being a father isn't going to play out exactly the way you think it will."

"Fine," I said. I waited a decade. A few more years to prove him wrong was no big deal, but even the thought of being a father terrified me.

"Good. Are we done here? They just rang the bell for the Cajun shrimp and crawdad boil, and if we don't go now, all the good bits will be gone."

When we returned with our plates, it was strange—there was no more tension. There could have been, but we'd both said what we had to say, and neither of us was angry anymore. The girls ordered another round of drinks, my father and I sipped black coffee, and Dad finally spoke to Jodi. For the first time, my father and I talked as equals. It was nice.

After breakfast was another first—I picked up the check. I expected my father to fight me harder over it than he did, but after he conceded, he removed something from his wallet and slid it to me down the table. "Here," he said. "I think you're finally ready. This is yours now. You have a wife of your own, and you're going to need it more than me."

It was a tiny, folded envelope as wide as my thumb and as long as my index finger that my father had made from the page of a book a long time ago. It took me a moment to recognize it. The words were mostly rubbed off, but I could just make out Gray's Anatomy. It was an old, crumbling, and scarred package that had layers of yellow tape in spots.

I remembered what was inside of it the moment he put it in my hand. I smiled at him. "Now what kind of officer would I be if I had to rely on luck to do my job?" I held the envelope for a moment before I slipped it into my wallet. It weighed nothing, but it felt enormous. "I can't believe you still have this."

"I told you I'd hold on to it, didn't I?" he said, scratching his nose. "We are part Irish, after all. These things come in handy."

He held on to that wrapped-up four-leaf clover for decades. Giving it back to me was his way of saying I'd reached a milestone. Maybe it was approval.

That was the last time I talked to my father. We exchanged a few letters. I planned to call him after I got back from survival school. I should have known better. I thought we had time.

Father always said, "Never start a fight; finish it." As a boy, without even thinking, you spout off what the grownups say. It's how we learn. It doesn't matter if you're a kid in a neighborhood or a lieutenant working for a general on a staff. It's why children say the damnedest things.

After the funeral, I had one fight left. I needed to finish my father's last chore; then I was going to kill his murderer.

Three and a half rows had been cut into what looked like a knee-high wheat field around Father's gray stone house. I followed the cut half row to where the fescue grass lawn was already growing over a mower that just didn't look right. It was a cobbled-together Frankenstein monster of a mower. The Franken-mower that murdered its creator. Truth be told, the massive stroke that killed my father could have come at any time. The mower just made it more likely.

Four different-sized wheels were connected four different ways to a wide, rusted-metal mowing deck. The Briggs & Stratton engine had all its protective panels torn off, so it looked more like an exploded diagram than an engine. I had to pull the mower from the tall grass to restart it. As soon as I moved it back, I realized I was standing in the exact spot my father died.

He could have easily bought a new mower or paid a service to cut his lawn, but paying someone to do something he could do himself would have never occurred to him. It took twenty minutes of pull starting and cursing before the mower gasped and came to life. It was one of the hardest things I ever had to do. Mowing the lawn my father couldn't finish. Following his footsteps, one row at a time, in the brutal Florida sun. It was more like plowing a field than cutting a yard, and the mower continued to buck and run in place for a few minutes after I shut it off.

It was sunset when I finished dismembering my father's murderer. It died with a soft whimper and soiled itself in less oil than I expected. I was done, and it finally hit me.

I grew up used to setting my feelings aside until I needed them. I was better that way, but my courage was all used up. My vision was blurry, and nothing was clear no matter how much I blinked. I was crying because I was alone and finally could. I was sad and resentful and relieved to be done. My father and I had both come a long way. He was my first survival instructor, and I worked hard to earn his respect, even after I told myself I didn't care about it anymore. At least, in the end, he was proud. I stood there like an idiot, squinting at the last rays of the sun, quietly sobbing my heart out. Like most things, it wasn't fair—it just was.

CHAPTER 7

I deployed to Kuwait to direct US communications at Ali Al Salem Airbase. It was autumn of 1998. Eight years earlier, Iraq had annexed Kuwait as its nineteenth province, where Iraqi soldiers looted Kuwait. Banks were robbed. Hospitals were emptied of patients, and medical supplies were seized. Valuables were confiscated and palletized. Cute girls were loaded onto trucks like cattle and shipped back to Iraq. At one point, Kuwait reported more than twenty-five thousand unlawful arrests, many of them of families with children.

When the UN Security Council was initially reluctant to believe the scale of atrocities occurring across Kuwait, videos of torture during interrogations were smuggled out and shown to them. Women and children were raped when they were found by patrols, and sometimes they were bound and left for other patrols to have their turn later. Young men were taken, gathered together, and chained naked in more secluded places, then raped in turns. Food was in short supply, public executions were conducted each day, and torture was random, frequent, and brutal. It was how Saddam ruled the nineteenth Iraqi province of Kuwait for seven months.

Four months after the invasion, the United States led a devastating air war, Desert Storm, followed by a decisive ground war against the border forces in Iraq and the occupying forces in Kuwait. Forty-two days later, the Persian Gulf War was won. The Gulf War technically ended when Iraq no longer had the ability to control their combat forces and internal affairs, and the war formally ended a few days after Saddam Hussein lost control of his army. At that point, out of options, Saddam sent Deputy Chief of Staff Sultan Hasheem Ahmad and Lieutenant General Salah Abbud Mahmud, the Iraqi III Corps commander, to negotiate a cease-fire with General Norman Schwarzkopf in a dusty US Army First Infantry Division tent in Safwan, Iraq. Saddam's generals weren't technically there to surrender, but after two hours of bluster, it was clear General Schwarzkopf knew more about the status of Iraqi forces and had more military control over Iraq than they did. The Iraqi representatives agreed to surrender and unconditionally comply with every coalition demand. One of those demands was that Iraq dismantle its WMD programs and allow UN inspectors unfettered access to all sites to observe and confirm it.

It worked for a while.

In the mid-1990s, Saddam Hussein was through with compliance and routinely threatened UN inspectors and denied them access to Iraq's WMD facilities. He drove his Republican Guard forces south toward Kuwait as part of a decade-long game of chicken he liked to play with the United States. He would ban inspectors and threaten Kuwait until we bombed him back into compliance. It was a decade of "do-overs," and that was about to change.

In 1998, everyone I knew celebrated Thanksgiving and Christmas in the Middle East, far from home. The Operation Desert Thunder II build-up had just ended, December was just around the corner, and I needed to have equipment I couldn't source in Kuwait to get flight and surveillance missions up and running before Operation Desert Fox kicked off. Tension was building. We were briefed that the operation would happen sometime soon, but at the time, the most concrete answer I could get for the new operation's timeline was, "If something happens, it will go down in a week or two."

We were thirty-nine miles south of Iraq at the "Rock," otherwise known as Ali Al Salem Air Base, Kuwait. The base was built on a sandstone hill, rising above the surrounding desert plain. In defiance to Iraq, it faced Saddam like a fist with broken middle finger. When sandstorms shifted the light spectrum toward red, the base looked like it was built on the surface of Mars.

We couldn't see many details in Iraq from the ground at the Rock, but we could hear Saddam's saber when it rattled. Saddam's army was moving toward us again; coalition forces were massing at the base, and the infrastructure and supplies on hand couldn't keep pace with our massive growth. People were stacked like cordwood. We scrambled to accommodate new arrivals wherever we could find the room. As the number of troops and working hours increased, we were reduced to one hot meal a day and easy access to MREs (military "meals, ready-to-eat" in sturdy plastic packages).

I lived in a Harvest-Expandable tent that had last seen action as a morgue during the Vietnam War. It was already beat up when I moved in. From the inside, the holes in the canvas shone like stars and moons in the sky, but the AC still ran cold. I patched the holes with layers of duct tape to keep out the wind and dust and camel spiders. For six months, it was home.

Camel spiders had a mythology all their own. They were ghost stories that persisted through every desert tour. In war zones across the Middle

East, there are nearly as many camel spider horror stories as there were Chuck Norris jokes. The rumor was that flesh-eating camel spiders ruled the open desert through stealth and an anesthetizing venom that allowed them to sneak in, attach themselves to their prey, and dissolve victims with their numbing drool so they could feed on you while you slept, never knowing you were being eaten alive. Even the Rock medical briefing mentioned them as a health threat.

Camel spiders move fast and silently at night, but I'd sometimes see them during the day in outlying areas, clustered in the corner of walls or in the shade of rocks. Tawny, spindly creatures with too many long legs, heavy jaws, and thick, segmented bodies that looked like rows of furry chevrons caked with sand.

Storytellers would recount the tale of the security-forces sergeant who decided to sleep out under the stars when the night was so clear the Milky Way was a bright fountain and you could watch satellites streak across the sky with your naked eye. In the morning, he woke and stood up, stretched, and then died when his guts fell out of him, camel spiders dragging what they could of him as they retreated into the desert.

If Chuck Norris had been that security-forces sergeant, he would have woken up after a great night's sleep, stretched, and found his cot surrounded by the twisted husks of dead camel spiders, some of them still smoldering, some still convulsing in pain, before they died upon tasting his blood.

I didn't pay the stories any mind—the spiders were generally small but fierce-looking with big orange or black jaws—but I didn't see the spiders often, only on the outskirts where people seldom went. The only unnerving thing was in the morning or predusk in remote places, when shadows were long and a particularly large camel spider would follow me. It would stay at just under a shadow's length away.

I walked, it walked.

I stopped, it stopped.

Stop and start. Always staying just out of reach.

Yelling and throwing rocks didn't faze them. In the end, it wasn't worth a fuss. You couldn't shake the tail, and they'd just ride your shadow, like an ugly cab fare, until they got off at some even darker, cooler destination. Otherwise, the stories about them were just stories.

Or so I thought.

We still had shower tents at the Rock. Dusty, olive-drab tents, each with a spring-loaded plywood-door entrance, a row of tiny stainless-steel airline sinks for washing and shaving, and two rows of compartments with pull valves that would give you about a minute of water per tug. Our shower water was nonpotable and came from massive, camouflage-covered rubber water bladders laid out on a concrete pad and filled regularly by a water truck. A shower at a bare base anywhere is a humanizing experience; a shower in a desert camp is a luxury. There was no mixed hot and cold water, so shower timing was an art. Shower in the afternoon during full summer sun, and you'd scald your skin off. Shower in the evening in winter, and you'd have to take comfort, after your teeth stopped clattering from the frigid water, that you really were a grower, because after the cold-water flash froze your parts, you certainly weren't a shower. Fortunately, the lost inches always grew back.

We mostly ate halal and kosher MREs because the other bases in the region didn't want them and we ranked lowest on the army resupply chain that brought us everything we didn't fly in. But we didn't have time to complain. We had to prepare for the ground battle that would come if the bombings planned for Desert Fox didn't disrupt Saddam's WMD capability and compel him to recall his troops. While our leaders at the Combined Air Operations Center (CAOC, pronounced *kay-ock*), far removed from artillery fire in Saudi Arabia, joked that our little operation was just a speed bump for the Republican Guard, they did put together a massive air campaign that would make Saddam regret crossing into Kuwait again.

While we made stone soup for the additional mouths we had to feed, the Kuwaitis brought in tanks and forward-deployed forces from across Kuwait to defend the base. Before the Gulf War, the Rock was overrun by Saddam's forces. It left a mark on Kuwait's culture, and they moved with a sense of purpose at odds with the glacial speed at which business usually occurred in the Arab world. Notwithstanding the underlying tension, we got a tremendous amount of work done and cleared an eight-month backlog of command and control improvements for the base in just three weeks. Despite the visible pain it caused our Kuwaiti hosts, some meetings were short, and one was even held without tea. It was the only time I can recall hearing a Kuwaiti apologize.

After getting to know each other, I had a great working relationship with most of my Kuwaiti counterparts on base and in Kuwait City. Mostly, they were my friends: Assad, Fahad, Abdallah, Yassin, Ali, Mustafa Bin, and Mohammed—from the ministry, not Mohammed from the airport. Mohammed from the ministry was a real man among men and a Kuwaiti patriot. Mohammed from the airport was a cranky, incompetent prick. We had cultural differences, and not everyone was who, or what, they initially appeared to be. The American drive to "get it done now" in the more leisurely *Insha'Allah* (if God wills it) world of Kuwait caused most of our tension, but with humor and friendship, we were able to overcome most obstacles, one cup of tea at a time.

Eight years earlier, Saddam Hussein had raped Kuwait. Now his forces were heading toward us again. We had a great plan, but some pieces were still missing, and we were running out of time. Tens of thousands of combatants from several countries were massing to send a message to Saddam Hussein and to ensure history didn't repeat. There was still a mountain of things left to do. It didn't make me feel better that the first thing I ever learned about military operations was that no plan ever survives first contact with the enemy.

CHAPTER 8

Things grew chaotic as we ramped up for Operation Desert Fox. There were many changes in direction and personnel, and the frenetic pace began to take its toll. I rushed across base to make my meeting in time. My new Kuwaiti liaison for the operation was a dour religious officer we'd occasionally see around the base, scowling at us. In addition to his duties as religious officer, he had been appointed as acting chief of Kuwaiti communications operations and infrastructure on Ali Al Salem, and I was required to work with him. We were operating on a Kuwaiti base, and I had to get his approval on all improvements or major changes we made on the Rock.

He and I couldn't have been more different. I routinely made him crazy and disagreeable as I did my job with my team, which was updating and modernizing the command, control, and communications systems around his base. He was all unhappiness and grinding teeth. Although he had a lot of ribbons on his chest, he had no technical background. He truly believed that the base should modernize as and when God willed it. While he waited for his orders to come down from his burning bush, I did my best to drive modernization forward, always aware that there was a lightning bolt somewhere out there with my name on it. I figured that if it were Allah's will, God would eventually stop me in my tracks.

Change pissed him off more than anything else. Most days, he was more of an adversary than a liaison. If he could have gotten away with it, he would have had me beaten regularly with a stick. I know this because his idea of a joke was to shake his head after every third or fourth thing I said and counter, "If you worked for me, *Na'qib* (Captain), I would have you beaten with a stick."

I didn't realize until much later that this was a real perk of being a religious officer.

I answered the way I always did. "Let us then pray, *Ra'id* (Major), that I do not get transferred to your command. It would be too painful for both of us."

That always brought a smile, and we'd move on to the next topic.

His name was *Ra'id* Andyit—Major Andy—but my British counterpart used to refer to him, over the cigars we smoked at night, as "that bloody bastard crown prince" or as a buggered *something* in British English that roughly translated to the brutal conjunction of the *ra'id*'s arse and an insanely large object.

Andy was what remained after he attenuated his full name to what he thought I could manage. The Arabic version on his approval stamp was both long and impressive.

Our host base commander had a sense of humor and set a standing meeting where both of us presented status updates every Wednesday afternoon over tea in his office. Wednesday afternoon was the start of Major Andy's and most Kuwaitis' weekend. The fact that the commander rarely canceled a meeting was a testament to his desire to improve his ability to share information across the combat forces on his base. The commander's job was not only operations but also to balance the needs of politics and religion in a manner that honorably made progress and settled differences over afternoon tea.

Tea could take two hours. For contentious issues, there were follow-on teas.

The commander liked piping hot apple or mint tea with enough sugar cubes to turn the contents of each cup to syrup. When he was happy with us, his staff would also set out snacks. If there were no plates of snacks, Andy would signal to his flight sergeant to cancel or slip his link time, as Andy was also a religious golfer.

When the commander was concerned things were going too fast or too slow, we would accompany him around the base, either driving in his big black Mercedes or on foot when the weather was agreeable.

It was during one of those walking tours, while the commander left to take a call, that Major Andy told me the story of the fall of Ali Al Salem with sorrow in his voice and pride in his eyes. "They fought and fell back," he said. "Fought and fell back until their weapons were empty and they had nowhere left to go." He pointed out the path they'd taken. As we walked, he grew animated, stopping to show me a doorway or an open area where they had sprung a trap. "Here the Iraqis fled, only to return later in force."

We traveled the long way around a wide area that was cordoned off by cables but still not cleared. The areas within and around Gulf War targets in Kuwait were still filled with unexploded ordinance (UXO) dropped by coalition forces during the war and, in some places, mines left by Iraqi soldiers. Paths had been cleared between them, and you didn't dare venture off. Bright-colored metal placards with either a bomb or a skull and crossbones hung everywhere and said in English and Arabic, *Keep Out, Do Not Cross, Danger, UXO.* Some said simply, *Stay Back,* with an orange face that had, for good reason, a frown.

"Here," he said. "It was here they were finally captured, then bound and set on their knees before Saddam's officers. They say an officer walked the ranks with a cricket bat, savaging them while his troops laughed. And that, before dark, a few men were released and hunted down like animals for sport."

Major Andy paused to light a cigarette. He offered one to me. I hesitated for a moment, then took it. It was a peace offering. I hated cigarettes, but refusing his offer would have been an insult. He gave me a light off his zippo and continued.

"You hear these things, but you never know for certain." He exhaled like a dragon and stared at me for a long moment before he continued. "We know many were beaten and shot before they locked away those who could still walk in the old officers' club.

"In the morning, they hanged the base commander from the flagpole over there. After being forced to witness it, my brothers who survived the night were lined up by the club entrance right there and shot until they were dead." He stopped again, and we smoked some more. "They did things to their bodies before they left."

Smoke curled tightly around us while we talked. Then the wind picked up, and it was gone. We must have smoked half his pack of Dunhills. I had been lost in thought, but there was a gust of wind, and I noticed the gathering clouds.

Footsteps crunching through the gravel broke the silence, and I turned to see the commander's aide, Fahad. He looked like a raven in a bespoke suit and wore a skullcap. "*As-salaam alaykum*," he said with a curt bow. "The commander has finished his business and was pleased with how your meeting is progressing, so he went home to avoid the rain. He suggests you do the same." Then he turned on his heel and quickly crunched back the way he had come.

"*Wa 'alaykum salaam*," I said as I waved. "Peace. Out."

As soon as he rounded the corner to his car, the rain came.

Rain in the desert starts out differently than anywhere else I've ever been. It falls in splats of mud until the air is cleaned of dust and suspended particles. Then, if enough rain falls, the dust and mud wash away, and afterward, in the sunlight, the sand is gold, and all the pebbles that a moment before were a dull and lifeless beige glow pink and blue and white and red and green like jewels. The air is delicious and alive for a moment until the water evaporates and the desert flows again. For a moment, it's like walking on treasure.

That was how the first rain fell in Kuwait one late November while the sun touched the earth through the holes in angry clouds, like an illustration from a child's Bible story. We took shelter under an overhang, leaning back against the same wall where the Iraqis had executed the last of the old guard of Ali Al Salem AB, while we waited for the mud to stop falling and for the rain to run clear.

Major Andy told me what the Kuwaitis needed and what he was prepared to give us to make it happen. We watched the sun stab at the rain as we worked out what we needed to do.

There were no rainbows. We didn't agree on a lot of points, but by the time we were done arguing, we had a working plan. We were going to build the first coalition operations center (COC) in northern Kuwait.

We had a lot to do, and we were already behind the power curve. As I ran my hands over the pockmarked sandstone, still radiating heat against my back, I realized the bullet scars crisscrossing the wall were all waist high or lower.

The mud was finally washed clean, visibility was high, and everything as far as I could see under the setting sun was gold and sparkles, but the breeze was dying, the rain was tapering off, and the dust was already reaching out from the desert to rebury its treasure.

CHAPTER 9

November 1998—Ali Al Salem AB, Northern Kuwait

It was a little before dawn when I finished fleshing out the steps we needed to take to build a COC with my team. It wouldn't be easy. It would be a temporary nerve center connecting US, UK, and Kuwaiti air operations, radar surveillance, forward-based ground forces, base defenses, medical evacuation, and special operations. It would also be our first go at sharing intelligence when and where we could with local UK and Kuwaiti forces.

I was tired, and the moon was a crescent on its side, low in the starry sky, that looked like a sickle or a smiley face.

The air was still warm and, due to the rain, unexpectedly humid for the desert.

I crunched through the gravel in my flip-flops, toiletries in the crook of my arm, a brightly colored towel wrapped around my waist, intent on a shower and a few hours' sleep.

I strode into the shower tent thinking about shaving before I went to bed, but the slam from the door startled something in the trash.

We'd had desert cats in the trash before. They were scrappy, slightly bigger and leaner than a house cat, and usually battle scarred. For a long time, a big, striped, torn-eared, half-blind survivor would sit and wait and stare down airmen leaving the chow hall with his one good eye looking for bits of chicken or fish. Rabies was a risk, and fleas still carried disease, so contact with feral cats was discouraged, and pets were forbidden in the field. Cats are smarter than we give them credit for. Simba never overstayed his welcome, and after defying gravity by snatching enough tossed food out of the air with all four of his paws, he would move on to the Kuwaiti trash, UK mess, and desert edges to hunt before making the rounds again. I had a smaller, more domestic version of him at home that I missed.

I figured live and let live as the trash rattled around. I couldn't care less. I was tired and getting ready to shave when the garbage pail fell over. Looking into the polished steel plate that passed as a mirror, I saw what came out, and it wasn't a cat.

What came out was a large, gangly spider that, in the fluorescent light, was bigger than my two hands if I put my wrists together and stretched my fingers wide apart.

I looked at it. It looked at me, and I figured it would scuttle off into the night and do whatever camel spiders actually do. Live and let live.

But no.

As I turned back to start shaving, I heard a sound like drumming fingernails on a table.

I turned back to see spider legs oscillating over the plywood floor as it rushed me.

I stomped my foot, yelled, and threw my can of shaving cream at it, expecting it to finally retreat into the night and let me finish up and finally get into the shower.

But no.

That just made it mad.

It squared off at me, reared up on its back four legs, and hissed.

Hissed.

That got my complete attention.

A spider hissed. At me. Now I was pissed off.

I grew up on Long Island and, while we have to be careful of black widows in the woodpile, our house spiders are the daddy-long-legs variety that eat mosquitos and, every once in a great while, leave messages like Charlotte in a web along the lines of *That's some pig*.

They don't pick fights, and they definitely don't hiss.

It became a primal conflict, one between a man and the beast blocking his way to a shower and then bed. Without even thinking, I pulled down the closest tent pole and advanced to beat the hissing camel spider to death so I could finally get clean and sleep.

As far as plans go, it wasn't a bad one, except that bug wasn't about to just be squashed and die. It leapt to the left and right, then charged at me in fast, foot-long hops that dodged from side to side as I swung wildly at it. First I missed it; then I grazed it with the *womph, womph* swinging of my tent-pole spear.

I knocked down everything not nailed down around the room trying to kill that bastard bug.

When I finally connected, I hit it dead center. It was like hitting a whiffle ball out of the park, and I was stupidly proud of myself as it sailed across the room in a leg-curled wad.

I stayed proud of myself until it hit the back wall of the tent, rebounded, and headed straight toward me.

The tent pole was again a wild *womph, womph* blur as I continued to clip it and miss it as it evaded in ridiculously fast hops and steps.

I was finally able to stun it when it dove at me during its final assault.

It continued to hiss as I beat it unconscious.

I think I actually laughed and made a guttural war cry of a noise when I finally managed to kill it, stabbing it through its middle with the metal tip of my tent pole.

I must have looked insane to the two airmen who walked in right at the end of my fight—me standing in front of the small, stainless-steel shaving sinks, a towel wrapped around my hips, leaning on a pole, panting, with trash strewn around me in the crazy light of a fluorescent bulb madly swinging on its cord.

There was an uncomfortable moment of silence as they stared at me.

I showed them the curled beastie impaled on the pointy end of my spear.

All I could manage was a breathless, "Watch out for the spiders," but they were already gone.

We pitched the plan for a COC designed to share information and intelligence across the Rock to the senior base leadership later that morning, and the US, Kuwaiti, and UK commanders said, "Make it happen."

That was how the first Joint Operations Center (JOC, pronounced *jock*) came to be in northern Kuwait. In reality, since it would share Kuwaiti, UK, and US operations information and intelligence resources, it was really a Combined Operations Center (COC, pronounced *cock*). But since no general officer will go on CNN and say his COC, being the brains of the operation, successfully mounted offensives that not only penetrated enemy defenses but pounded them into submission . . . JOC continues to be the word we use to this day.

It took us four days with six multinational teams working nonstop to get the infrastructure, computers, and approvals in place. Unfortunately, I was still missing the heart of the system to make everything work, and even after talking to our hosts, the State Department, and the other services participating in the operation, what we still needed wasn't in Kuwait. And the clock was ticking down.

CHAPTER 10

December 1998—Ali Al Salem AB,
Northern Kuwait, and Riyadh, Saudi Arabia

It was a frustrating thing. For the first time in my life, I was in a position where I had all the money I would ever need to buy anything I could ever want, but I couldn't get the one thing I absolutely had to have. Millions of US dollars and Kuwaiti dinars were immediately available when I could show how some as of yet untapped *noun* (person, place, or thing) could be used to kill bad guys better, save coalition lives, or paint a clearer picture of what our enemies were doing. The rub was that what I needed wasn't in Kuwait. What made it worse was that it was impossible to get it imported and installed in time to use it.

Today, you can pick up the high-end version of a network switch and router combination at your local Best Buy electronics store one aisle down from the new movie releases. Now one is small enough to carry around in your pocket until you need to conduct mobile business or hook up a few friends to play lag-free multiplayer games online. If you wanted one now, a router-switch infinitely more powerful than what we needed back then would set you back about $150.

In the late 1990s, advanced network devices were as big as backpacks, made to order, and cost somewhere between a new Mustang and a two-year-old Corvette with low miles. There were a few available at the factory, but even if we expedited one of them, with customs delays in at least three countries, the present we needed to open before Christmas would arrive as an Easter egg, if it arrived at all.

I canvassed every possible place a spare switch or one being replaced as part of an upgrade might hide. I posted a map behind my desk and drew circles around military flight routes and roads we could travel in relative safety after factoring in the time we'd need to install and test the JOC before we went live. The map included military facilities, businesses like banks and phone companies, diplomatic missions, and casinos as close as Bahrain and as far away as Monaco. After a few days, there was big red X on my map over Kuwait, Oman, Germany, Italy, Greece, Egypt, Qatar, and Turkey. Each X represented a failure to find the device I needed. I had one more day to send messages and call and follow up. After that, time was up. I was angry. I'd just finished a fallback plan that was pretty good, but moving data in real time had become critical to operations, and the Rock just didn't have enough network horsepower to do everything we needed for Desert Fox.

I was tearing down my map when my secure phone rang. It was the communications and technical services officer at the US embassy in Riyadh. The ghostly voice on the other side of all the switches and signal algorithms that kept our conversation private from our enemies said, "Captain Riley?" When I said yes, she said, "I'm calling to make your day."

I smiled when I hung up the phone. I had never been to Saudi Arabia. Fortunately for me, general officers tend to tour the downrange combat-zone facilities and functions they're responsible for at the end of one month and beginning of the next, so they can meet their troops working in harm's way and better understand the downrange missions. It also gets them two tax-free months of income for each trip they take every year, so there was already a standing milk run for executives in the theater. It was a one-in-a-million find—an hour or so away as the Learjet flies, then just a short drive to the embassy. With a high-speed pass through the markets to round out anything else we might need, we were back in business again.

I was excited by the prospect of a visit to the Kingdom of Saudi Arabia. It was the land of Aladdin, Scheherazade, Sinbad, Ali Baba, and at least nine hundred ninety-seven other Arabian Nights stories.

I couldn't wait to get what I needed and look around.

Until I got there.

It was a dizzying whirlwind, and I was a dervish gathering materials as I spun through Riyadh. The city was an exotic, nearly incomprehensible mix of desert heritage, boys with toys, men in white robes, and women dressed in black, whom I couldn't even acknowledge without severe Sharia law consequences.

The Saudis I met were a people bound by a strict set of rules but with specific exclusions and exceptions that seemed to allow them whatever they wanted almost whenever they wanted it.

At least for the men.

The women remain a mystery to me. But I suppose that's how it was meant to be.

It wasn't the fairy-tale land I half expected. It was the unspoken arrogance of "I can have my cake and eat it, too—but not you." A conceit that hounded me for nearly thirty-two nonstop hours of cultural turbulence in the not-magic kingdom.

With more time and some sleep, I might have found a better way to navigate that culture.

Everything in life comes down to the quality of our relationships, and I didn't have any in the kingdom beyond military and embassy channels. Traversing Riyadh was intense, and Saudi Arabian culture was complex, like Japanese society, but only polite to someone who wasn't me.

The Saudis are a rich, proud people torn between ancient nomadic tradition and concentrated wealth, fervent religious doctrine, and ridiculously conspicuous excess. At almost every moment, there was a palpable tug of war between the past and present, where image was everything.

A State Department official greeted me at the embassy and escorted me through public spaces full of wooden desks, ornate chairs, and firm couches. Past wide aisles where short lines of cranky Americans waited to talk to embassy officials at stations with thick glass dividers. She had bright green eyes and wore her black hair in a pageboy cut. She moved with the grace of a dancer as we navigated deeper into the embassy complex.

Her name was Anna, and she told me the word *riyadh* translates to *lush meadows* or *gardens*, and we talked over steaming cups of just-brewed German coffee before she pushed through a heavy steel door she had to open with a key card and a passcode. It was a restricted area, probably one of the most restricted areas in the compound. The air was ice cold, and our footsteps echoed on the hollow, raised floor that forced air through racks of telecommunications and network equipment. It was the nerve center of the embassy. For an IT guy on a restricted diet of hand-me-down equipment well past its prime, it was a walk-in freezer full of delicacies. A frolic through a compact space that opened up at the fringes, filled with enough communications equipment to run a small city. More important to me were the bins filled with components and shelves heavy with neat rows of apparatus I coveted, plus other bits of paraphernalia I could put to good use.

She leaned in to me then and spoke in my ear, so I could hear her voice over the din of ventilation and teletypes and other devices that clacked and buzzed. After months away from my wife, I was more conscious of women than I'd realized. I was keenly aware of her breath in my ear, how good she smelled, and how warm she was in that icy vault. I'm five foot seven and a half, and Anna was several inches taller than me. She had a runner's frame and wore a colorful silk blouse that covered her neckline and wrists with ruffles and made her look pixyish. My eyes followed to where she pointed. On a table was a sturdy box fitted with shoulder straps. Then she said the three sexiest things I'd heard since I arrived in the desert: "The equipment you requested is already packed and ready to go"; "You can take anything else you need that isn't bolted down"; and "There's more coffee where that came from."

My fingertips were blue when Anna escorted me back to the embassy entrance.

"I can't begin to thank you enough, Anna, you're a lifesaver."

She smiled and shook my hand. "Just make sure you put all that gear to good use."

"You know I will."

"Call me again next time you need help saving the world," she said as she unclipped the visitor badge from my chest. I shook her hand one last time, nodded, and watched her for a moment as she walked away. I left the embassy with that router strapped to my back, slightly aroused, with two high-end store shopping bags filled to the brim with geek swag.

The marine guards, who understood at a glance that I was robbing them blind, hesitated before they let me pass. Without looking back, I knew they were still frowning when I stepped out into Riyadh's blinding light.

CHAPTER 11

December 1998—Riyadh, Saudi Arabia

Today, Riyadh resembles a sprawl of sandcastles caught in a mesh of congested superhighways anchored between two modern towers, the sharp point of Al Faisaliah always visible in the southeast and the keyhole eye of Kingdom Centre always watching from the northwest.

In 1998, Al Faisaliah was a toddler of concrete work and construction delays and cranes, and what would become Kingdom Centre was a warren of tenuously connected empty space and district oases hidden within a canyon of blocky, crammed-together buildings. There weren't many visible landmarks, and crawling through the winding side roads and back alleys while I looked for electronics and computer shops was like treasure hunting in a dungeon.

Downtown Riyadh was disorienting, and I was scrutinized as I traveled through the streets and back-alley markets. My visit was treated as a barely tolerated incursion. I got to experience firsthand the reception white blood cells usually reserve for an infection as the Mutaween religious police assisted me when I was lost and tried to ask directions. They whacked me with sticks. Not just to enforce the decency laws but also to help me navigate Riyadh.

I was in the wrong neighborhood when *whack, whack, whack*, and I knew to turn around. During the salah call to prayer, if I didn't bow down, then *whack, whack, whack*, it was time to go, and I quickly left. A young woman brushed by me on the way to the market while her male escort was distracted, and *whack, whack, whack,* I was strongly prompted to turn right and perform a very nonsecular U-turn. In Saudi Arabia, the Mutaween were the corporal punishment version of GPS. When there was no clear violation, there was still the *whack, whack, whack* of recalculating.

Hitting Mutaween back got you jail or worse. They loved their work and would cite chapter and verse from the Koran while they smacked you.

I didn't understand it, so I made up translations in my head.

Whack, whack, whack, Bharuch Atah Adonai (blessed is the Lord our God); *whackity, whack, whack,* Jesus is love; *whack-a-whack whack,* Islam is peace.

I hated the indignity of it, but our leadership made it crystal clear before we left the compound that it was their country, their rules, and we were ordered not to cause an incident, no matter what, and so the fun continued. The compromise, on the Saudi part, was that only one or two Mutaween would "motivate and direct" us while hordes of Mutaween would come out of the stonework to "correct and detain" wrongful citizens or employees of the kingdom.

Our uniforms generally let our host nation more easily track us. It also let their security forces know we were partners or guests, but in Saudi, we were required to wear conservative civilian clothes outside of mission or diplomatic facilities to avoid upsetting the locals' more delicate sensibilities, and we were only to present our military ID if there were a major problem. I felt naked without my uniform. My white dress shirt, ball cap, blazer, and khakis didn't offer much protection, but they did allow me to somewhat stylishly execute the local policy of smile, grunt, and bear it.

The old men in red-and-white *ghutra* headscarves with their crazy Gandalf beards were more benign than the younger men in more modern sport coats. While the old guys favored headshots with their walking sticks, they yelled more and didn't connect as hard; the younger Mutaween used extendable metal batons. They would glare and start *whack-whacking* me across the back to a section of Koranic surah that sounded a lot like "I love my job, I love my job" before pushing me off in the direction I was supposed to go.

I got the impression Westerners annoyed them more than anything else, and they thought any more effort would have been wasted on us. At that point, I was more worried about the Styrofoam-encased router in the sturdy box strapped to my back that was now covered in tears and dings from all the whacking.

I turned in to a Saudi Arabian government office that looked like a modern-art version of a palace built as a thickly frosted, inverted layer cake. I showed my ID and was patted down while the guards argued about whether they could let me in with my gear. After an hour's delay, I was finally allowed in. Once I was changed back into my uniform with my equivalent rank in the Saudi Royal Air Force pinned to my chest, the guards lost some of their bravado. When they realized, with some distaste, that I outranked them, our relationship progressed from "Hands above your head, and get down on your knees, now" to "If you would please come this way now, sir." The words were different, but their tone stayed the same.

Another hour later, the guards had verified the story I kept repeating in bad Arabic that translated roughly as, "Me good servant, shop for big general, he meets with crown prince now. Me wait," and I was finally escorted from security to a large, comfortable chair in an ornate anteroom to join two small groups. Ours waited for our general to finish his last meeting before our flight back to Kuwait. The other waited for the Saudi royal our general was meeting.

Like most meetings, it went long, but there was tea and snacks for each entourage, and I was happy to rest there. I had what I needed, and our general had a driver that wasn't me. Driving in Riyadh is exhilarating. It's like playing bumper cars on crack with Ferraris, and I was finally winding down and looking forward to getting back. I'd been up for more than thirty hours straight, and I was approaching my limit.

I was trying to get my two shopping bags of assorted cables, cards, and specialty tools to balance on the floor so they wouldn't fall over when it hit me. I started laughing, and even after I realized I was disturbing the others waiting, I had trouble stopping. It was the first time I realized that Major Andy, if given the chance, would have really had me beaten with a stick. Before Saudi Arabia, I thought it was only a metaphor.

Saudi Arabian GPS aside, something deeper troubled me, but I still couldn't put it into words. At first, I thought it was just a strong desire to get the hell out of Saudi, based on my lack of cultural sensitivity and a real dislike of sticks, but it was something else.

An older Saudi child, not quite yet a man, finally put into words what was really bothering me. He was the young son of a dignitary I met by chance while we waited for that same meeting to end. The youth, still years away from real facial hair, was well appointed and spoke English better than I did. He was slender, with darker hair, skin, and eyes than mine. He wore a crisp white dishdasha robe that covered his wrists and went down to his Birkenstocks. Over it he wore a black vest with heavy (probably real) silver embroidery. If I had to guess, I'd say he was in middle school.

He was waiting for his father in the lounge for the same reasons we were waiting for our general. He noticed our uniforms and came over out of curiosity despite the advice of his servants. I thought he was going to lecture me on disturbing the peace with my laughter.

"You there," he said in clear English. "You."

I was surprised. No Saudi had talked to me directly except to ask for my papers, sell me something, or recalculate my position. "Yes?"

His bodyguard quickly inserted himself between me and the young man before I could say anything else. He grunted terrible English along the lines of, "You stand in presence of Prince So-and-So, Something of Something, Star of Big and Important Things . . ." It went on for a while, and I started to drift. Eventually, the bodyguard stopped talking when he thought I was ignoring him, because I was. When I stood up, he glared at me and brandished his submachine gun before stepping aside. Every time I looked at him, he'd feel up his weapon and, dental plans not being a big part of the minion benefit package, smile a big, blackened, semitoothy grin.

The Saudi youth startled me when he stepped in close and demanded, "Answer me, why are you here?"

I took a petty degree of satisfaction in being taller than him.

It was a broad question, so I started with the talking points. "Well, young prince, my people are here to work with our coalition brothers, the Saudi people, to ensure that Saddam's armies do not rise again to disturb the peace of his neighbors."

"You are our servants," he said as a statement of fact, not an insult.

"No, prince, we are not, but we are here to help."

"How does your service differ from that of our other servants," he said, motioning to his bodyguard, "who protect us, run errands, clean for us, or do the many other things beneath us?"

He didn't say it in a mean way. He just didn't see a difference between US military forces and his maids, bodyguards, or garbage men.

"Well, prince, technically, we're not in your employ. We're here because it's the right thing to do, and it serves both of our sovereign interests to work together."

"That still makes you our servants."

"Respectfully, you're wrong. A better word would be partners."

His mouth hung open in stunned confusion, some of his aplomb dissolved, and his voice quivered. "But . . . that's what all the fathers say."

Then he turned on his heel, dismissed me with a wave, and rejoined his entourage. Hassan caressed his weapon again in an inappropriately familiar way, snarled at me one last time, and loped away after his master.

Through that lens, all the arrogance, disdain, and whacking finally made sense. It was so outrageous I laughed again as I watched the young prince's group move themselves as far away from me as they could while still remaining in the anteroom. I knew I had to stop, but that laugh was a long time coming, and it took a while to get out. So, they saw us as servants. It made me laugh even harder despite the stares. It reminded me of an F. Scott Fitzgerald quote from *The Great Gatsby* I was forced to memorize in high school that I hadn't thought about again until that moment: "Let me tell you about the very rich. They are different from you and me. They possess and enjoy early, and it does something to them." I sat back down to wait for our general and to contemplate what I'd heard. I was certain that despite being painfully delicate and frigging diplomatic, I was going to get my ass chewed the entire flight back to Kuwait. Even that didn't quench my good mood. I'd gotten what we came for, and I'd learned something important. I absolutely hate it when people think I work for them when I don't.

I smiled, but the other entourage still looked uncomfortable. Out of the mouths of babes . . . but that's what all the fathers say. The US military was no servant of Saudi Arabia. We worked together when we had common interests, and while I understood the strategic value of predictable oil production, the ridiculous amounts of money involved, and the political pressure to mobilize the military to safeguard our interests, in my heart, I longed for a time when we wouldn't be called up so readily to bleed over foreign oil fields.

CHAPTER 12

December 1998—Riyadh, Saudi Arabia

We sped through traffic in a black armored Suburban. The polycarbonate side glass distorted the cars and streetlamps alongside us like a funhouse mirror. The drive to the jet waiting for us at Prince Sultan Air Base (PSAB) was everything I expected.

"Captain Riley, do you have any idea who that was?"

"No, sir, he had a lot of titles for a tween. His bodyguard said he was a magnificent star of—"

"Stand down, Captain. This isn't a conversation."

"Yes, sir."

"The Saudis are our insanely sensitive hosts. They influence global banking and have close ties to many of our past and present civilian leaders, not to mention their key role in oil production politics and our ability, or inability, to continue to operate out of bases here. What we say and do here impacts all of it. Especially if you're anywhere near Saudi royalty. Do you get me?"

"Yes, sir," I said, and I did; nonetheless, the lecture and ass pain continued, and he didn't relent until he ran out of breath just before we stopped for the ID check at the PSAB gate. The checkpoint was lit like a medical operating theater, where the white light of ten suns turned night into day and burned through every shadow. There was no place to hide.

By the time we parked beside our Learjet, the general got his wind back, and he and his entourage finally started to laugh. "Now then, my aide also told me the young prince said that US forces were his country's garbage men. And that you gently but firmly corrected him."

"Yes, sir, I did."

"That part was outstanding. We are not the maids and garbage men of Saudi Arabia. I am glad you were able to help educate their next generation."

"Thank you, sir," I said. Then the general boarded the jet and spoke with the flight crew while his entourage got everything stored and found their seats.

I thought a Learjet would be spacious, since captains of industry, rock stars, and famous athletes own them, but they aren't. They're more about the freedom to go anywhere in comfort.

I belted the banged-up router/switch package into the seat across from me as though it were a small child. It was the last missing piece in a mission-critical puzzle that would help give the US, the UK, and Kuwait a better picture of what was going on in the upcoming operation than we'd ever had before, although some assembly was still required.

The general's drowsing entourage filled the back of the jet, and I strapped into my seat. Even though my chair back was grounded against the multipurpose toilet / storage / spare seat bulkhead and wouldn't recline, I was leaving Saudi, and it felt like first class.

Before the general took his seat, he patted me on the shoulder and said, "It goes without saying, Captain Riley, you probably shouldn't return to the Royal Kingdom of Saudi Arabia for a very long time."

"Yes, sir. No question," I said.

The general nodded and took his seat; the hatch was sealed, the engines spooled up, and the small jet taxied toward the runway.

I looked at the lines of welts and bruises crisscrossing my forearms—never returning to Saudi Arabia was fine with me. I got what I needed, I didn't do anything wrong, and I got my ass handed to me for doing the right thing. I traced a welt with my finger. Last time I felt like that, I was a kid.

After the swelling went down from getting dragged back to fight, my face looked mostly human again, and Sarah and I took the ferry from the terminal in Patchogue to Watch Hill on Fire Island and spent the day swimming in the ocean and exploring the wilderness by Skunk Hollow.

Piles of driftwood washed up along the shore and collected together like a broken forest of black-and-white trees. We stretched out our towels, Sarah sat with her back to a split piece of gray wood bigger than a table, and I lay with my head in her lap, looking up at her. I answered all her questions about the fight, and the after-fight, as we watched the waves. It was mostly our beach for a few hours, and Sarah would pet my hair as if I were a cat curled up in her lap or turn my face and frown as she traced the lines where the cuts and stitches were still healing.

"Yeah, I'm a mess," I said. "Why do you even bother? I mean, you're smart and cute; you could be with anyone and go anywhere."

"You think I'm cute?" she said, smiling.

"Shut up, you are, and you know what I mean."

"We always have the most fun. I mean, look at this place. And you take good care of me. Ever since . . . Wait, don't tell me you don't remember how we met?"

"I can't remember ever not knowing you."

"I was in a bad car accident just before we moved here," Sarah said. "I still had a cast on my arm and bandages around my eye, and I was finally out walking around the neighborhood when I saw a bunch of kids that looked like they were playing. But when I got closer, a big boy was intimidating all the other kids. He was saying that this was his street now, and when a kid stood up to him, he'd swing his bike around and hit the kid with it until he backed down. When I tried to leave, he knocked me down with his bike, and all the big kids backed away."

"That was a long time ago."

"You were the only one who stood up to him. You told him that this was our neighborhood and to leave. Even though you looked half his size. He kept pushing you, but you stood your ground and kept telling him to leave. Then, he started punching you hard and laughing."

"That's not good."

"It wasn't, it was horrible, but instead of backing down, you grabbed him by the throat, and he couldn't pull you off. You didn't stop choking him until he passed out, and the adults came out of their houses to drag you off him. Even after he got up off the ground, you kept yelling at him. While the adults held you back, you screamed at him to go away and never come back, because the adults wouldn't be there next time."

"And then everyone lived happily ever after?"

"After the adults finished scolding you, you helped me up. I was so scared I couldn't move. Even though you had a black eye and a bloody nose, you weren't even mad. You walked me all the way home and joked around until I stopped crying."

"Did all that really happen?"

"You really do get hit in the head a lot, don't . . ." Then she stopped.

"Yeah. It's OK. I was pretty cool, huh?"

"Well, aside from that, you weren't very impressive. You didn't even tell me your name."

"Hmm . . . let me think. I remember when I said you looked like a cool pirate with that eye patch on, you cried all the way home. Then you hid from me and wouldn't even tell me your name. Even after your mom baked us cookies, you still wouldn't tell me your name, until she made you."

"You haven't changed at all," she said softly.

"What was that?"

"Nothing."

"It sounded like something. In fact, now, I'm more—"

"Shut up."

"But don't you—"

"Shut up. The best thing you can do right now is not talk."

"OK. You win. I'll be quiet if we can stay here like this for a little while longer."

Sarah patted my head some more. We stayed that way with my head on her lap, watching the waves and breathing in the salt air, until we had to run to catch the last ferry home.

CHAPTER 13

December 1998—Ali Al Salem AB, Kuwait

Local news reports showed Saddam's army massing near the border. Tension spread through Kuwait City with every broadcast. Graphics displayed major elements of the Republican Guard moving south. Stylized images of tanks and troops and scud missiles counted down the distance as Iraq's army inched closer to Kuwait.

The proximity of Saddam's forces induced hysteria, and waves of Kuwaitis began an exodus. Those who remained at work were pensive and distracted. They went through the motions, but they didn't finish sentences; barter stopped short of optimal profit; and tea was left untouched.

Détente was an international-scale child's game of red light, green light. The US moved carriers and bombers into place to counter Iraq's red-light blocking of inspector entry into suspected WMD facilities. Saddam would again green-light his forces and race back toward Kuwait, and his soldiers wouldn't stop until America drew another red-light line across Iraq with cruise missiles and bombs. Saddam would finally let inspectors return and bide his time while his army stomped back to Baghdad to prepare for the next round.

By December, for many Kuwaitis, it felt like déjà vu of 1991, the invasion of Kuwait, all over again. A hostile army was once again heading right at them. The Kuwaitis had lived through the murder and pillage of

Saddam's military once, and they weren't about to stick around and see how things turned out a second time. Many of them had been POWs, and they vowed that they would never, *ever*, be captured or treated like that again. The last Kuwaitis who could left the country in droves on open-ended "one way for now" tickets.

We installed the technical package we got from the embassy in Riyadh, stood up the first JOC in northern Kuwait, and we passed information and tactical intelligence to Kuwaiti ground forces, UK Tornado reconnaissance and bombing missions, base defense, and special and psychological operations teams. It was the first time we ever had real-time situational awareness of all those missions. We were even able to work with US intelligence analysts back in the States and provide limited reporting on UK Tornado targets to navy forces aboard the USS *Enterprise* and marines on the USS *Belleau Wood* afloat in the Persian Gulf.

Air-raid countermeasures were in place across the Rock, and every light was blacked out. From a distance, we were an indistinct stain on the sandstone jutting out from the desert. I was taking a break in the cool dark on our perimeter wall, looking toward Iraq and listening to the sounds of our encampment: the snatches of hushed conversation, the rustling of tents in the breeze, the hum of faraway generators, and the whine of jet engines on the flight line. Our defensive tactics weren't much different from what we used in WWII. To make it more difficult to bomb or shell us accurately, all exterior lights on base and in the surrounding town were powered down and locked off. Blackout drapes were strung at every entrance to block the light, window flaps and holes in tents were sealed, and military police patrolled the compound to ensure our light discipline was maintained, mostly through profession-alism, harsh language, and extra layers of duct tape. It was a sobering reminder that, at the time, we were the only air base in range of enemy artillery.

On clear nights, the city lights of Basra and the port of Umm Qasr in Iraq caused a glow in the northeast, but the haze that hung in the desert air made the view a rare sight. Under blackout conditions, from our highest perimeter wall, I still couldn't see the lights of Basra, just a lime-green smudge in a sky punctured by hard stars that made it look like a nebula. We'd been up a long time preparing, and the air tasking order said we were just moments away from launch.

I checked my watch and started counting down: three, two, one . . . Then it happened. Jet engines roared across base, and four-ship flights of Tornado fighter-bombers clawed their way into the night. To the east, a constellation of yellow stars slowly rose to the sky. Some disappeared, and some grew brighter as they moved our way like small formations of meteors. A few fell on Basra, but the rest continued to trace a path west in the darkness, growing fewer in number as they approached. The ones that touched the ground in front of us exploded in flashes of lightning and rolling thunder as Iraqi positions to the north, east, and west of us were pounded by Tomahawks launched from ships in the Persian Gulf and ALCM cruise missiles released from air force bombers. The closest targets were over thirty Mississippis away.

I spent the better part of the next three days in the JOC, coordinating requests for information and fine-tuning our communications across the spectrum of operations happening in and around the Rock. For days, the air held the faint smell of acrid debris and burnt metal. It hung over us in a persistent haze that was particularly thick at dawn. It was a nostalgic smell of victory.

— ★★★ —

Summer of 1978 was halfway over. I was on Long Island, and it was just before sunset. My best friend Sarah and I were in the empty baseball diamond on the hilltop behind our school. I gently slid the rocket lugs onto the launch rod and carefully inserted ignitors into each engine. I looked away and held my breath when I connected the wires to the battery. Our launchpad was an inverted pie pan held down by rocks with a launch rod hammered through it and into the bare spot between first and second base. With the shiny orange rocket mated to it, I thought it was pretty enough to make even the most cynical NASA engineer smile. The rocket was designed for one engine, but it had a wide tube fuselage, so I figured four engines would be better. It was tricky getting all the engines to fire off at the same time.

I thought it would look cool to have an engine at the end of each fin, but that didn't work out so well. Fins ripped off, rockets launched sideways, and sometimes engine ignition would delay and the rockets would tumble or zigzag across the ground. A few tried to hunt us down. Several bruises, burns, and apologies later, I realized that gluing and taping the four engines together and igniting them with a big lantern battery worked best. Three engines would have been easier to handle, but more was better. So, I modified the orange rocket and prepared it for flight.

Sarah wore a battered hardhat with red letters on the side that said LILCO, the Long Island Lighting Company, and the kind of goggles they hand out for chemistry experiments. Even though her hair was tucked up in it, the hardhat was so big on her it looked like it was trying to swallow her head. I wore a ball cap that was still a little big even on the smallest setting. We slowly backed away until all the wire was played out, and after I connected the controller, Sarah stood behind me and offered her encouragement. "You know, this isn't going to go the way you think it is."

"Why do you say that?"

"None of the test rockets survived," she said.

"That's why they were tests. This one will be different."

"If you say so."

"This one has to be awesome," I said.

"Why?"

"It's the only rocket we have left."

"Hmm," Sarah growled. "OK. Ready?"

"Mission is a go. Begin countdown."

"You are such a nerd ... three, two, one."

"Ignition," we said in unison as I hit the launch button.

There was a hiss, then a whistle, and the rocket was gone, just a streak of orange climbing straight into the sky. Sarah and I jumped and cheered, but after several moments of glorious flight, something went terribly wrong. As the rocket descended, smoke enveloped it, and it slithered back to earth like an angry gray snake. It sputtered as it chased us. Just as we jumped apart to avoid it, the parachute ejected. We looked at each other and sighed with relief. But as it floated down, our rocket erupted into flames, and the parachute swelled like the belly of a hot-air balloon, bobbing in the air just above us. For a weird, serene moment, we watched the fire eat our rocket in a tango of crimson and green-flamed destruction five feet above the ground. We crept closer until we could feel the heat of the billowing firestorm. Flames incinerated the parachute. There was the sound of a candle being blown out, and the remains of the rocket slammed to the ground with a bang. It was as if gravity had caught a touchdown and spiked the cremated flying machine in the end zone. After a moment of shock, we looked at each other, laughed, and began stamping out the grass on fire in left field.

"Well, that certainly was something," Sarah said as we tossed the remains of the rocket and launchpad in the trash bin. There was nothing

recognizable left. Just ashes, refuse, and hard bits of plastic slag molded in patches of scorched earth.

"Thanks, Sarah. I wanted to launch that rocket with my dad, but it was way more fun this way."

"It was awesome," Sarah agreed as she stretched out in the grass.

I thought so, too, and fell into the grass next to her. The air was still. The sun set in a swirl of red, and all that remained of our rocket was a bitter mist that clung to two kids in an otherwise empty field.

"I thought, with all the smoke, at least someone would have climbed up the hill to see what we were doing."

"I'm glad no one came," Sarah said, staring up at the sky. "This is our awesome."

I reached out for her hand, and her fingers intertwined with mine. A breeze rose up from the east, and there was an inevitable thumb war.

Part of me wanted to cry. My father had left after the divorce, my mother was crazy, and I was supposed to act like the adult my parents couldn't be, but Sarah's hand squeezed mine, the first stars came out, and I realized I was happy.

Sarah was right.

I didn't have to worry about any of that right now.

We made fire in the sky. It was our awesome.

President Clinton declared victory over tyranny, and the air force later reported that over three days and four nights, more than a thousand munitions had been dropped on almost a hundred targets. The operation was designed to inflict maximum damage on critical nodes of Saddam's military and WMD programs. Fifteen percent of the airstrikes came from British Tornado aircraft;[9] most of them flew out of the Rock.

In the US, the press reported the play-by-plays of Operation Desert Fox, swiftly followed by accusations that the operation had been orchestrated to distract the nation from the fallout of President Clinton's affair with Monica Lewinsky. Pundits argued that either Desert Fox was instrumental in forcing Iraq back into compliance, or it had no impact whatsoever on Saddam's ability to project power and deploy weapons of mass destruction outside of Iraq. I listened to their arguments, but none of the experts debating the issue were there. The operation was a resounding success, but we wouldn't understand how effective Desert Fox was until we found ourselves on the ground in Iraq some years later. The campaign savaged Iraq's military weapons research, production, and storage facilities. It forced Saddam to recall his army, and it once again enabled WMD facility inspections.

When the Kuwaitis did return, they massed in jubilant crowds in celebrations across Kuwait to relieve three months' worth of stress and uncertainty. There were street parties at every corner and even small, pre–Liberation Day parades.

The Kuwaitis we worked with throughout the operation and our vendors from downtown sent presents to the base as Saddam's forces retreated north. They brought pastries, monstrous donuts as big as my head, and fresh fruit the next morning for breakfast. Later in the afternoon, trucks began to arrive with platters of stuffed game birds, roasted with eggs on huge piles of rice cooked with nuts and dried fruit. It was a bewildering array of food, and there was so much of it we had to get

---

9   Capt. Gregory Ball, "1998 – Operation Desert Fox," Air Force Historical Support Division, August 23, 2011, https://www.afhistory.af.mil/FAQs/Fact-Sheets/Article/458976/operation-desert-fox/.

the commander's permission to set up a special buffet in the chow hall so everyone could enjoy it. It would have been a feast under any circumstance, but we were a sleepy little base and the last stop on an army supply line where, except for the food bought downtown with our commander's discretionary funds, we got the picked-through remains of the provisions no one else wanted. It was spectacular, and for the rest of the week, there were small exchanges and meetings to celebrate the victory and express gratitude. Their sense of national pride made it difficult for Kuwaitis to speak directly about the US role in their defense, but they were gracious in often indirect ways.

"My wife made these chocolates, you should try some."

"My cook, Haba, makes very delicious lumpia egg rolls. They are small bites of paradise. She wanted you to have them as her way of saying thanks."

"I just got a box of Cuban cigars in, come smoke them with us."

In private spaces, I was offered many excellent bottles of whiskey as presents, which I was, sadly, in accordance with General Order No. 1, required to politely and respectfully decline.

Tea and snacks with the base commander were lavish. Our Kuwaiti hosts were proud of their role in routing Saddam's army, forcing them back to Baghdad, and reducing the WMD threat.

It surprised me that most of the tea we drank in the Middle East was brewed from Lipton bags. The wrappers were a different color, the text was in flamboyant Arabic cursive, and the taste was a little different from what we got in the States, but it was Lipton all the same. What made it exotic was how it was served in the tall, thin tea glasses ever present in the Arab world with an air of ceremony and a pile of sugar cubes. That day, tea was special. After the hot water was poured over the leaves, they opened and formed beautiful flowers in the bottom of my glass. It was fragrant and delicious. The tea was like wine, and the accompanying snacks were the Kuwaiti version of royal high tea delicacies, pastries, and fruit.

Major Andy ate, mostly nodded, and agreed with his mouth full of snacks while I gave my report. He scowled, grumbled, and harrumphed a few times, but when I paused for him to speak, he just turned away and picked something else off a tray or held his glass out for more tea. It was the first day since we started working together that he made it to his golf club on time.

Everyone I submitted for decorations based on their actions during the operation received them, except for Airman Conner. The medal I recommended for him was declined at headquarters—not because of the impact of his accomplishment but because he was too junior. They felt only more senior personnel deserved that level of recognition. I appealed that decision and added testimony from the UK commander on why his actions had made a difference.

My commander frowned under his bushy moustache, then handed me a cup of coffee and a cookie and sent the award request back to headquarters. I felt like a kid in detention whenever I was summoned to his office, but he was a mentor from the days when that word had real meaning. The mystery was how his wife could make such beautiful, work-of-art cookies taste so nasty. I tried hard to believe that the butter just went rancid while they were held up in customs, not that she was trying to kill him. My appeal for Airman Conner's decoration came back almost immediately as *Declined, do not resubmit*, and I thought about what to do for a while.

As a consolation, my commander agreed to present a more modest decoration that he could approve for Airman Conner without having to go through headquarters. So, we did, but it still rubbed me wrong, and I couldn't let it go. In the end, I was able to get Airman Conner a VIP pass and helicopter ride out to the morale events held on the navy carrier *Enterprise*, still on patrol in the Persian Gulf. The pass let him tour the carrier and hang out with the comedians, singers, and a bunch of cheerleaders doing shows for the troops. He got to travel with the entertainers and their entourage. It was a magical place, and the ladies supporting the troops sometimes got caught up in the moment after hearing all the war stories of a fit young airman in uniform. Those are emotional tours for the entertainers, and it was easy to get caught up in the moment. Sometimes they could be a little more patriotic, and grateful for a man's service to his country, than they might otherwise be inclined to be, and Airman Conner returned from the *Enterprise* two days later with a ridiculous smile plastered to his usually serious face. Just looking at him was good for morale.

Whenever an IT guy comes back to work covered in the lipstick marks of cheerleaders, it's a victory for every IT guy everywhere.

CHAPTER 14

January 1999—Ali Al Salem AB, Kuwait

"Be aware of your surroundings. Take care on the road. There are reports of VBIED (vehicle-based improvised explosive device) activity along Dead-Sheep Highway. Remain vigilant. That is all." That was the end of the morning threat briefing, but food was disappearing from the chow hall, so the commander ordered a special update from the two civilians who ran the dining facility. It raised more questions than it answered, degenerated into a fistfight between the two of them, and they were restrained and escorted away. Due to mismanagement, we were out of everything at the chow hall except for a freezer full of chicken kiev, condiments, and the kosher and halal MREs no one else wanted to eat.

As soon as combat operations wound down, the Rock was drained of troops, and Ali Al Salem AB started to look like a ghost town. One of the few teams that rotated in that evening was for me. My replacement had come, so I met him at the airport and got him settled into a billet. That meant I was going home soon. Our group commander wanted a two-week overlap between us, but the new captain was a smart, take-charge kind of guy from my home unit. I figured that after more than a few days of introductions, Q and A, and working with me, I'd just be in the way. The first thing a new commander needs to do is take command, but orders were orders. While he acclimated, I got ready to do a few last things before I took the three-day pass my commander gave me after

Desert Fox. I was looking forward to a little R&R, I had plans, and my bag was already packed.

First thing on my to-do list was a mission to get upgraded equipment in case the Rock was ever used to forward-stage forces again. A new satellite dish and control van had just come in from the States, but the equipment was still parked at Kuwait International Airport and needed to clear customs. The new equipment would more than double our existing communication capabilities. That meant access to more data, the ability to support new operations, and better phone lines home.

I briefed my NCOs (noncommissioned officers) on what we needed to do, and when they left to assemble our convoy, I started making calls to put the pieces together. As expected, it was business as usual: Mohammed from the airport screwed us again and buried our customs paperwork. His secretary assured me that with a little luck, *Insha'Allah*, we should be able to pick the satellite equipment up by the end of next month—if God willed it.

There was nothing else I could do. I only had one option left. As much as I didn't want to, I had to convene an emergency tea.

I was leaving soon, so it was the perfect reason. A chance to say goodbye to my Kuwaiti friends. I called Mustafa Bin, who, among other things, oversaw airport customs.

"I apologize for asking with such short notice, but I'm leaving Kuwait soon, and I would like to say farewell to the friends I've made here. Is there an agreeable time we could meet today?"

"Yes, yes, my friend, we would like that very much. I will have my key staff there, and someone from my office will call you back with the time to meet."

"You're the best, Mustafa Bin. Thank you."

"Do not worry, my friend. How many times do I have to tell you, this is my airport. I will see you soon."

After that, I called Malcolm at the embassy, Assad and Fahad from the base, Abdullah the merchant, Mohammed from the ministry, and big Ali from the security office. I also invited Yassin from the military police, but he was out with a pretty girl he couldn't introduce to his mother, so he sent his regrets. I looked forward to seeing everyone before I left, but I was also counting on peer pressure and the opinions of superiors, which are important when conducting business in the Arab world, to help shake my equipment free. For the emergency tea, I loaded my best cigars, and a few small presents, into my Humvee.

I reminded everyone about the VBIED threat and made the call sign for our convoy FedEx, because we were absolutely going to deliver. Five minutes later, we left the Rock in a line of five tactical military vehicles painted camouflage to blend into the desert but covered in flashing amber lights with placards in Arabic and English that read, *Convoy—Stay Back, Do Not Cross.*

We traveled down Highway 70 with both the military precision of a convoy and the light show usually reserved for a Disney parade float. The airport filled most of the space between the sixth and seventh ring roads that radiated south from Kuwait City. It was a two- to three-hour drive depending on traffic, and our convoy was cutting through the desert, quickly and conspicuously. If we'd been heading north, we'd have connected with Highway 80, the highway of death, where Saddam's armored forces fleeing Kuwait had been cut down. Both sides of the road were still littered with bullet-riddled tanks, trucks, and personnel carriers. The picked-through remains of Saddam's war machine still stood where they fell as sand-blasted and sun-bleached reminders of the war.

Where the northern road was characterized by the carcasses of slaughtered vehicles, the southern road we traveled was littered with the corpses of sheep and camels. On both sides of the road were dead and decomposing animals. It wasn't something new. Fresh kills fell atop bone piles. The number-one cause of livestock death in Kuwait was motor vehicles. Any bit of wild grass was an open range, and up until a few years earlier, no formal driver's education had been required. We called it Dead-Sheep Highway, but there were actually several Dead-Sheep Highways located around Kuwait. Our convoy screeched to a flashing halt several times when animals stepped into the road or were herded into our convoy by shepherds just as we were about to pass by. We had to be careful. There was a security alert for VBIEDs, we needed to quickly and safely complete our mission, and accidentally killing an animal in the Arab world is a big, expensive deal. If we hit a sheep or camel, the US government was responsible not only for the dead animal but also for all the lambs and calves, milk, wool, and meat the deceased animal would have provided its owner over its entire lifetime. In the case of camels, there was also the stud fee that could be charged to breed racing camels and all their future progeny. Based on the claim forms Kuwaiti camel ranchers filed with the US government, every camel killed in an accident with a US vehicle was the virile lothario camel equivalent of Secretariat. So, most of our convoy safety briefings ended with, "Whatever you do, *don't hit livestock.*"

Mustafa Bin, chief of customs and airport operations, pulled out all the stops. He was a little taller than me, and he had a huge, perfectly waxed handlebar moustache that made him look a strong man from the thirties. I shook his hand, introduced my replacement, and we talked for a few minutes before he took my hand again and led me to a large conference room that was set up like a buffet. Almost all the customs officers were there, along with Mohammed from the airport, who looked miserable even before he saw me. Mustafa Bin led me to each of his staff, and we talked and shook hands, and afterward, he said something nice in Arabic that roughly translated to *You're leaving, so let's eat and drink and smoke to our heart's content.* Then Assad and Fahad from the base grabbed me and steered me toward the food.

First, we ate and told stories. Mostly they were jokes about me.

Then we drank tea and smoked. Once everyone was mellow and relaxed, I gave Malcolm and the Kuwaitis small gifts I'd brought and thanked them for all their support and help. When I gave Airport Mohammed his gift and shook his hand, his mouth made the requisite smile, but there was a barely perceptible screech, like iron bending.

After, the party began to break up. Mustafa Bin took my hand, and as we walked out, I said, "It's a shame that we can't take that air force satellite equipment that came in the other night with us. It would help us protect the base, and, *Insha'Allah*, we already have trucks here and we're going back that way."

Mustafa Bin's brow furrowed. "Mohammed has not released that yet?"

"I am just now getting time off after we all worked so hard together during that last operation. Is it possible I misunderstood? It would be a great relief if that were so."

"Excuse me just a moment, my friend," Mustafa Bin said as he locked on to his Mohammed.

I nodded to Abdullah the merchant and shook hands with the good Mohammed from the ministry and big Ali from the security office before they headed out. Big Ali slapped away my handshake and hugged me so hard I thought he cracked a rib.

"Thank. You. Big. Guy," was all I could squeeze out as I patted his back like I was trying to tap out.

"*Ila-liqaa.*" *Until we meet again*, he said. Then he released me and stomped away.

After I finished a bout of coughing, I turned to see Mustafa Bin.

"It does appear you were mistaken, my friend. Mohammed left right after tea and is releasing that equipment to your men as we speak."

"You're a good man, Mustafa Bin. Thank you for allowing this get-together. It meant a lot to me, and I will miss you," I said as my right hand touched my heart.

His smile stretched from curl to curl under his moustache. "You are, I think, part Kuwaiti now, Captain Riley. Enjoy your rest, and may Allah grant you a safe journey home."

Abdullah the merchant put his hand on my shoulder as I was leaving, and I slowed my pace to give the others a long lead. Once we were alone in the corridor, I asked, "What can I do for you, old friend?"

"We still good for tonight?"

"Absolutely. Look forward to it." We parted ways there, and I headed out to the storage yard.

Abdullah wasn't really his name. Truth was, I'd known him for years, and I still only knew him as John. Abdullah was a spy, a covert operator who specialized in collecting information for the US and advising friendly forces. Occasionally, he'd take an interest and recruit or mentor others in the community. He was a huge Beatles fan, and after I worked a job with him and his protégé Lucy in what's now Croatia, he gave me my first call sign, Ringo, when I was a new air force sergeant. John was the first person to meet me when I arrived in Kuwait. He'd been collecting valuable information on Iraqi forces by posing as a local entrepreneur named Abdullah who ran a thriving electronics business with offices in Kuwait and just outside of Basra in Iraq. With John's help, the Kuwait army was able to deploy their artillery and armored units more effectively. He also provided updates that made the ground and air orders of battle for Iraq more accurate. Right after we got the JOC up and running, he used our secure lines to transfer video and answer questions for decision makers back in the States. A few hours later, additional targets we'd had trouble pinning down had pictures and coordinates that the air force and navy added to their tasking orders and destroyed.

I walked the cantonment area to the row of vehicles parked in front of the customs checkpoint. My Humvee and four M-Class deuce-and-a-half trucks were hitched to a satellite dish and support equipment. It was a heavy load; our maneuverability, speed, and braking would decrease.

We gathered at my Humvee. Airport Mohammed was waiting for me with an administrator carrying a clipboard and stack of papers.

"I didn't expect you'd see me off in person, Mohammed; I'm honored," I said with my hand over my heart and a nod of my head.

"I had hoped to see you one less time, but as they say, the devil is cunning." He motioned, and his assistant presented a pen and paperwork for my signature. Before I signed, I looked at my NCOs, and they nodded so I knew everything was accounted for. I unscrewed the pen cap, and just as I was putting pen to paper, I had a thought.

"Mohammed. You don't mind if I flip through those transportation documents before I accept this shipment, do you?"

"Certainly, but I was told your time was short."

"And you are correct, as always. However, it would be disrespectful if I didn't ensure the accuracy of the papers my subordinates gave you."

"Fine." Then Mohammed motioned to his assistant, and I was presented with the bills of lading, equipment inventory, and, most importantly, the customs release forms.

"Thank you for your kind indulgence," I said, flipping through the documents and handing the papers back to Mohammed's assistant.

"Then you are satisfied that everything is in order?" Mohammed said with a predator's smile.

"Yes. The papers are perfect. Now once you affix your official seal to the bottom of the releases, we'll be on our way."

In an instant, Mohammed's smile bent back to a frown.

We stood there for an uncomfortable moment. He stared daggers at me; I smiled; my airmen shuffled uncomfortably from foot to foot.

Then he said something beyond my very basic Arabic, and his assistant pulled out a stamp. *Click, click, click,* and a colored seal was affixed to each of the release forms, and I signed off on my papers. We were good to go. I reached out, Mohammed had his assistant shake my hand, and then they quickly left. I smiled for a moment longer, watching master and minion stomp away before I finally let out a long sigh and felt my shoulders crumple. Without those seals, we could have been detained or, worse, arrested for theft.

My guys just laughed.

"Doesn't it get old, sir? Don't you get pissed off?" asked Master Sergeant Parson.

"It wears me out, but I've actually learned a lot about business here. If you're going to work with the Kuwaitis, there's an old Arabic proverb you have to know. 'Before you let fly the arrow of truth, always dip its point in honey first.'"

I showed our paperwork at the checkpoint, and our convoy was waved through. Then we turned on to the road and headed back to the Rock. For safety, our convoy was lit up like the Vegas strip.

We were about a quarter of the way back, on the outskirts of Kuwait City, where the road began to skirt oil fields and the shanty towns where laborers lived, when I got the radio call.

"There's a vehicle on our six. It's accelerating toward us and maneuvering erratically."

The road was getting congested, and we were in a bubble of traffic, trying not to get too close to our convoy.

"FedEx-1. You're lead now. Don't stop; drive on. I'm falling back."

"Copy that, FedEx leader."

My driver dropped us out of the convoy, and I scanned behind us. It was all crazy Kuwaiti rush-hour traffic. As we fell in behind the last truck and reeled them out, everything looked copacetic.

The road would reach a bottleneck about five miles ahead of us, where construction dropped two lanes down to one in both directions and stretched around a wide median. Drivers were jockeying for position, but that was nothing out of the ordinary. Then I saw it. Approximately a mile behind us, a dark gray BMW sedan broke from the traffic, fishtailed wildly on the shoulder, and accelerated to well over a hundred miles per hour, passing other vehicles until the shoulder ended. Then he darted back into traffic, almost knocking a small white car off the road.

"I've got visual. Stay in close formation. Don't stop for anything."

"Copy that." All four other vehicles checked in and tightened their spacing.

The BMW continued zigzagging through traffic until it was just behind us. For a moment, it slowed; then the driver tried to pass us on the left. We blocked the way, and the driver snapped back in behind us, fishtailing and almost losing control before darting left again. We moved to block him once again, but it was only a feint, and as soon as we started to break left, he swung around and passed us on the right. My driver tried to adjust, but the BMW was quicker and more agile than a Humvee. He slipped by and closed the distance to my convoy.

"FedEx-4. BMW fast approaching on your right. Stay in formation. Maintain speed. Don't try to maneuver pulling a trailer."

The road narrowed to one lane with a walled shoulder on each side, but the shoulders ended after the merge, and the right shoulder was disappearing fast. The BMW shot forward to pass before the gap closed.

"FedEx convoy. BMW passing on right shoulder. Maintain speed."

That was when the right shoulder ended. The driver tried to cut off the convoy the way he had cut into traffic earlier, but he wasn't fast enough. The BMW clipped FedEx-1, and the grey sedan's front quarter panel crumpled. The BMW rotated; then it hit the construction barrier and bounced into FedEx-2, and its trunk and rear compartment were crushed. It bounced off the construction barrier and into the convoy again in a shower of sparks. Then FedEx-3 hit the grey sedan in the front ahead of the engine and spun it around once more. The shoulder opened up again, and the BMW bounced off FedEx-4 and tumbled until it skidded to a stop on the side of the road.

"FedEx convoy, report in. Is anyone hurt?"

The convoy reported no injuries or major damage, and there was no explosion. We were clear.

"Sir, FedEx-1, should we pull over?"

"Negative, maintain formation. Press on and return to base. I'll catch up after I check the wreck and talk to the local police."

"You sure about that, sir?"

"Sure, yes; happy, no."

"Copy that, FedEx convoy, rolling on."

I watched their flashing lights fade in the distance; then we circled back to the smoking vehicle on the side of the road. We stopped a short distance behind the crashed BMW. I double-checked my sidearm; the safety was off, and a round was chambered. The BMW had come to a stop on its tires and ground to a stop against another section of barrier wall. The rear side windows of the vehicle were gone, the front and back glass was shattered, and the driver was cursing and struggling in his airbags. I didn't think anyone would survive that crash.

A pair of police officers arrived in a sand-and-black-colored SUV with flashing blue lights. They wore tan uniforms and berets and approached the BMW cautiously as they spoke to the driver in Arabic. I holstered my weapon, exited the vehicle with my hands up, and walked over to them. The smell of gasoline was strong.

"Officers. I have to report an accident. Do either of you speak English?"

They both looked at each other and laughed. "Some English, us both."

"Is he OK?"

The policeman said, "*Insha'Allah*, he is mostly. Unharmed and after medics come, he can go home."

"I'm *Na'qib* Riley, US Air Force. He ran into my convoy."

"We followed him through traffic. He saw the lights. He saw signs. This was God's will."

"About that," I said. "I'm going to need a note for my commander."

After the ambulance came and took him away, the officers took Polaroids of what was left of the BMW, and we sat in their car and smoked some of my cigars. After twenty minutes, I had an original and carbon copy of a surprisingly small accident report not much thicker than a US traffic ticket. One copy each for the host and US commanders, by way of the JAG. Between their English and my bad Arabic, I was almost certain it described the accident and said I wasn't to blame, but prison in Kuwait wasn't something I was keen to try. When I told them I'd have to call Malcolm at the embassy, one officer held up his hand, and they spoke quickly in Arabic. Then, he added a line to the top of the tickets in English block letters: *NO FAULT U.S. FORCE*. That made me feel better, and when they wrote their names next to it and stamped both copies with a green ink seal, I gave them a couple more cigars, vigorously shook their hands, and fled.

The rest of the trip back to base was uneventful.

While my guys staged the equipment and unloaded our supplies, I headed to our host and group commander's offices to brief them on how my convoy had cut a new BMW in half but no one died and the police report said, I was pretty sure, that it wasn't our fault. I wasn't 100 percent sure until our host commander read the form, looked at me, gave a thumbs up, and said, "Everything is A-OK." The meeting with the US command staff was mostly laughter at my expense. Most sentences started with, "Now let me get this straight," and my commander kept bringing in other commanders and making me retell the story. But we were able to pick up the new satellite facility, no one got hurt bad, and despite destroying a civilian vehicle, our trucks only had dings and a few scratches in the paint. Looking at the twisted remains of that once-ultimate driving machine, *Insha'Allah*, it could have been worse. I was walking out the door when I got summoned.

CHAPTER 15

January 1999—Ali Al Salem AB and Kuwait City, Kuwait

I had evening plans in Kuwait City. I changed into my Arab church clothes—the khaki slacks, white cotton dress shirt, and standard-issue navy blazer I'd last worn in Saudi Arabia—checked my M11 sidearm, slid it into the holster under my right shoulder, and adjusted my jacket. When I was satisfied it wouldn't bulge, I put on my old NY Mets ball cap and grabbed the leather backpack crammed full of my stuff. I took one last look around, and there was a knock at the door.

Standing on my doorstep was a Kuwaiti flight sergeant. We had a sharp exchange of salutes, and he left after delivering his message. Major Andy awaited me in his office, at my earliest convenience, which was a honeyed way of saying, "Come now."

I could feel my three-day off-base pass ticking away.

I was annoyed, but I got most of the really vile comments out under my breath as I hiked across base to the middle of a nearly dead grass field, to the wart of concrete that led to Major Andy's lair. I stepped into the cave-like enclosure that shaded a blue steel door, took a deep breath, pushed the call button next to the speaker plate, and announced myself. Then, I smiled at the camera mounted over the door and gave a peace sign, and a moment later there was a loud metallic *click* that released the lock. Major Andy's office was down a ridiculously long flight of stairs in an underground bunker. It grew colder every step down.

There was no handrail, and after the heavy steel entry door closed, I had to pause. It took my eyes a moment to adjust from the harsh light of the desert to the string of naked bulbs that dangled from pipes that ran along the ceiling down to Major Andy's domain. I began my descent with my right hand against the wall. My boots echoed off the steps before fading into the mechanical sounds of air conditioning, forced air, and buzzing electrical equipment. I always looked forward to the place where that stark corridor spilled into the one section of partitions and old wooden desks set on the patterned wool carpets that defined the area where the Kuwaiti communications staff worked. Until the Kuwaiti base commander appointed a new communications liaison to fill the vacancy, Major Andy would continue both his religious and communications responsibilities and maintain offices at his headquarters, the base mosque, and in the communications bunker. When I stumbled out of the darkness, a flight lieutenant put a cup of hot tea in my hand. Then his staff gathered around and stowed my things, and we exchanged pleasantries and talked shop.

After I finished my tea, someone was dispatched to confirm Major Andy was ready to see me. When everything was set, it would get quiet, and someone would point across the ocean of computer flooring to the one large wooden door that led to Major Andy's office. In the middle of that expanse of flooring, only one rack of high-capacity, state-of-the-art network equipment clacked and flashed. I always thought it was a shame it only connected the five PCs in that vault and five other computers across the Kuwaiti side of the base, but I wouldn't have much use for email either if I had the luxury of sending runners to get me anything I needed, like Major Andy did. How we did things was so different, but we did work well together during the last operation. His office in the bunker always reminded me of a tomb in a ruin.

I collected my thoughts, inhaled sharply, and knocked on Major Andy's door.

I thought the summons was to chew my ass or to explain that we really would have to compensate that Kuwaiti citizen for his BMW.

"Good evening, Major Andy. I was just heading out. What can I do for you? If this is about the accident this afternoon . . ."

Major Andy chuckled. It was a new sound to me, and it disturbed me enough to stop me in my tracks. "Oh, that. The estimable Mr. Shah made a bad choice, but he survived, *Insha'Allah*, and has, as a result, learned a valuable lesson. Do not worry about that incident. He does hate you now, so if you see him out with his brothers in Salmiya, it would be best not to stop and chat. Otherwise, I would not worry."

"I'm relieved to hear that. Do you know him?"

"Yes, but I have only met him a few times."

"The way he was driving, we thought he might be a terrorist."

Major Andy laughed. "He is mean and arrogant and impatient, but he is from a good family. Too many people saw what he did. It would be inconvenient for him if he did not drop this. Besides, he is no insurgent. He is already driving another nice car, very badly, not far from here. He is what you Americans would call a . . . bag of douche?"

"A douchebag?"

"Ah, yes, that. A douchebag. So impolite and yet so specifically disgusting. Such an American phrase. But, as he is a well-connected . . . would you say, feminine hygiene product?"

"We'd just say douche."

"Yes. Since he is a well-connected douche, it's better for everyone to simply ignore that this accident ever happened. He will not seek compensation from you, and we will not make an issue for you or your government. More proof of our superior civility."

"You are too kind."

"Yes, we are. Now that your concern is put to rest, it's time for business. You will come with me now."

"You just said I wasn't going to be punished."

Major Andy smiled. "If I had my way, I would have you caned for disrespect, for being an infidel, and for . . . just being you, but as that would exceed my authority . . ."

"Sadly, a missed opportunity."

"Sadly, yes. But now we go to my car. There is something happening you should see."

We walked back where his staff worked, and my bag was returned. Major Andy gave an order to one of his flight sergeants in rapid Arabic that included my name. After a nod and salute, the young NCO briskly left. "He will inform your commander that I have taken you away with me on business. Now, we go."

The sun was already setting when we got to Major Andy's big Audi. It snarled to life, and we glided past the gardens planted around a cluster of sunburned buildings. I opened my window and waved to the workers in gray-and-blue coveralls tending the palm trees and planting roses as we drove by. They stood up and saluted back.

"You shouldn't indulge them," Major Andy said sternly, lighting a cigarette. "It distracts them from their work."

The sun was so dimmed by the dust hanging in the air that it looked like the moon in a tiger-striped sky of fuchsia and gold. I kept the window cracked to let out some of Major Andy's smoke. "How long will you keep them working here? It's been, what, eight or nine years since the liberation of Kuwait?"

"They are free to return to Iraq whenever they wish, just as they are free to stay here and work until all the damage their army did is repaired."

"But weren't they your enemies?" I asked, confused. "They have free run of your base."

"Let me ask you this, *Na'qib*. Do you believe that anyone who goes to war is wholly righteous or evil?"

"No, *Ra'id* Andyit, I believe most who go to war just do the best they can to accomplish their missions and take care of the people around them. Afterward, they should be judged by what they did."

"Then, as long as they are believers who do good work and good things, it matters not to me. Here they have mosques and food, barracks and medicine. There is no shame in bringing life to the desert and making it green."

"I didn't expect such an enlightened philosophy."

"More proof of our cultural superiority," said Major Andy with a grin. "It is called *tawbah*—what you might call atonement."

We cleared the base entry control point and headed toward Kuwait City, smoking in silence, watching dusk turn to night. Desert nations don't really come to life until the evening. As a rule, the only people out during the hottest parts of the day are the foreigners, servants, laborers, or others whose duties absolutely require them to work during the light. Generally, there is a siesta-like lull after lunch, and then Kuwaitis return to work to conclude their affairs as early as possible, so they can return home again to get ready for the evening. After the heat breaks, the evening in Kuwait is about seeing and being seen, entertainment, and the real business conducted between friends and family in large groups over food with music, tea, and smoke.

The big Audi purred as we increased our speed under the bright ring-road street lamps. The colorful lights of Kuwait City were to our left, and the ribbon of asphalt we drove on suddenly became as smooth as glass as it bisected the rolling desert.

"Don't you think it's about time, *Ra'id*, to tell me why you abducted me?"

"Maybe I don't understand the word as you do. Perhaps in America abductees ride in the front passenger seat smoking with their captors? I, for one, don't think that would work so well. If I abducted you, I think you would be crowded in the back seat between at least two very unprincipled men, or even better, beat unconscious and in the trunk. That might appeal more to your New York mafia disposition."

"You're really getting too into this."

"My preference would be to have you tied with a mouth gag and, I think . . . yes, a hood over your head."

"Just a normal Friday night for you, *Ra'id* Andyit?"

"I wouldn't use the word 'normal.'"

"I need to be at Marina Mall by 9:00."

"No problem, *Insha'Allah*."

"So where are we really going?"

"I'm taking you to a party. You'll like it."

"*Insha'Allah*?"

"Of course. But I promise you will like it. At the very least, it will move you."

The streets were overflowing with people, and from the moment we left the car, we were swallowed up by the crowd. We were in a park just past Messila Beach walking toward Anjafa, and the roadway along the beach was set up like a festival. There were food stalls under tarps and tables in a long row interspersed with piles of things for sale. The atmosphere was more like a gigantic tailgate than a carnival. Musicians played string solo instruments I didn't recognize on corners, and small groups formed ad hoc bands that accompanied the people singing and chanting in the crowd. Children ran from thing to thing with their faces painted black, green, white, and red like the Kuwait flag.

Major Andy stopped in front of one of the stalls and, a moment later, handed me two skewers of prawns just dipped in tamarind fish sauce, then grilled until they were still juicy and had just the right amount of salt and funk. They had been wrapped up in thin flatbread and handed to him as both package and edible plate. I grabbed napkins and walked beside him as he ate fish kabobs that looked similarly prepared.

"Thank you for dinner. So, what is all of this?"

"Can you not tell?" he said between bites.

"It looks like a small version of Liberation Day, but that's not for a few months."

"Yes. Tonight, we celebrate this most recent defeat of Saddam Hussein and dance because our people remain free and happy."

The prawns and bread were delicious, and I munched while I walked along the boulevard. As we got closer to Anjafa Beach, we passed kids dancing in beautiful, brightly colored traditional clothes and mothers holding babies swaddled in the Kuwait flag. Everyone was laughing and joking and smiling. Green-white-and-red-iced chocolate cakes were passed throughout the crowd on huge platters that you just couldn't say no to. We eventually reached a high spot overlooking the street next to the long paved stretch across from Anjafa Beach, and there was a loud PA screech and feedback wail.

"Turn around, *Na'qib*, and watch. This is what I wanted you to see."

A moment later, there was the crash of cymbals, and the Kuwait national anthem began to play. People throughout the crowd, especially the children, began to sing along. We stood there together for about a minute, and then the anthem faded into a moment of silence. There was an announcement over the loudspeaker, and then a sound like cannon fire, and around the corner raced a dozen sheiks in white robes riding camels. Some of them held scimitars in the air, others huge Kuwait flags as they galloped toward us. When they got to the edge of the park, they slowed and fell into a line formation of pairs and rode proudly past the crowd. They were followed by a color guard that led a platoon of soldiers that marched slowly by. After the soldiers walked the citizens. The announcer said something, and the crowd erupted with applause. As I watched the first groups pass, I started to notice. There were a few young men and women, but the parade was mostly made up of teenagers and tweens. They waved and smiled at the crowd, and the crowd cheered them on. Many of them had scars and burns I could see through the black, red, green, and white paint under the streetlights from where I was standing. Some were missing arms.

There were a few young adults, but they were mostly kids. Kids with braces on their legs and kids walking with prostheses who sometimes leaned on attendants but didn't stop. The crowd cheered louder when they saw their determination.

The rows of children marching by went on and on. The children who couldn't walk rode in expensive convertibles and waved to the applauding crowds.

At one point, Major Andy leaned over to me and said, "This is a parade to remember and to honor the POWs from the invasion of Kuwait and the Persian Gulf War."

I tried to do the math in my head. Most of the kids in front of me had been POWs when they were captured by Saddam's army when they were between four and ten years old. They had been just little kids. Some of them were still little kids.

"It is solemn, but I thought you should see this, because you may not see something like this ever again. They went through many terrible things. They had so much taken from them as children, but we got them back—and look, they can still smile. This is the strength that children have. This is why we must never forget. This is why we must protect them. This is why we must do everything in our power, so this never happens again."

He had tears in his eyes, and I didn't know what to say. I patted his back and squeezed his shoulder. We stood like that for what felt like forever, and I tried hard not to cry but to cheer for them and applaud as row after row of kids smiled and waved as they passed by.

CHAPTER 16

Major Andy dropped me off at the Marina at 2100 hours, and I wound my way through the mall to a café that overlooked a crescent-shaped inlet of piers, where multi-million-dollar boats were docked in strings like jewels on a necklace.

It was a comfortable place to catch up now that the Kuwaitis had returned and the world had moved on from the US battle with Iraq. Conversation shifted from the unrest and massacres that made war almost inevitable in Kosovo, and what NATO would do, to the Y2K bug and whether the world truly would stop next New Year's Day when every computer clicked from "99," for 1999, to "00" and the machines got confused by what the zeros meant. The opinions were passionate and divided.

The café was packed. Men were clustered together, lounging at full tables, trading stories, while Pakistani and Vietnamese waiters performed a complicated rondo of service between the customers and kitchen. Young boys in white vests and headscarves tended a hardwood fire at a barbeque pit near the edge of the broad, covered patio, where they assembled bowls of *shisha* tobacco per each customer's order. The oldest boy stoked the flames and arranged the wood with long metal tongs, picked perfect-sized coals out of the fire, and set them atop the foil he'd wrapped around each clay bowl full of fragrant tobacco. Then, he'd set the prepared

171

bowls on a metal plate, with extra embers on the side, and poke just the right number of holes in the foil so the hookah draw would be perfect. Perfection meant just the right amount of air passing through burning coals, smoldering the optimal mix of tobacco and something sweet and fragrant, then pulling that smoke through water, where alchemy and physics turned the vapor into something cool, nicotine impregnated, and delicious with every inhale. When the oldest boy was finished, he'd hold the platter up, and a small boy would appear, whisk the plate away, and mate the *shisha* bowls to the hookah pipes at tableside. Sometimes, they balanced five platters of *shisha* and embers at once and danced through the crowd like circus performers spinning plates.

The night was hazy, and the lights strung across the marina and around the masts of the docked ships glowed like soft, white globes. The thick, tall concrete roof that provided shade during the day briefly held and concentrated the smoke. Then, night breezes pushed the gray tendrils out through the open space that allowed a perfect seaside view. From the bar area, the men clustered around the flickering coals at each table gave the café a cozy, tribal campfire feel, and the glow from the coals flickered in their eyes. I ordered tea and began to relax. The hard edges of the day continued to soften, and if I squinted, the café on the water became a watercolor painting.

It took a few minutes of people watching, but I finally found him smoking in the crowd.

He was at a table next to a petite woman with big brown eyes that looked out from a sapphire blue burka. Abdullah was dressed differently than earlier. He'd traded in his suit for a more relaxed gray *thoub* robe with a white-and-black-patterned *shemagh* headscarf he secured with a double *ogal* band.

I took the long way, so he'd see me coming.

"*As-salaam alaykum*," I said—*peace be upon you.* It was a more relaxed, general greeting to his party since I knew them.

"*Wa 'alaykum salaam*," replied the girl with pretty eyes. *Upon you be peace.*

"Say all the words. Properly," Abdullah said with a scowl.

I paused to collect my thoughts, walked over to him, held out my arms as to greet my brother, and said softly and clearly, "*As-salaam alaykum, Abdullah. Toz Feek, Shitan. Tel has tee zee, Masaa' al-khayr. Ya ibn ashar'moota,*" which I believed translated roughly to *Peace be upon you, Abdullah. Screw you, Satan. Kiss my ass, and have a good night. You son of a whore.* I don't have a talent for languages, so for me, that was a best effort.

He stood up like he was going to punch my face. Then he grabbed my head and planted a big *ma-smooch*-sounding kiss on both of my cheeks. "Your pronunciation and diction are atrocious, *Na'qib.*"

"Not my job to blend."

"Still, such language."

"What can I say? The army wrote my phrase book."

"That's no excuse for being late."

"Don't give me that crap. Nothing starts on time in the Arab world. What happened to 'don't stand out'?"

"So, you show up wearing a Mets cap? That's just sad. Lucy—you remember Lucy, right?"

"Yeah. Hi, Lucy." Lucy was older than she looked, but she was short and had a gymnast's frame. People tended to treat her like a child and ignore or underestimate her; it was a mistake she used to her advantage. Lu and I had been together, on and off, for a while. She weighed maybe a hundred pounds soaking wet, but she'd grown up in a martial arts family, and if I absolutely had to fight her, I wouldn't with anything short of a shotgun. I only ever beat her in a fight once, and I had to use chocolate.

She was an exotically beautiful mix of ethnic Japanese, Philippine, and Cherokee features, and she was the second-worst joke teller I had ever met in my life. I was always happy to see her again. Now, I was married, and she was with Abdullah. We were good, each happy the other was happy. Not in that bullshit way people always say they are when they still have regrets. We had no unresolved issues. There were no ghosts in our romantic afterlife. Our relationship was still as warm and casual and comfortable as old jeans. I trusted her with my life. She saved my ass in Zagreb when I was there briefly in the late eighties and Yugoslavia was unraveling. I was in the wrong place when police stormed in to suppress a Serb protest. It went big-time wrong, and blood got splashed across a city block. If she asked, I would do anything.

"Lucy, don't we still have that thing? Kufi?" Abdullah asked.

Lu nodded, dug through her bag, and handed me a black crocheted skullcap.

"Put that on."

I sighed and stowed my Mets cap in my bag and stretched the Muslim prayer cap onto my head. "Better?"

"Yes," said Abdullah, slapping my cheeks and then motioning for me to sit. "Now you at least represent a team with some chance of winning." Then he motioned for a waiter and ordered a pot of coffee, an assortment of fruit and sweets, and bowls of a *shisha*-producing smoke that tasted like cigars and crème brûlée.

It was a beautiful night to sit out. We munched on layered filo pastries baked with honey and nuts and ate dates while we chatted and watched the random fireworks shot up by boats out in the bay. I told them about the parade, and they nodded their heads as they listened.

"Don't make that face," Lu said after my story ended. "If you like, I can ring up a few girlfriends to come out with us and keep you company."

"As nice as that would be, I'm heading home soon, and it would make my wife sad."

"Suit yourself. It makes me happy we get you all to ourselves for a couple of days. Who knows when we'll ever get to do this again."

"Me too." I waved to the waiter and ordered another pot of coffee.

"So, *Na'qib*, did you finally get Airport Mohammed to give you your equipment?"

"Yeah, but he still tried to screw me going out the door. He set my guys up with improper papers that would have likely gotten them detained for stealing. Especially after he tipped off the police. What a dick."

"At least he's consistent. What did you do to piss him off?"

"Nothing."

"He's an asshole to everyone, but he had a real hard-on for you. So really, nothing?"

"Thanks for that image," I said, sipping coffee from the fresh pot before deciding to add sugar to it. "When I first got to the Rock, equipment was disappearing at customs. Nothing major, but sometimes they were hard-to-get components we really needed. So, I might have tagged a couple of choice items, and when I found his brother selling them back to one of our bases later . . . it's possible I may have had a talk with him."

"I would love to have been a fly on the wall for that talk," said Lu. "I hope you really busted his balls. He never missed an opportunity to get handsy."

"I don't think anyone ever talked to him the way I did. He was livid, but he did set up a meeting with his brother. After I gave him some date-stamped photos and documents with serial numbers and MAC addresses, he offered to look into the matter. Mohammed called me a few days later to let me know our missing gear had miraculously turned up. A 'clerical error.' And, *Insha'Allah*, I squeezed a friends and family discount out of his brother, so we finally started getting better quality equipment."

"Nice. You're lucky his brother, Faisal, didn't try to kill you. He loves money more than God and women."

"You know him?"

"You can't trade in electronics in Kuwait and not cross paths with him."

"I didn't have enough evidence, and the air force didn't want to make waves with the Kuwaitis, but I had enough of a hold to keep Mohammed, grudgingly, honest. Fortunately, he was sloppy with his bookkeeping, and Faisal didn't want anyone looking into his lucrative contracts with the US."

"So, you bluffed?"

"I just appealed to Faisal's sense of patriotism."

"How so?"

"The usual. What's good for Faisal is good for Kuwait . . . and with Saddam heading south, it would be unfortunate if those contracts were delayed due to a terrible misunderstanding."

"So, blackmail."

"What a vulgar thing for an Arab merchant to say. I had enough evidence to make him sweat, but nothing to make it stick when he lawyered up. But if I made a public allegation, he'd have to answer awkward questions, orders would be canceled, and payments might get delayed. Allegations of corruption are inconvenient when you've got an invader on your border. I simply gave him the opportunity to be a patriot for the cause, at a discount."

"Intimidation and extortion, then."

"If by that you mean how business is conducted in the Middle East every day, then yes, *Insha'Allah*, our negotiations bore fruit and concluded well. The air force saved a few million dollars, and I'm sure he wrote me off as pest control."

Coffee and fireworks led to walking through the night markets, which required Indian street food, which gave us the energy we needed to take a boat out into the Gulf.

The boat was a forty-foot white-and-blue cigarette boat docked a short walk away from the café. We stepped aboard, and Abdullah started the four engines while Lucy and I cast off the lines and pulled up the fenders. It was a still night, and with a rumble, we pulled slowly away from the pier and maneuvered through rows of docks to the narrow channel that led into Kuwait Bay. Usually, the boating season ends in September, and while water traffic never stops, it does taper off. Due to the beautiful winter weather and Saddam's rout, the bay was thick with boats, and going was slow. While Abdullah threaded the needle, Lu and I watched the breathtaking night skyline of Kuwait City as it surrounded us then began to recede.

After a few jinks and hard turns, we left the congestion of party flotillas in the harbor, the moon and stars became more visible, and we could see the twinkling lights of offshore oil rigs in the distance. We passed through several lines of young sheiks racing each other and playing at what looked like jousting in expensive sport-fishing boats. Once we were clear of other shipping, I switched with Abdullah and piloted the boat in the more open water so he could change and take a break. Once he was changed, I'd start calling him John again. It was more familiar, and we were finally far enough away. Lucy wasn't Lu's real name either, but Lucy was the name she was using when I first met her, and I liked how it felt nostalgic.

The center of the boat had a row of three seats at the controls, but there was also an *L*-shaped group of seats aft and a set of seats and loungers built into the bow over the cabin. Lu traded her burka for a turquoise-and-black string bikini and an oversized yellow sweatshirt with the sleeves rolled up. She navigated and kept me company while John trolled for fish. After catching up for a while, I asked, "Why are you mad at John?"

"Why would you ever think that?" she said with a wink and a smile.

"Well, because it's not nice to take other people's stuff," I replied. Her long black hair was pulled back with a couple of clips and secured with my ball cap so it wouldn't whip around. The shirt was also mine.

"Don't worry, we'll definitely make up. Probably soon. Just not yet."

"Hell hath no fury . . . This is why I hate PSYOPS."[10]

Even at lower throttle, the four massive engines hummed, and the long boat sliced through the water at ridiculous speed. The boat controls had a yoke like an aircraft instead of a steering wheel, and I expected the hull to chop and buck on the water, but with a slight adjustment to the trim, piloting the big boat was like driving a Porsche on the autobahn in sixth gear.

After several hours, we dropped anchor in the sandy part of a reef just off the coast of a small island with a lighthouse. Our GPS display put us not far from the Saudi Arabian border. After I killed the engines, the only sounds were John reeling in his line and the soft slap of water against our hull. I confirmed there was no traffic near us, shut down the radar, and turned off most of the lights. After a good stretch, I rotated the seat around to talk to John.

"Catch anything good?"

John locked his rod into a vertical rack, stood, lifted the top of the seat, and said, "Take a look."

---

10   Psychological operations. In the military, they're used to influence or change enemy decisions and morale.

Under the seat was a huge cooler full of recirculating seawater, and swimming in slow circles were a red snapper that barely fit, a couple of bream, and a fish that matched the color of the seawater so well it almost looked transparent.

"Nice. Now how much of this did you really catch trolling?"

"That snapper while you were still going slow, trying to get a feel for the boat, and that clear one bit when we got here and I was taking in my line. I think it's called a *jesh umalhala*. Pretty color, but it's got the wrinkled face of an old man with jowls. It was so ugly, I had to keep it to show you."

"I was just glad you let me drive."

"You should try your hand at fishing tomorrow. Is Lucy still pissed?"

"You know she is. Take a look."

Lu was sitting at the highest point on the boat, straddling the radar arch, her hair flowing behind her in the slight breeze, looking out over the water, still wearing my sweatshirt and Mets cap.

"I don't know what you did, but you should apologize."

"Why do you think this is my fault?"

"Because it is. It doesn't matter to me either way. I just drove a cigarette boat to a desert island reef drenched in moonlight, where a beautiful, half-naked girl is wearing my clothes. I'm not a man with a problem."

"Fair point." John closed the lid on the fish and climbed up to Lucy.

I turned my back to them and looked at the gulf. As my eyes got used to it, the water was glowing all around us. It was bright enough to make out the rocks and sand under the clear water, and I could see a luminescent trail from the back of our boat. When I leaned over the side, I could see swarms of what looked like green fireflies swimming all around us.

John, the spy, was wrapping things up as Abdullah, the merchant, and then he was heading in for debriefing and reassignment. When I first started in military intelligence, he was an occasional voice on the other end of a secure phone that pointed me in the right direction and gave me advice on how things were going in the Soviet Union or how political changes might affect nuclear surety. Every once in a while, he'd call to see what Strategic Air Command was doing about an event or to request reconnaissance. In that early part of my career, I only knew him as Sir. He tried to convince me to stay in air force intelligence when my enlistment was about to end, but I was heading back to Long Island to finish my bachelor's degree because I believed in my heart that if I delayed any more, I would never finish it. He came to my going-away lunch in Omaha, Nebraska, and I was touched when I saw him. No one just winds up in Omaha by accident. Either you go there with a purpose, you live there, or something's gone terribly wrong.

"Hi, Ringo."

"Hi, John. This is a surprise. You should have let me know you were coming."

"Then it wouldn't be a surprise."

It was the second time John and I had met in person. The first time was in Yugoslavia in the late eighties, when we traveled through Sarajevo, Zagreb, and Ljubljana. During the last year of my enlistment, I had a lot of time off I had to use, and I wanted to see Europe. Since we had regular missions flying to bases across Europe, getting there was easy. I started in Greece and worked my way through Turkey, and, after Italy, I wanted to spend some time in Yugoslavia because it was the first time we'd been allowed to visit a Warsaw Pact country, the sites were breathtaking, and the exchange rate was mind-blowingly good. I didn't know John was there. I didn't even know what he looked like.

But I'm curious, and one day I encountered something unusual on a rail siding in Belgrade. I took pictures and notes and debriefed with an OSI colonel when I got to an air force base, because that's what I was required to do. The colonel was extremely patient and distinguished, but he didn't think the activity was significant, so he saw me off with the kind equivalent of a pat on the head and a cookie. But he did submit a report, the activity was significant, and John found me a few days later drinking coffee at a café outside my hotel in Sarajevo.

That was when I met Lucy. I'd like to say it was love at first sight, but even after working together for two days, she hated my guts. John wanted to retrace my steps, and Lucy thought dragging me around was a colossal waste of time. She didn't say a word to me the whole time. Her part of our conversation came through in glares, hisses, and body language that clearly said, "Go now." In fact, the first words she ever said to me were, "Get down. Now."

The day we finished our work together, it was already dark. I said goodbye, John shook my hand, Lucy hissed, and I headed out across the city to my hotel. The atmosphere in Zagreb had been apprehensive all morning. Restaurants and shops were closed in the afternoon, and the streets were almost empty. There had been increasing tension between the Serbs and Croats, but I didn't know things had come to a head until I turned a corner into a plaza and ran into a mob that looked like the scene from a Frankenstein movie, with angry people carrying pitchforks, knives, and old hunting rifles. The only things missing, as they pushed against a police line, were the torches. There was shouting and chanting, and the crowd worked itself into a frenzy. I skirted a raised area of plantings; then I saw someone from the crowd hit a policeman with a bottle, and it was anarchy. The mob surged, the police fired submachine guns into the crowd, and I heard screams, breaking glass, and, "Get down. Now."

I dropped down, and an axe just missed my head. Its handle glanced off my shoulder. I turned to see Lucy break the arm of a large, shaggy man. The axe fell to the ground and clattered against the cobblestones. Lucy spun the man into the crowd, and I picked up the axe.

Lucy finally smiled at me. Then she said, "Prove me wrong," and we worked our way through the chaos of crowd and the police. We avoided the fights we could, but our clothes were torn, and we were both bleeding by the time we crossed the city. Our communication had improved, and Lucy spent the night in my room.

The next day, John collected us with two huge guys he said were George and Paul, and they took us to the train station. Lucy was talking to me, and when my train to Ljubljana prepared to depart, she kissed me. John hugged me and said we'd meet again. A lot happened. John gave me the call sign "Ringo," and my vacation was only halfway done.

The night after I completed my enlistment in the air force, John bought me a steak dinner in the Omaha Old Market, and we got caught up over glasses of whiskey.

John was the kind of guy who could walk into a roomful of strangers, in any city anywhere in the world, and by the time he left, you felt like your best friend was heading off to war. It was hard to say no to him. He was a kind of hacker, but instead of manipulating code, his medium was the needs and aspirations of people. John had a talent for finding and connecting unlikely people and then reprogramming them to be more than they were on their own. He was, for lack of a better word, a spy. He was the first person I ever met who I knew was brilliant. In a different context, he was the perfect entrepreneur and mentor. Spy, for some reason, has a romantic connotation, until you break down the job description. There's an adage that explains it well enough. Soldiers kill for their country; spies betray for their country. The trust they betray the most is that of people who truly believed they were friends. I didn't have the skill or stomach for it. I was better suited as an analyst who occasionally helped with collection.

I saw John off at the airport. Then I drove through the Dakotas until I crossed into Canada to meet Lucy in Winnipeg. After a few days of catching up, our road trip continued through Ontario, where, in a small village somewhere between Sandy Lake and Thunder Bay, the engine in my VW Rabbit caught fire, and we came to a stop in the middle of the town square. After I popped the hood, people came over to point at the flames and say things like, "Look at that. She's burning pretty good." Eventually, someone was nice enough to get a bucket of sand, and after the fire was out, we left with the locals for a nice lunch of grilled doves and Moosehead lager while the car cooled off. After a new set of plug wires, a couple of hours of soldering, and several rolls of electrical-tape first aid, the car started, and we were able to drive it to Montreal for surgery. We were in love. We enjoyed Montreal while my Rabbit recovered; then we spent most of that winter in Quebec City.

I saw John again four years later. It was another surprise. After I finished my first degree, I worked a lot of different jobs. Eventually, I wound up near where my father was living. I was working my last days on a thoroughbred horse farm in Florida before heading to officer training school and back to the air force as an officer when I was asked to shuttle VIPs from various airports to the farm for an event.

John was the last person on my list to pick up. I was holding a card with a different name at the terminal, but then he walked up.

"Hi, Ringo."

"Hi, John," I said after a moment. "What are you doing here?"

"This must be fate," he said. "Let's go."

I turned the card over. "I like John better."

"Me too, but this is the Alex show until the ritual slaughter is complete."

"Copy that. It's nice to meet you, Alex. Have you been to Ocala before? If you're staying a while, I can recommend a few great restaurants and interesting attractions you won't find anywhere else."

The ride to the airport takes several hours from Tampa, so Alex and I got to know each other as we drove out to the farm.

The affair was hosted by my boss, Max. He was a successful lobbyist and businessman with strong ties to many companies, but he had a real passion for thoroughbred horseracing. For a short time, he was the deputy director of the Central Intelligence Agency.

People seemed to be having a good time. It was a wonderful catered event for a select group of business luminaries and former ambassadors. They were assembled, as near as I could tell, to destroy the career of a prominent executive from a major telecommunications company.

There was champagne in crystal flutes and elegant toasts. Gulf shrimp canapés and heaps of caviar on puff pastry filled with onion and egg were walked through the room by mostly blonde waitresses. While some introductions were made, the guests seemed familiar with one another. The ladies wore pretty summer dresses with bright, heavy jewelry. The men wore unbuttoned dress shirts and tailored silk blazers that cost more than I made in a month.

Eventually, a bell rang, and everyone moved to the table. I was seated in the chair farthest from the head of the table, but still at the adult table. Other tables were set up outside of the dining room for staff, and there was a row of chairs with side tables along the back wall for the security details of the guests who brought them.

I was wearing the nicest jacket I could find at Dillard's and having flash-backs to the first time I traveled through Italy, where, as I sat on the train, I'd realized that everyone, from businessmen to farmers, had been more well dressed than I had ever been.

The first course served was flounder with lemon butter and herbs. Before the plates were cleared away, Max raised his glass and lauded the executive's accomplishments. Everyone applauded. After the fish course was finished, but before a brace of game birds was served, the executive was fired. I watched the executive nod along with the toast and smile, then freeze when our host's next words were, "But you are, unfortunately, no longer the right person to lead that or any other division in the company. That is why we're terminating you, effective immediately."

"You're joking," he said. But looking around the room, no one else would make eye contact with him. To make matters worse, many of the other guests at the table were the movers and shakers of other major companies in his field.

Max was the only one in the room who smiled. "No, I'm afraid not. When I hired you, the first thing we discussed was loyalty. You cut a side deal. Good for you, bad for us. You didn't think we'd notice? You should have paid more attention." Then Max looked at me, "Bill?"

"Yes, sir?"

"Sorry to cut your dinner short, but our guest has a flight to catch."

"Yes, sir." I took my place next to the executive to escort him out.

"I'm not going to stand for this," the executive said. Then he actually stood up, which I found ironic. There was a note of hysteria in his voice. "How dare you treat me like this!"

Max just looked at him like he was a monkey in a zoo whose antics no longer amused him. "Do what you want, but if you say another word or don't follow Mr. Riley out immediately, you will find any severance you thought you had gone by the time you land in New York. There's a jet waiting for you. Don't let me ever see you again."

The executive spun around; he looked to the other guests for support; but after a long, uncomfortable moment, he snapped his mouth shut and followed me out to the car.

Conversations started at the table again before we were even out of the dining room. Alex was engaged in an animated discussion with the attractive woman sitting next to him.

I brought the executive through a side gate to where the car was waiting. I opened the door for him, but he stopped short, looked back, and just stood there. After I counted twenty-five Mississippis in my head, he still hadn't moved.

"Sir, we need to go, or we won't make your flight."

He stayed frozen. I figured he was still in shock, so there was no harm in giving him time. The truth was, the jet would wait until we got there.

"Sir, it's time to go now."

He regained some of his composure, turned away, and stepped into the car, and I closed the door with a satisfying thunk.

I didn't know his story, but he did just get his throat cut in public, and I could tell he'd had no idea it was coming. It was more than a career slaughter; it was a public shaming. I'd never seen anything like that before. I'd ask Alex if he could tell me more when I got back to the farm later. I did know that since I'd picked him up that morning, Mr. Former Executive had been rude to everyone who worked at the farm. His gold watch cost more than all the cars I'd ever owned combined, and people like him never starve.

He made a few angry calls. Then, the poor bastard cried the rest of the way to the airport.

My boss was nothing if not a man of action. He was tough, smart, and direct. I learned a lot in the short time I did odd jobs for him. He tried to talk me out of going back into the air force. "You're never gonna make any money in public service. You've got other options. Let me help."

"I know, Max. Thank you. I really mean it. I can't explain it, but this is something I just have to do. If you really want to help me, please, support me on this."

Max must have told me a hundred times how foolish I was, but he sent a strong recommendation in support of my commission to the air force.

Max had a reputation for being complicated and difficult to work for, but I never saw that. There was just one rule you had to follow. Your word was your bond. Either you did what you said you would do, no matter what the cost, or the earth you lived on got scorched.

I heard Lu call me. She'd set up a table between where the seats built into the bow formed a *V*-shaped sofa. She was all smiles, and her hair was in a braid. "So, you won. Did you put my stuff back where you found it?"

She just hummed as she set out tumblers and dropped a few ice cubes into each glass. John cracked the seal on a bottle of Little Boy Blue—Johnnie Walker Blue Label—with a flourish and filled the three glasses with amber gold.

"*Naz'dro'vyeh*, to the president, *ee Za Milyh Dam*," I said, raising my glass, in rough pidgin Russian. *Thanks for the drink, to the president, and,* motioning to Lucy, *to pretty girls.*

"*Naz'dro'vyeh*, to the president, *ee Za Milyh Dam*," they repeated, then we clinked glasses and drank.

"So, how's business?" I asked. "You said it was growing fast. Are you finally out?"

"Yeah. It grew too fast. I'm more of a startup guy, but there was just so much money to be made. We just had to ride the wave," John said as he freshened our glasses. "Quality electronics are hard to get in Iraq, and Iran has a lot of influence in Basra, so there's a lucrative black market as long as you show your support for the local officials and enforcers with dinars."

John sipped his whiskey, and Lu continued. "With the buildup in Kuwait, the price of our inventory skyrocketed. Some components even had bidding wars, and the profit was ridiculous. We paid back our investors after our first three months of business, and my workforce in Kuwait and Iraq grew so much there was actually pressure to keep me here. The local news ran articles about the success of our business in Iraq, and we won a best new business award in Kuwait. Can you believe it?"

"But this was the right time to sell," John added. "I started the two companies with just under five million Kuwait dinars, and, even taking some losses on the Iraq side, we cleared just over thirty million in sales."

"Not bad for a part-time CEO. Congratulations," I said, finishing my drink.

"Needless to say, the shareholders are happy. It's a nice chunk of seed money for other ventures, and I'm ready for a change," John said, swirling his drink in his glass. "It's nice to finally be able to take a break."

Conversation and whiskey flowed and combined. I made it through "cheers," "prost," and "*salut*."

By the time we got to "*kanpai*," I was done.

I woke up midmorning in the chill air on a deck lounger with a thick wool blanket wrapped around me. It was overcast. I hadn't slept long, but it was a deep sleep, and I felt refreshed. I still remembered a fragment of dream in which I was flying through bad weather.

Then I felt it again. Turbulence—that's what it felt like. Like an aircraft flying through turbulence, but there was no engine drone, just pitching and rocking like flying through a storm.

That's when I realized I was awake, and my friend Johnnie Walker was gone.

The turbulence I was experiencing was my friends John and Lucy rocking the boat from their cabin. Epicenter right below me, two meters down. *I guess John is really forgiven.*

I focused my eyes. There was a light mist slowly burning off the dull azure water. We were moored just offshore from a small island that looked like a green, grassy hill surrounded by a circle of yellow beach with a few buildings and a lighthouse on a metal tower. It couldn't have been much more than a mile wide.

I banged on the roof of the cabin and shouted, "Stop, we're capsizing." After a pause, and childish laughter, the turbulence continued, more vigorously. For at least another minute, anyway.

I stretched, stood up, and walked aft. The fish John caught were still circling in the saltwater cooler, although one of the bream was missing. I hooked the red snapper and gutted and scaled it over the stern. Then I scored and filleted it. After rooting around in the galley, I put most of the fish in the fridge and took the seasonings and lemon I found, along with plates, out to the small gas hibachi mounted at the back of the boat. At far as breakfasts go, you can do a lot worse than fresh-grilled fish on calm water.

When "While My Guitar Gently Weeps" started playing, I knew John was up. His love of the Beatles bordered on fanaticism. He came out on deck just as I finished smoking the fish with tea and was setting the fillets on the grill.

"She's going to be pissed," he said, looking at the cutting board.

"I know, but she'll forgive me."

"How come she always forgives you?"

"I know what she likes to eat."

Lucy came out a few minutes later, wearing a bathrobe that looked like a white *yukata* covered in cherry blossoms. "Where did you get that knife?" She almost dropped the coffee cups she was carrying but just managed to make it to the table. "That's my favorite knife."

"You know I got it from your sheath, in the harness you keep by the entrance to the cabin."

"You shouldn't just take people's stuff without asking."

"That's the pot calling the kettle black."

"Now it's ruined, and it's always going to smell like fish."

"No. It's not," I said, checking the red snapper and turning it over.

"You are so dead."

I pulled the knife off the cutting board, rinsed the blade in the gulf, then sprinkled it with salt and used half a lemon to scrub the blade down. "It's not my fault that all the kitchen knives on this boat are just for show. None of them even have a good edge." After I finished with the lemon, I rinsed the blade in seawater again, dried it, then rubbed it down with a little peanut oil until it glimmered again. "Here."

She took the knife, turned it, examined every inch of it, and finally brought it to her nose.

"See, I told you. No fish smell," I said as I started assembling plates of fish, dried fruit, and warmed-through flatbread John had brought up.

"I can still smell the fish," she said under her breath.

"No, you can't. I'll trade you for that cup of coffee," I said, holding out a plate.

It was like a prisoner exchange. She sniffed at the blade of the knife again, then grudgingly handed me the coffee and snatched away the plate.

190

And we all sat down to eat.

"So good," said Lu, between big mouthfuls.

"I have plenty more if you're hungry," I said, refilling my coffee.

"So good. OK," Lucy said, reaching for another piece of snapper. "I forgive you, just this once, but no more touching my knives."

I smiled and looked at John, who managed to shake his head, roll his eyes, and scowl all at the same time. "OK, but thank John. The fish is so beautiful. If I'd found rice first, breakfast would have been sashimi over rice."

"Thank you, John. Can we have *chirashi* sushi for dinner?"

"Do we have rice?"

"Yes, and shoyu and rice vinegar and horseradish, but no wasabi."

"Will you sharpen a knife for me?"

"Yes."

"I don't see why not."

"Yay."

That was the rhythm of our next two days. We spent the moments together like they were our last. The island was called Umm Al Maradim, the mother of boulders. Terns nested there. There were differences, but each tern looked like a small gray-and-white seagull with a black face, wearing a black crown of feathers that looked like a comb-over.

The water was a brisk seventy degrees, but it was warm enough to walk barefoot in the sand and splash in the waves. A few times, sea turtles swam so close to the boat I could reach in the water and touch their slippery shells as they passed by. While we fished, Lu worked on her tan.

After another night spent catching up, followed by a late lunch, it was time to head back. John took us on a slow lap around the island, then killed the motors when we were a short distance away on the far side. We looked at the island's green grass and the mottled reef surrounding it.

A few people walked around near the lighthouse, and there was a huge green turtle on the beach just above the breakwater.

"I'll never forget these last few days." I said.

"Me either," said Lu.

"I thought this would be private enough to relax a bit," John said. "But the other reason I wanted you to see Umm Al Maradim is because this little island was the very first territory in Kuwait we liberated from Saddam after the invasion."

We followed the coast back north to Kuwait City. Most of the shipping traffic we passed was container ships and supertankers bigger than our "mother of boulders" hideaway. Along the way, we passed open stretches of desert dunes where sand poured into the green gulf. The port of Mina Saud, with its oil terminal, spread out like a gas station for titans, with fat smokestacks and massive power plants that looked like the cityscape of an alien world. Then refineries rose up like cities of pipe and hose with cylinders like rockets wrapped in scaffolding. When we reached beaches studded with date palms, we could see Kuwait City in the distance.

John and I played chess and talked in the shade in the *L*-shaped seats on the stern while Lucy piloted us in. We were playing lightning chess, where each player only had ten seconds to make a move and hit a timer to start his opponent's clock. If you ran out of time, you lost your move that turn. With taunts, it was like a combination of chess and dominoes.

During the trip, mostly while we were fishing, we'd talked about parenting, the changes to expect, the good and bad parts, and my fears and concerns. John and Lu were happy Jo and I were having a baby. While we played, John offered a few last bits of advice, probably because he knew it would distract me.

"It's going to get harder for you when he's older. He won't understand where you came from, so don't even try to explain how good he's got it, because if you do your job raising him, he won't even be able to comprehend the world you grew up in. Hell, he won't understand what you do now. Your world isn't his world. His world is a safe and secure island, with happy meals, clean water he won't want to drink, good schools, and few natural predators. How do you explain hungry if he's never been?"

By the time he finished his thought, we'd traded six moves. "It's a perception versus reality problem, isn't it? So, how do I pass on the lessons I want him to learn in a way he gets?"

"That's the better question, isn't it? You picked up some tricks surviving the world. Life threw a lot at you, and you turned out OK. Your boy will learn how the world works by watching you. How you solve problems will be how he solves problems, at least at first. How you talk to people, handle adversity, show that you care, all your good and bad—he'll model what you do. By the time kids can make conversation, they already have you figured out anyway. When they're finally old enough to need your advice, they'll gladly take it, from anyone who isn't you."

We traded another five moves, and John was starting to push past my line on the chessboard. He had taken more pieces, but I was still OK. We were still building up our strength and getting into position. "So, you're saying he's going to see through me from day one and act like I do until he decides he knows better?"

"Exactly. Children are amazing. Sometimes, I think kids teach us more than we teach them. Just look at infants. Why do they fall down over and over? The answer is because they want to walk. Give your kid the confidence to try and fail at a million little things and the resilience to keep picking himself up, and he'll learn how to not fail at what's important."

"It's a little overwhelming." We were just past the middle of the game, and I slapped down my bishop to exploit an opening. "Check. How will I know if I'm getting it right?"

"That was weak. Never threaten a king. Kill him, or die," John said, taking my bishop and slapping the timer. "Honestly, if you just do the best you can and learn from your mistakes, you'll be fine. Kids are tougher than we think."

"Any other advice?"

"Yeah, don't fuck this up."

"That one I worked out myself."

In a straight game of chess, John was virtually unbeatable. In our lightning game, cheating wasn't only allowed, it was encouraged if you didn't get caught or if your opponent didn't call you on it. It was John's rule, and the reason was simple: life isn't fair. Cheats could be as simple as distraction and moving a board piece or as elaborate and obvious as my plan.

John could palm pieces, so if I glanced away for an instant or didn't focus on his moves, pieces disappeared from both sides and reappeared in tragic places for me. If I focused too much on his cheats, it ate away my time for strategy and moves.

When confronted by a superior adversary, you can't attack him where he's strong. You have to hit him hard where he's weak, or you'll always lose.

I tapped John's hand, and he returned the rook he stole to the board, but he still made his move in time. Then I made my move and hit the clock.

John picked up his knight, and Lucy changed the music from the Beatles to Paula Abdul, and John almost missed his move. Lu and I had a deal, and changing the conditions of the battlefield can change the momentum of a battle. I made another move, called, "Check," and hit the clock. Then Lucy stood up and began to dance as she steered. John's movements slowed, but he was still able to block my advance and even drop an extra piece on the board in a bad place for me. Two other ways to beat a superior foe are to achieve overwhelming mass and surprise. Mass was Lu and I ganging up on him.

Lucy did a finale of gyrations when the song "Straight Up" played, moving her arms over her body and sliding her bikini around, but I fell into my own trap, and we both missed a move as we watched. But I knew what came next, and John didn't. When Lucy pulled off her top, turned around at the end of the song, and blew a kiss to John, the element of surprise was achieved. He knocked half his pieces off the board, and I smacked my queen down for checkmate. It was a beautiful execution. Defeat was acknowledged, and Lu and I smacked hands in double high fives while John retied her top. It was the first time I ever won a chess game against John, and he acknowledged it as the best cheat seen to date. The cost of Lucy's collusion was I had to cook a final meal for us to eat together before we returned to Kuwait City.

The trip back took as long as *White Album*, *Abbey Road*, *Revolver*, and *Yellow Submarine*. There was a short reprieve after Lucy put her foot down and played songs from Tone Loc and my new favorite, Paula Abdul, but it didn't last. We docked at a pier where the boat could be refueled just as the song "A Day in the Life" from the *Sgt. Pepper's Lonely Hearts Club Band* album ended.

Lu and I waited in the cabin while a dock crew tended to the boat. I watched out the window while Lucy changed back into more conservative afternoon wear for Kuwait. John, now Abdullah, was in his robes, directing traffic as we took on fuel, supplies, and water. There was even a crew that cleaned the windows and sprayed off the salt accumulations on and around the hull.

Once the crews were gone, I slid open the door, but before I could step out of the cabin, Lu wrapped her arms around me and held me back.

"I know you're scared," she said in a gentle voice, "but you don't have to be. There was a time when I wondered if there was a future for us with a house and a baby, but it just wasn't in our cards, but I'm so happy for you. That's why I can say this, because I know you, and I thought this through—you'll be a great dad."

I turned around, and she kissed me. She was a little teary eyed.

I smiled, but she was pissed off. "When a pretty girl kisses you, you kiss her back."

"Yes, you're right," I said as I tilted up her chin and kissed her good-bye. It was sweet but brief. One Mississippi, plus a few heartbeats.

"I'm glad we caught this break. Next time you're in the States, I want you to meet Jodi and hold the baby."

"I would like that very much," Lu said.

"Watch your back, and take care."

"Me? You're the one who always needs watching over. You're lucky I'll always be your guardian angel."

"You know, by default, that makes you a stalker."

"A cute, well-armed, highly trained stalker with a benefits package."

"Awkward," said Abdullah, walking over with a clipboard full of papers. "Amusing as it is to see you two behave like children, before you get to the 'I know you are but what am I' phase of this debate, we've pushed our little vacation to the wire, and now we need to go. We probably won't meet again for a while, but as soon as I can, I'll see you around."

We said our last round of goodbyes, and they set off.

Lu blew me a kiss, and I waved. It was surreal. There was a rumble, a few boats passed by, and they were gone. If I couldn't still taste Lucy's ChapStick, it would have been like they were never there.

CHAPTER 17

January 1999—Ali Al Salem AB, Kuwait

"Captain Riley, have a seat." My boss's office smelled like fresh coffee. It was more crowded than usual because he was getting things organized for his replacement and sorting through what to ship home. "Coffee?"

"Thank you, sir."

"Cookie?"

"No thanks."

"I'll get to the point," he said, sitting down in the chair next to me. "I've been asked to see if you'll extend in Kuwait to act as liaison between the other services and Kuwaitis."

"I don't understand; my replacement is already here."

"This position will entail more than communications, and because of the additional requirements and duties, both the air force and army would like this to be a new position."

"What are the additional requirements and duties?" I said, sipping at my coffee.

"Formally creating a base support plan for the Rock, deconflicting what we can offer and what will be required by the other services to stage forces here, taking the JOC to the next level in terms of levels of security. Liaison with Kuwait and the surrounding sovereign nations. It's a joint job, and you'll work for the army."

"Hmm. The coffee's good. It sounds like a great opportunity for a logistics officer who's already a major or a lieutenant colonel. Especially with the sensitivities to rank some of our Arab coalition brothers have where everyone's a prince. The air force should be able to shake that tree easy enough. Joint political jobs are good for promotions; majors will kill each other for it."

"You were requested by name."

"May I ask by whom?'

"Two Kuwaiti base commanders, the embassy, oh, and a certain army one-star at Doha."

"Isn't he the one who keeps us in chicken kiev and halal MREs?"

"That's the one."

"I hate that guy. Permission to speak freely, sir?"

"Of course."

"My wife is having our first baby in two weeks, my tour is over, my replacement is here, and the biggest operation we're likely to see in Kuwait for the next few years has already happened. What they want to do can be handled with regular troop rotations over the next twenty-four months. Now, having said that, I do believe consolidating the air and ground ranges around the Rock makes a lot of sense, and if we think of build up and bed down using a scaled-down South Korea model, this could be an ideal jumping-off point for interesting surge missions."

"So, is that a yes?"

"Respectfully, sir, that's a no. It's important work, but not urgent, and there are probably a hundred other guys more suited to logistics planning than me."

"If you stay at least six months more, the army is willing to consider rolling your accomplishments here in with the liaison work and submitting you for a combat decoration."

"Like I care about stuff like that."

"You cared enough to make a big deal out of it for Airman Conner."

I sighed. "I've already been recognized as the best at a lot of things by the air force; dangling a shiny medal doesn't do it for me. I'm good. Recognize my officers and NCO instead."

I wasn't altruistic. I liked praise and acknowledgment and advancements as much as anyone else. I really liked being considered "among the best" at what I did, but I was only as good as my team, and after testing myself and seeing what I could do, those recognitions simply didn't motivate me anymore. Earning the right and authority to have access and control and solving big, complicated problems was what gave me a rush. And my next big, complicated issue was right in front of me—seeing my son born. Me becoming a dad. God help us all.

"I didn't think you would go for it," my boss said, taking a bite of the cookie on his plate and grimacing. "But the general specifically told me to mention it. He seemed to think it would set the hook. So, now that I have delivered his message, what will you do?"

"As I see it, this is just the army posturing, because even though they're responsible for this part of the world, they didn't get to play this time, and the air force and navy got all the headlines. So, now they're going to show that they can take charge and that they're important."

"That's a good assessment, but it's not an answer."

"I get what they want, but what do they really need right now?"

"There's a planning session for the base starting tomorrow. You'll be attending it as the Rock's representative with two lieutenants to support you. I'm sure you can figure it out if you start there."

"Copy that, sir, but my answer is still no. There's no imminent threat, and my skills aren't ideal for what they say they want to do. Unless there's something I'm missing, my mission's over. We won. It's a great job for someone else, and my best choice is to head home and see my first child born. If the air force extends me and orders me to take this position, I'll salute sharply, and I will do my best, but I'm no volunteer."

"I'll pass your decision up the chain. Keep in mind, this may turn into a 'beatings will stop once your morale improves' situation. For my part, I respect your decision and agree that there's no urgency to keep you here and that we have professionals whose job it is to plan things like this. Just understand, the air force may still order your extension and transfer to army command."

"Understood, sir."

"Dismissed."

Assembling at 0400 hours is almost always cold, dark, and short of coffee. My lieutenants were chipper, which pissed me off, but they were talented and enthusiastic and knew where we were going. We ran through our plan of attack on the ride over to the army headquarters compound, where the planning conference was taking place.

The army hosted all the other services. We three represented the air force. All the other services came out in force, and their team leads were all lieutenant colonels. We had territory and capabilities they wanted, but the discussions were mostly collegial. A few hungry alphas came out swinging, wanting to dictate terms and take everything we had with nothing in return, but they weren't as hard to negotiate with as the Kuwaitis. We went a couple of rounds of, "I am sorry, sir, but your list of wants exceeds my authority in this matter. Let's work on satisfying what we absolutely need from each other, then I'll get you on our general's schedule, and perhaps you can work out the rest."

There were no takers for the meet with the general, but after that, we met as small groups of horse traders in meetings that usually ended with, "OK, if you can give me this, I can guarantee you that." After the first day was done, we debriefed with the army leadership and handed in our write-ups. Then, during the evening, they would print off new drafts for the attendees, and we'd return to horse trading until all the questions were answered and every blank in the agreement template was filled in. After dinner, I met with our host and asked the obvious questions: "If we're in Kuwait, and we rely heavily on Kuwaiti infrastructure, why were there no Kuwaitis? If we're cobased with UK forces, why aren't they playing?"

The colonel in charge of the conference ran his hand over his jaw, looked at me, and replied, "Good points. See what you can do."

Those were my nights. After dinner, I'd send my lieutenants off with light homework and orders to make new best friends, figure out what everyone attending really did, and then get a good night's sleep. Once it was quiet again, I'd coordinate with the Kuwaitis and Brits and try to hunt down decision makers in the Beltway, where it was still daylight before they left for lunch. It was more than forty-eight straight hours of work, but the colonel detailed six soldiers to me so we could complete our night coordination and so they could finally meet their Kuwaiti counterparts. We finished our base support plan, host agreements, UK basing and support agreement, and some sensitive negotiations with the State Department and DIA. In just two long days, we covered a lot of ground, and I was exhausted by the time all the hand shaking was done.

Flight Lieutenant Jason Roberts and I were smoking cigars in the shade of a courtyard full of palm trees. Jason was my opposite number on the UK side of the base. He was tall and had bright blue eyes and a wind-burned face. He was an impressive engineer.

"You looked knackered, mate."

"Is that the queen's for 'like shit'?"

"A fair approximation."

"Thanks for your help with the conference. Sorry it was last minute, but you really came through," I said. "It looks like the air force intends to keep me here another six months working for the Army."

"You worry too much, mate. Your army looks at the world as the army and the Coalition, not like we're one coalition. My wing commander was just glad you called. It was nice to have a chance to help build the future together. Isn't your missus ready to give you your first?"

"Not my army," I said. "I'm happy to help, but we separated from them in 1947 for reasons that don't seem to have changed." I enjoyed the cigar. Jason came by the best Cubans. "Yes, she should deliver in about one more week, depending on when the baby decides it's time."

"Congrats on that. It's a boy, right? Good on you, mate. Sorry your army's stirring things up after the fight. Now that everything's over, they lost the plot, and they're falling all over themselves to make a show."

"Thanks, Jason. It's not a done deal yet, but she's been going through all this without me and I feel like I'm letting her down." I stopped to relight my cigar. "It hasn't been easy; she's had a rough go of it."

"At least you were there for the conception."

"Yeah," I said, smiling. "There is that."

It was late after I got back. I showered and returned to the tactical morgue that was going to be my home away from home a while longer. My tent mates had already rotated back home, and the lieutenants that bunked with us during the surge were long gone. It was a rare luxury to have private space on a deployment, but as soon as my orders came through, I'd have to move to an army headquarters billet—a room of my own and a shared bathroom with indoor plumbing. That was moving on up, I supposed. It's not like I slept much anyway.

I took a moment to organize my things before I went to bed. I read for a little while to relax, but I felt strange not having an office to go back to or a team to lead. I could stop in, but I'd already handed my duties off, and their new commander was in charge. In advance of rotating back home, I had already shipped out all my nonessential gear. What had become a comfortable space was again back to basics. A pillow and issue sleeping bag, a cinder-block end table holding up a bottle of water, a stack of tattered hand-me-down books, a flashlight, and a metal-framed picture of my wife, in her flight suit, smiling. Under my cot was a bag of the MOPP gear designed to protect me from chemical, biological, or nuclear environments, a bag of issue equipment, my weapon, and a knife Lu had given me. I had a backpack prepped in case I had to bug out and an empty bag big enough to fit everything else not already packed away. My world was reduced to the twelve-foot-by-twelve-foot bay of a four-bay expandable structure, with a center space my former tent mates had filled with salvaged chairs, a cable-reel table, and two threadbare sofas with missing feet.

When it was quiet, I always wondered what Jodi was doing. Jo was the worst storyteller I ever met in my life. Listening to her tell a joke or describe events was as fascinating as it was uncomfortable. Watching her enthusiasm while she told stories was like watching a B-movie version of a ten-car Hollywood pileup full of buckets of blood, orphans, explosions, misplaced sound effects, and poorly cast bystanders shedding fake tears. It was so awful, I could never look away. It was annoying, but somehow it was also endearing.

We hadn't been able to talk for a week. The last time I'd been able to get a call through, she wasn't feeling well, and we'd argued. Then she told me she had to go to the obstetrician for more tests because there were complications, and I still didn't know what that meant. In the dark, I felt uncertainty and regret. Things were going to get harder for her, and there was nothing I could do about it. I was frustrated. I always believed I could figure anything out, and for a while I had a pretty good run. Maybe there really *is* no rest for the wicked.

All I could do was confirm once and for all if I was staying or not, then figure out my next steps. But it didn't make me feel better. Maybe the best thing to do was to sleep on it. I missed Jodi. The only upside was it was the first night since I returned from my three-day pass that I could sleep for as long as I wanted.

I woke up, and I didn't know why. It was pitch dark. I was still groggy, and people were talking just outside my door. I thought maybe a new arrival had come, and I was about to get a roommate. Then, someone held open the door, and a six-person team entered swinging their flashlights back and forth in the dark, searching for something. I had my hand on my sidearm. It took me a moment to realize what was happening. When I saw the silhouette of our first sergeant in the door, I understood something was wrong. I snapped my weapon to safe and slid it back to the holster under my cot. Then I sat up and called out, "Shirt, I'm over here."

He came over to me. "Captain Riley. Good. You're awake. It's your wife."

"Is she all right?"

"Yes, and the baby's fine, but there were problems, and she's not out of the woods yet. Her doctor wants you there. The Red Cross sent a request to get you home, and the commander just approved it."

"They're sending me home?"

"Yes, your boss was persuasive. How long do you need to clear out?"

"Now. I'm ready now."

I pointed to my stuff, grabbed my backpack, and retrieved my weapon, and in the time it took me to slide my wife's picture into my bag and zip it up, my guys had completely packed me out. By the time I got to the door, they already had my bags stowed in the Humvee.

I was taken to the Kuwaiti headquarters building. In a brightly lit room, Major Andy was sitting at a table flanked by two of his flight sergeants, standing at parade rest.

"You are having a daughter, I suppose?" he said with a sneer.

"No, a son."

"Finally, in the end, *Na'qib*, you show some promise." Then he pointed to the NCO on his right, and a stack of papers was set in front of me. "Sign where he points. We will conclude our business, and you may go."

After all the papers were signed, the other NCO collected and reviewed them and began to stamp them.

"Where is your security badge?"

"Here," I said, holding it up for inspection.

"This you may keep to remember your time with us."

"Thank you," I said, putting it back around my neck.

"That will be five KD," he said, referring to Kuwaiti dinars.

"You're charging me?"

"It's a bargain price for a memory."

I sighed. Even on the way out, there was always business. "Here you go," I said, putting a five-KD note on the table. Major Andy smiled as the NCO to his left took it and wrote out a receipt that he added to an envelope full of papers I'd have to take to customs.

Then Major Andy stood, came over to the other side of the table, put his hand on my shoulder, and said softly in my ear, "Learn well from what you've seen here. If you disappoint me, *Na'qib*, I will find you and have you beaten."

"I'll miss you, too, *Ra'id* Andyit." We clasped hands. "Thank you for everything."

Then the first sergeant handed me airline tickets, but when I looked at the departure time and the clock on the wall, I realized, "There's no way I can make this flight in time."

"If you miss it, the tickets transfer, and they'll get you on the next flight out of Kuwait," the first sergeant said. "The thing is to get you there so you can get out as soon as possible."

I was disappointed, but he was right. When I got to the door, I turned back one last time and rendered a salute to Major Andy. He and his NCOs returned the salute, and I felt like my work was finally done. As I walked out the door, I heard him say, "Do not be glum, *Na'qib*. Allah may yet grant you a reward."

We raced through the desert, my Humvee sandwiched between two military tow trucks with flashing lights that seemed to move cars out of our way. The first shirt was sitting next to me. He'd been fiddling with something since we got in, but I was caught up in my thoughts and didn't notice what it was until he handed it to me. "Talk to your wife," he said over the whine of the Humvee transmission. "I don't know how long the call will last."

I took a large satellite phone from his hand, and when I put it to my ear, the long antenna bent back against the vehicle's canvas roof. "Hello, Jo?" I said and heard my voice echo softer and softer until she replied.

"I'm OK, and the baby's OK." And I listened to the soft echo as the signal was delayed and repeated with every satellite jump.

"I'm coming home." Pause, two, three.

"I know; your first sergeant gave me your flight info. The baby's coming early." Wait, two, three.

"Are you really OK?" Pause, two, three.

"Yes. Just get here safe. I hate to say it, but I'm going to need some help with this." Wait, two, three.

"I'll be there soon." Pause, two, three.

"That makes me happy. I—"

And the signal was gone. I handed the phone back. "The call dropped, but we were able to talk. Thank you."

"Just doing my job."

"It meant a lot."

Our convoy screeched to a halt at the curb in front of British Airways / Lufthansa departures, and they downloaded my gear to a cart and assembled to say goodbye.

"Good luck, sir. It was an honor. Get home safe."

"I couldn't have asked for a better crew; you are the best. It was a privilege to serve with you." We exchanged salutes, and I entered the airport.

The clock over the British Airways desk showed my flight had departed almost an hour earlier. For international flights in the region, you usually had to check in at least three hours early to clear customs and security or you'd miss your flight. I'd have to take a Lufthansa flight to Heathrow and transfer to British Airways for the flight back home. There was no line, but a representative was waiting at the check-in desk. When I approached, the Scandinavian blonde attendant smiled and said, "Good evening, Captain Riley. We've been expecting you."

"You have?" I asked as I set my papers on the counter.

"Yes," she said as she printed off labels. "Just the three bags and your rucksack?"

I nodded.

"Very good."

I felt a hand on my shoulder, and I turned. Mustafa Bin had walked up behind me. He made a dismissive waving gesture, and two of his guys stepped forward and wheeled my bags away. Then he stepped behind the counter.

"Hello, my friend. I didn't expect to see you again," I said. His handlebar moustache was heavily waxed and spread out wider than I had ever seen it. He glanced at the monitor and then picked up my tickets and, with a smile almost as wide as his moustache, tore my tickets in half. Then in half again.

"What are you doing?" I asked in a hard voice. "I don't understand." I could have understood it if it had been Airport Mohammed, but with Mustafa Bin, it didn't make any sense. For the first time since I came to Kuwait, I felt a surge of panic.

"Perhaps you didn't understand me, then, when I said this was my airport?"

"I understand, but I'm confused."

"Those tickets were no good. *Ra'id* Andyit informs me you are having a son."

"Yes, but I've missed my flight."

"Do not worry. *Insha'Allah.* You'll be home as soon as possible." He looked up at the attendant, and she put new tickets in his hand. "A son as a first child is a blessing. For that, I believe we have an upgrade to business class for you. If you were Kuwaiti, then the upgrade would be first class."

He stepped over to my side of the desk, and we exchanged tickets for customs form.

"Thank you, Mustafa." I looked down at the first ticket, but except for the seat number and my name, nothing else was printed. "The dates and gate are blank."

He laughed. "Of course. That is because we held the flight for you. Was I really not clear? This is my airport."

I hugged him on the spot. He stiffened up, then patted my back, put his hands on my shoulders, and said, "This may be the last time I see you again, my friend. Remember Kuwait well."

He walked me through the airport, and we took a car to the front of a ramp stair that was attached to a jet parked alone on the tarmac. As I climbed the steps, people pressed their faces against the windows to see what was going on. When I got to the top, I waved at Mustafa Bin. He lifted one of his hands in acknowledgment, and his car drove off.

An attendant met me and guided me to the only open seat on the airplane, and the other passengers murmured as I passed by. It seemed they were expecting someone famous, or important, or taller.

They were visibly disappointed, but the big jet spooled up its engines, and we took off.

I watched the golden lights of Kuwait recede. After we leveled off, there were cheers when the pilot announced they were opening the bar. I read the paper for the first time in nearly six months. Gas prices were back down to ninety-eight cents in the States, due in great part to our recent efforts. A conscientious flight attendant poured a generous whiskey for me, and I started to relax. There was a lot to think about. Thanks to the effort of a lot of people, I was heading home.

I lived in a different, bigger world than I once had. I saw firsthand what Saddam Hussein did to Kuwait by traveling it from end to end, and I touched the scars he left behind. I also spent time with survivors of the invasion who were building a good life for themselves and a better Kuwait. There was something to be said for building relationships one cup of tea at a time, and I saw a different Kuwait leaving than I did when I first arrived.

The thought of raising a child still terrified me. I'd learned a lot about what not to do growing up, but I'd also learned valuable things from those harsh lessons. I wasn't a scared little boy anymore, and I wasn't alone. I had a wonderful wife and amazing friends. If they thought I would make a good dad, maybe I really would. I would see Jo soon. I had new friends and enemies, and I'd seen and done so many things that I couldn't wait to tell her. With a baby in the house, our life was about to change. It was really happening, and I couldn't wait.

I was going to be a father.

PART III: TO BE A MAN

The wanton Boy that kills the Fly
Shall feel the Spiders enmity . . .
A Truth thats told with bad intent
Beats all the Lies you can invent
It is right it should be so
Man was made for Joy & Woe
And when this we rightly know
Thro the World we safely go
Joy & Woe are woven fine
A Clothing for the soul divine.

—William Blake, "Auguries of Innocence"[11]

---

11   Blake, "Auguries of Innocence," lines 33–34, 53–60.

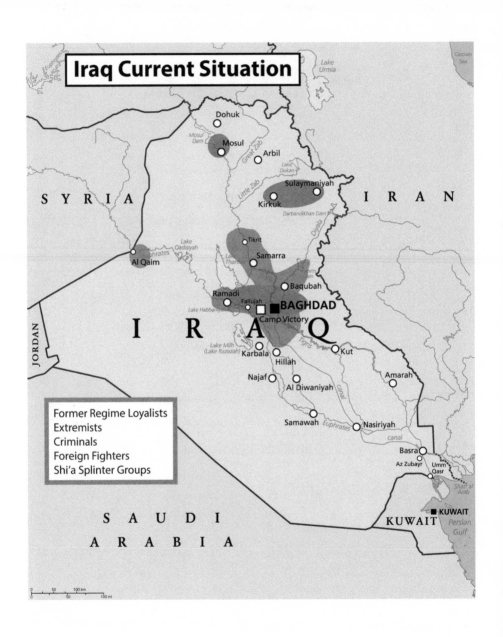

Iraq Current Situation

Former Regime Loyalists
Extremists
Criminals
Foreign Fighters
Shi'a Splinter Groups

CHAPTER 18

I remember every detail of the day he was born.

I raced back from Kuwait to Norman, Oklahoma. If it weren't for the efforts of the leaders at the Rock and the kindness of Major Andy and Mustafa Bin, I would have never made it in time.

Flying halfway around the world gave me time to think, and I was nervous. I didn't know if I could love this long-awaited stranger. I just didn't know.

I didn't want to hurt him. I didn't think I would, but I really didn't know. I'd read a lot of books about raising kids and about being a father. What I got out of it was kids are resilient, but there were a few fundamental things I'd have to get right.

I didn't want to be my father.

I wanted to be what my father *wanted* to be but couldn't be when I was a boy.

I wanted to help my son grow up to be smart, with the right tools for a good life. I knew wanting it wasn't enough. But I sincerely wanted it. I thought that might mean something. I could feel that want twist in my stomach and beat in my heart. That had to at least be a good start. I didn't have great examples to draw from, and I knew making it work would be hard.

I didn't see a best-dad-ever mug/T-shirt combo in my future. I'd be happy someday sitting down to dinner with my son and his family and

213

enjoying a pleasant meal. If he were happy and confident and could look me in the eye and say that even the bad parts of growing up really didn't suck that much, I'd take that win. For me, that would be enough. The anxiety reminded me of pole vaulting in school, when I wasn't ever sure of the right height to set the bar, and I had almost no chance to make it over. Where I missed and fell bad for months, all for the one time I got it right, made it over, and the bar stayed up. It was a weird thing to think about.

I'd have to unpack a lot of baggage to be a decent dad.

I got home in time to comfort Jodi as she gathered herself for one final, life-bestowing push. I urged her on, I told her to be brave, that everything would be all right. As soon as the words left my mouth, I knew I was a hypocrite. I really didn't know everything would be OK. I knew if it weren't for her digging her nails into my fingers with each contraction, my hands would be shaking and sweating. As she hung on to me for strength and endured the pain of childbirth, I was afraid.

We wanted this. I didn't at first—I had a lot of good reasons to be afraid of fathering a child. I was the reluctant one. Children of abusive parents tend to become abusive parents. That's what everyone tells you. It's not a self-fulfilling prophecy, but people generally do what they know.

As an adult who'd grown up in a rough place, having my own child always seemed to come down to an argument of fate versus destiny. Was I fated to follow in my parents' footsteps because I was formatted that way, or could I, through effort and will, choose a different way? I didn't know. For me, it was the same as asking, What happens after we die? I had faith, but I really didn't know.

— ★★★ —

I remember the day we had the talk. Jodi held my face in between her hands and told me I wasn't my mother or father, that we worked hard and had a lot to offer a child. She wouldn't let me look away from her big blue eyes no matter how hard I tried. Then she said the most important thing anyone ever told me. She said she believed in me, and one day our kids would, too.

"You'll be a great dad," she said. So, we formulated a plan and committed to a baby-making regimen, with the dedication of athletes preparing to compete for Olympic gold medals.

"Are you really sure?" I asked.

"Yes."

"But, are you . . ."

"Yes. Now shut up, and give me a baby now."

So, I did. It was the best possible combination of primal, powerful magic and New Orleans hurricane punch. After so many had warned me not to reproduce—ever—I did.

Jo screamed, and a little more of our son grew visible. Just the top of a little pink head crowning. He was coming out a lot bigger than he went in. That was a plus.

Jodi squeezed my hand and screamed once more.

He didn't cry when the doctor pulled him out of her.

He didn't cry when I cut his umbilical cord.

He finally cried when the nurses put drops in his eyes and washed him off.

After he was swaddled and wrapped and stuffed into a silly-looking hat, the nurse asked me if I wanted to hold him.

It was a good question. I did, and I didn't.

The screaming went on.

Jodi watched me closely as the nurse maneuvered that soft bundle into the crook of my arm. Behind her sweaty, expectant joy was the lingering cloud of *Would I love him?*

I wanted to.

I thought I could, but I didn't know.

I'd just flown twenty-four hours to meet him, and now that I was standing there, I wasn't sure.

There was no guarantee or warranty, no field manual to consult.

Just her and him and me.

The nurses hovered. I nodded, and they steadied his tiny body in my arms. I looked down at him, past his silly hat, into his moist, limitless eyes. Just as I touched the side of his face, his tiny hand rose up warm against my cheek, and in that instant, I finally knew.

Xander stopped crying in my arms and calmed to my frantic stream of happy gibberish. I stood there gently rocking him, and we stared into each other's eyes. It was one of the few perfect moments in my life. All that mattered was right in front of me.

I loved him. I don't know why. I just knew I did, and he loved me. My first child. My son. Xander, short for Alexander. It was a good name with big shoes to fill. He was named after the great warrior-leader who conquered the entire known world.

After Jo caught her breath, I relinquished Xander to her bosom.

I watched them negotiate nursing for the first time, and I wanted everything a father wants for his son: happiness, success, a long and healthy life, and, at the end of each day, the deep, easy breath of a peaceful sleep. There are all kinds of wars, but at one point, everyone was someone's baby. New to the world, hungry without knowing what that really meant, and freshly swaddled, wearing a stupid hat. Looking at him, I prayed bringing children into my world was a good idea.

CHAPTER 19

November 2003—Baghdad

After 9/11, the US mobilized forces to capture Osama bin Laden and destroy the Taliban and Al-Qaeda's ability to project terrorism. Their home bases in Afghanistan, Yemen, and across the Horn of Africa were destroyed. The mission expanded to pursue terrorists and break the financial and logistical chains that enabled their operations. There was a rapid increase in intelligence operations and capabilities, and the number of US special operators and their teams slowly grew. While we searched for Osama bin Laden in Afghan caves, on November 8, 2002, the UN Security Council adopted Resolution 1441,[12] giving Saddam Hussein one last chance to comply with disarmament. But Saddam continued to hinder those inspections.

After twelve years of diplomatic efforts to disarm the Iraqi regime without war, Saddam Hussein still refused to comply with his agreement to disarm after the Persian Gulf War. On March 17, 2003, President Bush gave him an ultimatum: Saddam and his sons must leave Iraq within forty-eight hours, or the US would go to war. Saddam refused. On March 20, 2003, the Iraq War began.

---

12   Frederic L. Kirgis, "Security Council Resolution 1441 on Iraq's Final Opportunity to Comply with Disarmament Obligations," *ASIL Insights* 7, no. 12 (November 10, 2002), https://www.asil.org/insights/volume/7/issue/12/security-council-resolution-1441-iraqs-final-opportunity-comply.

In his May 1, 2003, speech[13] from the USS *Abraham Lincoln*, President George W. Bush declared major combat operations over and that we would help rebuild Iraq. Six months later, I landed in the middle of an insurgency.

I was the captain in charge of a highly specialized multinational communications unit with the seventh Combined Joint Task Force (CJTF-7) operating out of Baghdad. CJTF-7 existed to neutralize threats and secure the area so the Coalition Provisional Authority (CPA) could do their job as the interim government of Iraq. We also provided support in the form of expertise and manpower to help the CPA rebuild Iraq. At the time, the US led a coalition of more than one hundred thirty thousand troops from more than thirty-six different countries, and Iraq was a perilous place.

I was at the crossroads of who I could be and who I would be, and I was running out of time. The month before, 44 US soldiers and marines had been killed and 413 wounded in combat operations in Iraq. The November casualty report wasn't in yet, but improvised explosive devices (IEDs) were getting more sophisticated, and that was a problem. Wireless doorbell components, garage-door opener parts, and cell phones were being used to precisely trigger bombs. That meant the parties you were trying to reach were increasingly disconnected from their lives. Armor, both for vehicles and bodies, was already difficult to come by. For vehicles, we improvised what we could from junkyard scrap and sandbags; for personnel, we cobbled together what we could from whoever we could whenever we went outside the wire.

We were caught in the transition from the previous decade's very little ground combat to a massive mobilization, and that meant delays

---

13   "Bush Speech: Full Text," BBC News, May 2, 2003, http://news.bbc. co.uk/2/hi/americas/2994345.stm.

until manufacturing caught up with modern warfare. At that moment, demand was kicking supply's ass. My body armor that morning was made up of loans from a UK warrant officer a foot taller than me and a barrel-chested Dutch marine a foot wider than I would ever be. I looked like a sand-colored turtle surveying the plaza through the narrow gap between my high collar and low Kevlar helmet brim.

As promised, this brings us back full circle to where we began.

It was still hot mid-November. Heat radiated off the stone buildings, and we were in an unfamiliar place, slowly moving through a thick, enthusiastic crowd along the broken pavement and dirt of a large plaza. Clusters of dead trees and low, smashed structures were all that remained of a city park. We were hemmed in on four sides by multistory concrete buildings divided by congested alleyways, and the stench was overwhelming.

Children played on debris piles the size of small hills composed of broken concrete and garbage. After weeks of terrorist bombings in government buildings, cafés, and popular meeting places, there was finally a lull in the violence, and the markets were open again. Within the square was a thriving bazaar filled with the sound of merchants hawking their wares and shoppers bargaining for deals. The pent-up frustration of curfews and caution and fear was giving way to laughter, commerce, and song. It was nice to see people being people again. More of that would mean we were winning.

Our Humvee slowed to a crawl as a swirl of humanity opened and closed around us.

It was our last mission of the day.

We were trying to find a fire station.

Baghdad never had an effective 911/first-responder system. After years of corruption and intimidation followed by recent fierce fighting, looting, and bombing, the fire stations we did find were left damaged,

221

abandoned, or unusable. It was still impossible to make a phone call across Baghdad, so firemen relied on smoke, family, or neighbors to lead them to the fires that broke out every day. Very few fire stations responded quickly. Most didn't respond at all.

We were weaving through the masses, and then it happened. In that crowd, framed by buildings I'd only seen before on CNN, I recognized someone walking toward me in a sweat-stained suit that had seen better days.

It had been a while.

In the moment it took my driver to negotiate the central market stands and rubble piles in the plaza, I ignored the merchants trying to attract our attention and the children selling trinkets, and I concentrated on that familiar face. After I made eye contact and before he turned away and disappeared into the crowd, I was sure of two important things: I knew him, and he knew me.

Although he was dressed like a local businessman, he wasn't one. He blended in, but he didn't belong. I knew him as John.

Then our moment was over, and in the shuffling of bodies, he was gone, lost in the crowd and clamor. Seeing him brought back memories I didn't have time for. A long time ago, he'd been my mentor. Over time, we became friends. He introduced me to an amazing girl, and I wondered if Lucy was still his partner. I hadn't heard from her since Kuwait. But I didn't have time to think about it. I was suddenly aware we were vulnerable.

We were stopped, caught in the open, and a chill ran down my spine.

Our unarmored Humvee was a fine vehicle. As long as we kept moving, it was a lot like a chariot, but we were outside the safe embrace of the Green Zone's walls, ground to a halt, surrounded by rubble hills and windowless six-story buildings, with no doors, no roof, no nothing on our Humvee to stop a bullet. We were overrun by children hawking their wares. Despite the heat, I shivered. It wasn't fear as much as a sense of déjà vu that caught me off guard.

I felt like I was out of time.

Father taught me how to tell time. It's the last memory I have of him helping me with homework. I was six and had just started the first grade.

"Get up, and try again," boomed the giant.

I climbed back to the table and sat upright in my chair. I was sweating in the cool room. I focused as hard as I could on the words my father was saying. We sat knee to knee at the kitchen table, papers with drawings of blurry clocks stacked between us. After-school cookie crumbs and shards of broken plate littered the otherwise pristine yellow-and-white linoleum kitchen floor. My cheeks were hot, and tears ran down my face.

I swore I would try harder and get the next answer right.

Father pointed to another drawing with a blank line next to it. "What time is this?"

"Eight fifteen?"

"Are you asking me or telling me?"

"Telling. It's eight fifteen."

"Good," he said in a growl. "What's another way to say that?"

My heart sank. "I don't know."

His hand moved fast. He was tapping the pencil on the table, and there was a pause after he carefully set it down. Then his arm moved, and my right cheek hurt, and my shoulder and head bounced off the wall.

I sat upright again in my chair and looked him in the eye, because that was important. I looked him in the eye and focused on what he was saying.

I would get the next answer right. My jaw was tight from my swollen face, and my throat was dry, but it didn't matter. It wouldn't stop until I got everything correct.

I was ready. He looked back at me and drummed his pencil. Then he stopped and asked, "What's another way to say eight fifteen?"

My heart stopped.

I sniffled, then shouted, "I STILL DON'T KNOW!"

He again set the pencil down. When his arm moved, my left cheek hurt, and I tumbled from the chair. The linoleum over concrete was still cold and unforgiving.

"It's a quarter past eight. Don't you know anything? Get it now?"

But I didn't get it. I tried to scream, "But a quarter is twenty-five cents, and there are only fifteen minutes." My indignation came out as a whine.

Snot ran out my nose as I climbed back from the floor and sat upright in my chair. I was sweating and focusing as hard as I could. Tears made it hard to see. Looking him straight in his blurry eyes, I swore I would answer the next question right.

"That's just the way it is," he said. "Again. What is another way to say eight fifteen?"

I swallowed hard and said as clearly as I could, "A quarter past eight."

My father nodded and pointed to the next drawing with a blank line next to it. "What time is this?"

I squinted until it was in focus, then I answered.

It took three hours, but I learned to tell time.

It was the very first lesson my father ever taught me: time would never be my friend.

CHAPTER 20

November 2003—Baghdad

Stopping was trouble. I surveyed the mob. Shook my head in a violent no and shouted, "Away, get away!" I didn't get the response I was looking for. Hundreds of people surged in closer. They flowed in like a tide, holding up baskets of merchandise. I ignored the M-14 between my legs, chambered a round in my 9MM Beretta, grabbed a helmet bag full of donated candy, stood up, tapped the handgun on the windshield glass, and said as loudly as I could, "Step away. *Now.*"

When they hesitated, I directed the crowd to part, pointing and waving the tip of my weapon in the directions they needed to go with a steady cadence of, "Step away from the vehicle, make a hole, get a move on, get out of the way."

The crowd dispersed, leaving only baskets held aloft by giggling, expectant children. We admired their perseverance and tossed handfuls of candy to them. The boys and girls smiled and clustered together, checked to see what they got, and started making trades. I settled back into my seat and waved as our Humvee lurched forward.

In the early days of reconstructing Iraq, I relied on skilled drivers familiar with the ins and outs of Baghdad. There's a reason the air force didn't make me a navigator. I have no sense of direction, but my driver that day was an exceptional guardsman from Tennessee who was heading home in a few weeks and then leaving the army. He had watched his friends get torn apart by IEDs detonated in the middle of two of his convoys. Soldiers had died. Some of the wounded survivors had formed a defensive line, but no more attacks had come that day. They'd had to pry the casualties from the vehicles they'd become part of and line up their remains in the sand while the rest of the convoy circled around them. They'd worked covered in blood that mostly wasn't their own. My driver said his friends who'd lived were never the same. The young soldier had eight months in country already and knew his way around downtown better than I ever would. His name was Private First Class (PFC) Tom Burke. He wanted to act on TV and loved to practice karate, which he pronounced *kay-rah-tay*, every morning at dawn. Tom was counting the days until he was out of the army.

Earlier in the day, we'd finished a mission to test out jamming equipment the services were fielding to counter IEDs. When we reached the fringe of the Green Zone, we waved off our gun-truck escort vehicle so it could return to base and support another mission. Finding a fire station in a haven of relative security should have been a cakewalk.

Our parting was premature. We were still within sight of the Green Zone wall when our vehicle reached the edge of the plaza. We pushed past the market crowd and slowly circled a small hill at the grid coordinates the Ministry of Communications had given us for the firehouse, but there was nothing there. Then we were mobbed again, this time by dozens of sullen-faced children. This time, it was different. This time, they weren't hawking wares. This time, they weren't smiling.

First, no one was there; then they ran out of the alleys and surrounded us. It was like getting caught in a flood. The children locked arms and pressed against our Humvee's bumpers, and a horde of tweens wedged their bodies into the wheel wells and wrapped themselves between the tires and exposed pieces of our suspension. I stood and looked over the windscreen at the patchwork of tattered clothes, dark hair, and hard faces. Small, thin bodies gripped each other and sought hand and footholds in any gap the Humvee allowed. And we couldn't move without crushing them.

I yelled for them to get away. I shouted at a boy with thick white scars running down his arms to move, but he just dug himself deeper into our front wheel well. I tried to wrench away a girl whose forehead and jaw were a mass of puckered gray burn scars, but her arms entwined the bars that attached the side mirror, and she did not move. In front of the Humvee, a little boy just stood there a few feet away from the bumper, staring at me with blank wet eyes. Snot and tears streaked his dirty face as he struggled to be brave. I couldn't reach him, and he wouldn't move. He just stood there, willing himself to stand his ground.

It was a look I knew as he fought to steady himself and look me in the eye: I knew that standing there, as he shook from fear, was important to someone he loved.

They clung to us, as an ever-tightening human net. We couldn't move forward, and we couldn't move back without running them down.

Then someone behind us started shooting. There were screams as the plaza emptied out.

Shots kicked white powder and chips off the buildings where they hit. But the debris pile protected us. Another shot ricocheted off the street and hit the underside of our bumper with a solid *thunk*. If we'd been moving, it would have sounded like a tire kicking up a rock. But we weren't moving, and it wasn't a rock. I shouted for the kids to get away and get to cover. But they held on.

They were packed tight around the vehicle, and we couldn't make them move. My driver tried to inch the Humvee forward just enough to move them back, but they still wouldn't let go.

Rounds came in faster behind us. They hit closer, all around.

The market was in chaos, and we couldn't back out without clearing the rubble pile sheltering us from the shots. But it didn't matter because we couldn't move. We were pinned down, couldn't tell where the shooters were, and couldn't risk firing blindly back across the plaza.

The kids wouldn't budge, and bad became worse.

CHAPTER 21

November 2003—Baghdad

I felt how a pheasant must feel flushed out and in the open, lined up for the shot.

The only difference between me and the pheasant was I knew what came next.

It was the worst kind of trap: we couldn't go back, and we couldn't plow through.

I shouted as loud as I could for the kids to leave, but they wouldn't go. I brandished my weapon, but they wouldn't move. I pushed the kid nearest to me away, but he had wrapped his arms around the doorposts and pushed his legs deeper into the wheel well.

As far as I knew, we were five Mississippis away from taps.

I fired a shot into the sand behind one of the kids, but it didn't spook them at all. When PFC Burke pushed one kid back, he was replaced by two more.

The gunfight on the other side of the hill reached a climax.

There was an explosion. A blinding pillar of flame filled the sky. A concussion wave of molten grit washed over us, and I saw what looked like the front of a pickup truck hover for an instant above the debris hill before it crashed in a pile of noise and screaming and fire. Right where the first group of kids had stopped us.

I was out of options.

I pressed the muzzle of my 9MM pistol into the head of the boy next to my door and pushed him back away from the Humvee with it as I stepped out. He was exactly the same size as my boy. His hair and eyes were dark brown, like Xander's.

"Tell your friends to get the fuck away from this vehicle."

His eyes blazed with a kind of hate I'd never seen before.

I pushed harder and growled, "*Now.*"

Thank God, he and his friends started to back away.

I shouted the Arabic words for, "Down, down, get down!" and waved my gun at the kids still in front of my Humvee. They looked from me to a man punching numbers into a cell phone down the alleyway. When I snapped my gun around to shoot him, he dropped the phone, raised his hands as if to surrender, then spun around and disappeared down the alley. I was enraged. I started to chase after him to put two bullets in his head, but as soon as he left, the children scattered. "That's right," I barked after the cell man. "Keep running."

I looked around one last time and raced back to the Humvee. The snaps and cracks of rounds ricocheted all around us.

I shouted, "Go, go, go!" as I swung back into the vehicle. It was clear ahead. Tom Burke didn't need me to tell him to go. We raced away through the alley.

Bursts of gunfire continued behind us as a line of men with rifles crested the debris hill. I owed whoever had bulldozed all that war detritus into piles in the plaza.

For all I knew, it was the remains of the fire station we were looking for.

So much happens in so little time. The entire encounter with the kids surrounding our Humvee and the cell phone man turning to run could have been measured in heartbeats. It felt like a lifetime.

"You OK?" I asked PFC Burke. The Humvee transmission wailed as we screamed down Airport Road. We were eight minutes out from Camp Victory.

"Hell, yeah!" he shouted. "This was my last mission. I'm so fuckin' done with Baghdad."

CHAPTER 22

November 2003—Camp Victory, Baghdad

Tom Burke talked nonstop until we pulled over to clear our weapons after we entered Camp Victory. I don't remember much of what he said until we shook hands and parted company. He gave me a half hug and double pat on the back with his M-16. Then he banged his Kevlar helmet into mine and snarled, "Keep your head down, air force."

We saluted, and he walked away. He didn't get five steps before he turned, arms behind his helmet, walking backward, and said, "Oh, yeah—and don't die."

Then he turned and crossed a small bridge over a dry irrigation channel. When he was out of sight, I looked around and found myself alone in the small cantonment area where we staged vehicles. I sank against the Humvee, took off my helmet, and allowed myself a short, controlled burst of meltdown. I'd stayed calm, focused, and on task for as long as I needed to. It's important to wait. People relied on me. I had to be strong for them. So, I pushed past the pain, shock, and realization until it was safe to crash. People won't follow you into bad places if they don't believe you have the ability and disposition to get the job done and get them back safe again. No one likes to watch a grown man come unglued, but I learned it was much worse when I kept it bottled up inside. Timing a meltdown wasn't indulgence; it was scheduled maintenance.

I sat there in the shade, my back against a hot tire that smelled like burnt oil and rubber in the middle of a maze of vehicles, and I clamped my hands over my mouth so I wouldn't make a sound as I screamed.

It wasn't the gunfire or the explosion. It wasn't the stench, or fear for our lives. What put me over the edge was getting trapped and the only solution I could come up with was to push a boy out of my way with a gun. I'd threatened more than a dozen other kids with deadly force. It was an awful day. I played it over in my mind, and I couldn't find a different way out.

I still saw the abject hatred in that little boy's face, my son's wide brown eyes, and a terrorist yelling at his phone before smashing it to the ground and running away. I screamed again.

How proud would Jodi and Xander be of me now?

No one died. No one got hurt. Everyone walked away. One day closer to home. There were more pluses than minuses, but it didn't matter.

Every night when I'm home, after my son is tucked in, I check to make sure he's all right, and I listen to his breathing. Sometimes I sit on the floor, my back against the foot of his bed. On good nights, our old, blind orange cat, Fairfax, curls up in my lap and purrs as I listen to the gentle in and out of his breaths. In the still night, listening to the soft ins and exhales, I say the Shepard's prayer silently to myself. Alan Shepard's prayer, that is—"Lord, please don't let me fuck up."

I couldn't get it out of my mind.

I'd put my Beretta 9MM handgun against a boy's head.

It was unimaginable.

Acid clawed at the back of my throat, and I clenched my jaw.

There were no other good choices. Every choice left us dead, kids broken, kids dead, or us as hostages. No ROE (rules of engagement) addressed kids as shields and traps.

There should have been a second IED. There was no other explanation. Why else go to such lengths to stop us in that spot? It was no coincidence a pickup truck exploded where we'd been mobbed in the market just moments before. It was no coincidence they'd used children to stop us a second time.

We were alive for no other reason than a delay in connecting a call or because their equipment failed. We got lucky. We got a happy ending. It's easy to forget that before Walt Disney came along, even fairy tales didn't have a lot of happy endings.

We got a next time.

But it left me asking: What kind of sick fuck uses kids like that?

I don't know.

I also had to ask: What kind of sick fuck puts a pistol in a kid's face?

Dissecting it didn't help. I was covered in cold sweat and shook in the dusk.

By the time I picked myself up off the ground, it was dark, and the call-to-worship prayer warbled from the speakers of a scarred minaret one-half kilometer from our gate. I realized I was walking. I didn't care where, but I had to keep moving, or I would keep thinking.

I stepped past the destroyed bridge behind the Al Faw Palace, a gilded jewel of a stronghold on its own island in the middle of a lake. It was surrounded by presidential villas clad in coarse white stone that glowed in the moonlight reflected off the water. Myriad decorative pools, stagnant irrigation waterways, and still fountains glistened among the disarray of untended gardens that were somehow both overgrown and dead.

The bridge's shattered stone and broken iron bones remained visible in the half-moon light like the decaying spine of a serpent from a myth. I shambled past it until I was at the far edge of the Al Faw compound, in the middle of a twenty-acre field, at the ruin of a massive fountain. It had been grand once, but its stone columns and statues had been pulled down and broken. What remained lay half-submerged in a wide black pool. I found it by following a nearly invisible path of cracked stones. I walked for a long time past date palms, through scrub, and over soft sand until my path abruptly ended at a curb of blue-veined white marble. I stared at it, wanting to push forward, but I couldn't. My path was gone, and the night was dark beyond the intermittent bluish-green puddle of light from the one still-working bulb in an ornate iron lamp.

I sat on the edge of the wide fountain basin. It was still half-full, and the liquid that remained inside looked like a pitch-black oil slick. In that flickering light, my reflection looked like a corpse staring at me from the bottom of a hole. In that black mirror, I still saw the family resemblance—my grandfather's bright brown eyes, my father's wide nose and prominently creased forehead, my mother's Sicilian olive skin.

But I couldn't see myself.

I locked eyes with the face in the still water, and I looked away first. Very few things frighten me, but I recognized something in the hard face I saw in the water that did.

I walked back to my tent, wishing it would stop, but my mind kept taking me back to my son and the boy who resembled him. My son and a boy who hated me even before I scraped him off my Humvee with a loaded, round-chambered weapon. My son and a boy who wouldn't disengage from his mission to kill me and my team until it was clear his mission had failed and my finger had moved to the trigger of the pistol and pressed a barrel mark into his forehead.

All I wanted to be was a good father. To do that, my boy needed *me* to come back home, not that thing that stared back from the dark water of that basin.

The last of my adrenaline was gone, and it left a bitter taste in my mouth. The wind rose, and I shivered as I wound my way back to my tent. The howls and high-pitched cries of hungry dogs roving in packs on the fringe of the camp were mournful and shrill like coyotes.

This is what I do, not who I am. I must have said that to myself a hundred times.

It was an agreeable thought; comfortable at first; but with overuse, I wore it thin, and its warmth got lost. I knew the moment I wrapped it around myself that it was a lie, but for a time, I liked the way that mantra felt. It was my armor, and I clung to it.

I wanted to retreat behind the comfortable familiarity of *This is what I do, not who I am*, but I couldn't. Not anymore.

The truth is we are what we do, and we are capable of so much more than I could imagine. What I might be in a year frightened me. I had to get home before that happened. That much was clear if nothing else was, and time was not on my side.

My family was my compass in Iraq when I was lost and alone, when things went wrong, and it was hard to tell the good guys from the bad, because sometimes they're the same. I had to make the right choice at the next crossroads: I needed to get back to my family. I had to survive for them. I would do the best that I could. I would return with honor.

That was the promise I made to myself.

I had forgotten about the familiar face I'd seen in the crowd on that first drive through Baghdad. I completely forgot about John. In fact, I didn't think about him again until he showed up on my doorstep holding a bag open, like a kid playing trick or treat.

CHAPTER 23

After clearing the second checkpoint, the CPA[14] complex felt like a college campus compared to the military fortress that was Camp Victory. The CPA operated out of Saddam's former Republican Guard Palace compound in central Bagdad. It was a two- and three-story sweep of ornately carved beige-and-white stone with porticos, a huge swimming pool, and a large verdigris dome. The complex occupied the wide stretch of land between a coil of the Tigris River. In addition to the palace, the bend in the river was filled with palm trees, orange groves, sandbagged trailers, and support buildings. The palace was defined by four massive bronze busts of Saddam Hussein wearing the battle helm of Saladin, the Muslim-Kurd who'd battled European crusaders and united the Middle East into one sultanate. Saddam was a master of appropriating the legends of various Middle Eastern cultures to symbolically legitimize his rule as the heir apparent of history's great empires. His busts stood on towers, where Saddam's countenance looked out across Iraq with four mustachioed frowns. They were about thirty feet tall each if you measured from the top of his thirteen-foot head to the bottom of a wide, abstract pedestal of a chest with epaulets. The second bust had already been removed from the palace tower with a heavy crane. I stepped past

---

14   Coalition Provisional Authority, the US interim government that administered Iraq until sovereign power was restored.

the demolition into the palace to attend a briefing as Saddam 2 was being eased facedown in the dirt next to a dour, standing Saddam 1.

I was at the CPA to learn the lay of the land and help the Ministry of Communications with infrastructure problems they were having. The CPA was the governmental organization tasked with running and rebooting Iraq. Ambassador L. Paul Bremer led a lean mix of State Department, military forces, contractors, and other multinational agency staff to run Iraq, coordinate her rebuilding, and create the infrastructure and controls necessary to transition the government back to her people as a democracy. They leaned hard on CJTF-7 for security and to fill holes in their manning and expertise. On the best of days, their job was like herding cats with rocket launchers instead of claws. The Iraqis saw us as both liberators and oppressors. They badly wanted something, but they hadn't found the right voice, or chorus, yet to articulate it.

I wondered if we just weren't listening.

During the briefing, over a videoconference link, General Abizaid said, "This is not an occupation. We're here to establish a safe and secure government, a safe and secure environment that will be transitioned over time to Iraqi security forces. And when we are no longer needed, we will leave. It doesn't mean we'll rush out. It means that we will, in a careful and in a certain manner, train and provide for Iraqi security forces to be responsible."

Ambassador Bremer served as chief administrator for Iraq, and General Abizaid was the commanding general of US Central Command.

Then Ambassador Bremer said, "We have received reports of Iraqi insurgents using women and children as human shields."

I got that message too late to need. They definitely were, but knowing to expect it and having rules to deal with it were two very different things.

The ambassador wrapped up with, "The governing council announced that Iraq would have a fully sovereign Iraqi government by the end of next summer, and the occupation would end . . ."

With delays in fielding the Iraqi Defense Force and New Iraqi Army units, it seemed like there was a lot to do in too little time. I had no idea what fully sovereign meant—maybe functional? Since CJTF-7 wasn't allowed to use the occupation O-word, I assumed coalition support would continue until at least the new Iraqi government could assure a measure of security and deter invaders.

Then it was feeding time. CPA briefings always began as solemn affairs, but by the end, reporters jockeying to make a name for themselves approached the Q and A portion of the briefing like hyenas circling a kill. It was impressive to watch general officers hold them at a professional distance without getting angry, but the behavior of some of the reporters—who rarely did more than film from the roof of the Al Rasheed hotel—was just too disrespectful to stay and watch.

I left just in time to ride with one of the CPA communications advisors to one of the Iraqi Ministry of Communications (MoC) offices. We were going to meet a team of project managers and telecommunications engineers working to solve a problem that hadn't gotten better since the end of the war. I was in a good mood as our nontactical civilian vehicles (NTVs) rushed through Baghdad's side streets to the former National Phone Company of Iraq. As I watched Iraqis on the streets flash by, I thought just maybe the CPA "Could Provide Assistance" and help them.

We were let out in an underground parking garage and walked through a massive security double door, flanked by Iraqi guards in body armor armed with submachine guns, into a spectacular modern lobby. The seal of Iraq was set in the floor in mosaic tile that was bordered by a curved reception desk made of dark wood and chrome staffed by four women. Behind them, guards stood in front of four cypher-locked doors. We were led through door number three.

Passing through the door was like going back in time. While the entry was grand, the operations area was a military building from the 1940s that had been bombed, rebuilt, and patched back together multiple times with concrete but never repainted. Cables ran everywhere like black roots that covered most of the floor and twisted through the ceiling. It was like a building the jungle had spent decades reclaiming. The only things clean and updated were the black-and-white pictures of the former phone company directors. They were a perfectly aligned row of stern-looking men with fierce mustaches staring out past their dark wooden frames with eyes that seemed to follow us as we stepped around cables and moved through the corridor. We emerged in a large room with an ancient central switchboard that a work crew in hard hats was removing. It was the original, still-functional central switchboard for downtown Baghdad. It had been installed by Nazis during WWII, and it was covered with swastikas and iron eagles. The CPA was replacing it with a modern digital switch, which allowed thousands more phones to connect to the phone system and allowed subscribers to place direct calls. The bad news, we would come to find out, was that many of the old rotary phones used across Iraq weren't compatible with it. Even worse, many senior Iraqi officials wouldn't admit that they didn't know how to make official calls to other Iraqi offices without the assistance of an operator.

After walking past the crew installing the new phone switch, we stopped in a corner of the huge room, where two men, surrounded by a group of women, were shouting at each other.

The crowd parted, and I walked up to the two men with my hand out and introduced myself. "Hi, Jack. Thanks for inviting me over. I don't know your friend." Jack Mosley was one of the CPA officers in charge of telecommunications infrastructure. Their argument paused. Jack was a big Swede from the Midwest with dark blonde hair and Viking-like features who, like most CPA officers, dressed like he'd bought the entire L.L.Bean catalogue before moving to Iraq. He was a good guy. In my short time in Iraq working with CPA officers, I'd come to sort them into one of three categories. First there were the patriots, who were idealists and wanted to make a difference; they were the uncompromising good guys, but sometimes that made them hard to work with in the gray areas of Iraq. Then there were the careerists, who came to Iraq only because that was the only way they would ever get promoted; they were incapable of making decisions without a boss making them for them, and they used their powers for good and for evil, depending on how the political winds were blowing. Finally, there were the criminals, the CPA officers in Iraq because they were being disciplined or on the verge of being fired at the State Department or in their military units and had been given a chance to serve their country in lieu of prosecution and to plus up the number of boots on the ground. They also could use their powers for good or evil. How they swung depended on how you could make their lives easier, and that made them simple to deal with.

Jack was a good guy—he was a patriot, and that made him a ballbuster.

Our translator said something in Arabic that sounded like a little more than what I said, and the crowd nervously laughed. After I shook Jack's hand, I offered mine to the gentleman in the patched jacket with thick brown skin and graying black hair.

Jack sighed, "This disagreeable man is Sami Bishara. It pains me to say it, but he's one of the best field engineers in Iraq. He was in charge of phone and network troubleshooting for Baghdad's civilian command and control infrastructure."

"Sami, *As-salaam alaykum*. I'm Bill Riley."

"Bill is the new chief of frequency management for the task force," Jack said. "In addition to his military obligations, he's here to get Iraq's version of the FCC up and running again. Also, Sami here speaks better English than he lets on, so be careful."

"So, Captain, upon you may there be peace. Are you here because you are our new master engineer?"

"No, Sami, I'm not. In fact, you're a better engineer than I'll ever be. I'm here because I have a talent for figuring out what good engineers need to be successful." Our translator interpreted that last part accurately, and the other engineers began to murmur. One of the good things about IT guys is that despite our arrogant pride in our work, the languages we speak, or the satisfaction of knowing that we are the smartest expert in the room at what we do, we're driven to make each circuit work. If they don't work, we work together until they do.

"No one else here can do this job," Sami said.

"Well . . . We've hired a lot of engineers," Jack said. "I think we can take it from here."

So that no one could sabotage his infrastructure, Saddam Hussein allowed no standardized, modern maps to mark the locations of plumbing, gas mains, electrical cables, sewer pipes, or telecommunications lines. Repairing a broken country without the right treasure map is almost impossible. Documentation that lets you know where things are is required whether you're urban planning, running cities, or repairing war damage. We found few records after the main fighting stopped, and they remained incomprehensible even after they were translated. Each system was written in its own unique code, and rebuilding the phone and data systems across Iraq progressed slowly.

"I can't do it, Sami," Jack said.

"Then you will never be able to make the repairs, and you will fail."

"Gentlemen, a moment."

"Sami, this is my first time meeting your staff—can we have tea and make introductions? I will be in Iraq for a while, and I'd like to get to know the people I'm working with."

"Yes, of course, *Na'qib*." Sami motioned to his staff and said something in Arabic that was too fast for me to catch.

"Thank you for your hospitality," I said.

"Bill, we don't have time for this."

"I have a little more time, Jack, and I'm thirsty. Let's sit at the table. One quick question while we're waiting for tea. How many holes have your engineers dug in the streets so far looking for major phone and network nodes and cable vaults?"

"Nearly a hundred."

"And how many times have you found what you were looking for?"

"Twice," Jack said in a very soft voice.

Sami began to laugh. Then I asked, "Mr. Bishara, how long were you in charge of critical civilian infrastructure and command and control for Baghdad?"

His smile disappeared. "I was the operations and maintenance deputy for ten years."

"And your director was politically appointed?"

"Of course. I served under four of them."

"So, then, to the real issue here: What was your rank in the Ba'ath Party?"

Sami turned pale, and Jack started to protest.

"Gentlemen, there are only two problems here, and you've both been talking around them. Let's address them both. Sami, you couldn't possibly have survived these last ten years doing what you do if you weren't a member of the party. Am I right?"

Sami stared at me for a moment, collecting his thoughts. "Yes, *Na'qib*. I was a minor party member, but it was necessary."

"And was Iraq a tough place to live and keep a good job in if you weren't a party member during Saddam's rule?"

"Yes. As you say, all professionals had to swear allegiance to the party, or there were consequences. No one likes to talk of these things. People who made light of or questioned the party disappeared. Their families suffered. It was the way it was."

"I understand, Sami. Thank you. That must make it hard for you, Jack, since you obviously want to hire him, but you can't because CPA order number one bars all former Ba'athists from government employment."

"Bill, I—"

"Ah, tea, thank you . . ."

"Sami, who is this?" I asked of the young woman with the brown, almond-shaped eyes who was setting out our cups of tea with saucers full of sugar cubes. Her dark hair was pulled back under a red silk scarf. She sneered at me like I smelled bad. It had been a long day—maybe I did.

"This is my lead engineer, Marjani Nassar. She is the wife of my nephew, and she has a fine mind."

"Is it common for engineers to be women in Iraq?"

"More so now than when I was a boy. Many, many men went to war. Fewer returned. Bright women took the jobs that were necessary."

"Mrs. Marjani Nassar, it's nice to meet you. The tea is good. Thank you."

"You're welcome. Now, if there isn't anything else . . ."

"Wait," I said. "How's your English?"

"Much better than your Arabic."

246

"Marjani," Sami said. "I apologize, she—"

"No need, Sami. I'm a big fan of honesty. Marjani Nassar, how would you like to help Iraq get back on her feet?"

"I will not work for your military."

"Good. Jack here is about as far removed from my military as possible."

"What would you have me do?"

"Me? I could use another cup of tea, but Jack here needs an engineer he can hire that can work with experts like Mr. Bishara to help find the locations of phone and communications equipment so he can restore services across Baghdad. You weren't a member of the Ba'ath Party, Mrs. Marjani Nassar, were you?"

"No. It was mostly a club for boys."

"So, that fixes your first problem, Jack. Sami, if members of your staff also worked for the CPA, your organization would get a small percent of each of those wages as a finder's fee, right?"

"That is the custom in our business."

"Jack? That should solve the issue of expertise without violating your orders. You willing to make that deal?"

"Yes. You and I are going to talk after this, but yes."

"Fair enough. Sami, now that business is done, what can you tell Jack about his problem?"

Sami smiled. "You have all the directions you need. You have simply started out on the wrong foot."

"We have notes on infrastructure, but they use some coding that we can't make sense of," Jack said after finally sipping his tea. "It seems like each one is different. They get us in the general direction of what we're trying to find, but the records are incomplete, and each is so different that we wind up wrecking a street to make a single repair, and the repairs are going too slow."

"Would you like to know why?" Sami said with a smile.

Over the next few hours, more tea was drunk, snacks were eaten, additional people were fetched, and a small corps of engineers and technicians was hired. The strange markings and annotations that led to the critical infrastructure points we were looking for weren't measured in yards or meters. With Sami's help, we discovered that the locations of wires and switches and junction boxes were based on the number of paces from heel to toe, or the length of an arm, or the distance from the heel of a palm to a fingertip. Turns to the left and right were left to the individuals originally hired to service specific areas. The problem was that everyone is built differently, and the right size of each person's stride became a critical issue. So, we found and hired back the original network installers and maintainers, and Iraqi systems were finally restored and improved.

Locating critical nodes wasn't a matter of walking in another man's boots; it was a matter of having the other guy's exact boot size, inseam, and reach. After thousands of years of progress, our success or failure was measured in paces and cubits, only instead of building an ark, we were rebuilding Iraq's damaged and neglected WWII-era infrastructure. Building an ark would have been easier, but we finally had a working pirate's treasure map. Arrrgh.

It was cold again. It always surprises me how cold the night can get in a desert. Temperature extremes in a land of extremes. If I held my breath a moment longer than regular breathing, I could see the plume of my exhalation before it dissolved in the dark, dry air.

I made it back to my billet at the CPA just in time to take a quick shower before the start of a mortar attack. Sirens went off, and I rolled to the floor in the bathroom as explosion after explosion shook my trailer. After the mortars subsided, some Arabic prayer echoed through the campus. It was a bad mechanical reproduction, like the copy of a copy of a once-pretty song. It started out mournful, then turned hopeful before it was drowned out by the *whomp, whomp, whomp chug* of heavy machine-gun fire.

Normally, I would have reached for a book to read at that point, but I'd looked around earlier, and there wasn't anything that really interested me. Most deployment buildings had a book-share area, but at CPA billeting, the periodicals were more . . . specialized. Someone had gone to the trouble of installing beautiful, handmade bookshelves and magazine racks—and filled them with gay porn. I stayed in three different billets there; they were all the same, and I have to say, I felt a little left out. I didn't really expect straight porn from the State Department, but there wasn't even any nice lesbian porn to more fully represent LGBT. That made me a little sad as I listened to nearby exchanges of gunfire.

Lying on the floor next to a beautiful bookcase with nothing to do and no book in my hand was a strange feeling. I've almost always had a book within reach since I learned how to read, and I have Sarah to thank for that.

May 1973—Long Island, New York

Reading came hard to me, and Sarah was my best friend. She had blue eyes and fine blonde hair, and that year, I think, she was taller than me. She lived down the street, and she taught me how to read. I loved the lilt of her voice as she read to me and helped me to pronounce words. We would meet after class each day, climb up the ridge that curved around our school, sit beneath the elms and scrub oaks that separated the sport fields, and read stories together.

Our second-grade teacher, Mrs. Rachne, would lose her patience with me, and the other kids would laugh. It was a regular cycle broken one day by Jimmy O'Conner, the biggest boy in our class at a towering fifty-five inches of mostly arms and legs. He was making fun of me and knocking me in the head with a book I couldn't read. Our teacher ignored it.

Sarah didn't have any patience that day. She came out of nowhere, shouting, "Shut up!" and ran into that boy so hard she knocked him over a desk. The reader he was smacking me with flew out of his hand, and Jimmy hit the floor like a sack of rocks.

The class exploded with laughter. They chanted, "Girls fight Billy's fights," and, "Jimmy got beat by a girl." I was mortified, and I knew I would never forgive her, especially because, at that moment, it was true. She had fought my fight, and somehow that was more embarrassing than getting teased. Jimmy and I moved back toward our seats, avoiding eye contact with everyone.

Mrs. Rachne silenced the class and scolded Sarah. Sarah looked indignant; her face was red; but she set her jaw and didn't say a word. Mrs. Rachne stared at Sarah from under her mass of black-and-gray hair, divided by clips that made it look like a giant spider was draped over her head, then finally sent her to her seat.

As if it couldn't get worse, when I picked up the fallen book Jimmy had dropped, Mrs. Rachne called on me to read.

"Billy, what does page five say?" The teacher's voice was overly sweet.

I looked down and read the first line without thinking. "The yellow duck quacked and spread her wings and flew away; ripples spread across the cool blue water in her wake."

"Hand it over," the teacher said, glaring at me, but after rereading the page, she conceded, "So it does," clearly perplexed by my sudden adequacy.

Just like that, I could read.

A week earlier, Mrs. Rachne had stood me up in front of the class and told me, in a constructive tone, that I lacked the aptitude necessary to read well. Years later, I found out I was dyslexic. While she may have been right, I kept up with the class from that day on. Her curt, annoyed acknowledgment of each of my subsequent successes was sweeter praise than all the satisfactory marks I finally made on my progress reports.

I grudgingly made up with Sarah and thanked her for teaching me how to read, in exchange for her pinky promise to not beat up boys for me anymore.

CHAPTER 24

We were in the Hayy Al-Shurtta neighborhood, at an outdoor café in the open space of a building with an exposed twenty-foot-wide gap in the first three stories. An explosion had sheared away the entire corner of the building and destroyed the original café, but they'd rebuilt, and people still lived on the other floors. We sat at one of the picnic tables in the shade, just under the jagged concrete edge of the second floor, drinking sweet tea with mint, talking, and watching people go by. They stared back and watched us strange airmen closely. How we were treated depended on the mood and recent history of the neighborhood. We were as respectful and nonconfrontational as we could be, armed to the teeth and in body armor.

At that point, Ramadi was a passionate, transitional neighborhood where every adult male was also armed to what teeth he had. So, while we didn't blend in, we did have things in common. There were still good areas by day, but at night, insurgents took hold of shops and housing areas with devastating consequences to the local people. At that moment, though, it was still possible to purchase more tea or *shisha* than you could use and tolerable enough for street artists, businessmen, local police, or Iraqi defense officers to sit with you in public and talk. If only to ensure that good tea or *shisha* didn't go to waste, as was God's will.

"Boy on girl. Two boys on girl. Girl three-ways. Girl on girl. Best three dollar you ever spend. Banned in France," a little girl said in a singsong voice that echoed down the street as she hawked DVDs from a basket.

The girl caught me by surprise, and I choked on my drink and couldn't stop coughing when I heard the incongruous sound of an Iraqi tween peddling porn. Everyone at the table laughed at me.

She had come over to the café with two older boys flanking her, each carrying a basket of porn. We said no, and the two older boys walked on to other tables, efficiently showcasing their wares to nearly every patron and passerby within eyesight. But she stopped in front of me, presented a reed basket full of porn, and asked, "What's the matter, soldier, you don't like girls?" She couldn't have been much more than twelve years old. Her dark, wavy hair was pulled back with a shiny ribbon, and she was wearing a clean yellow dress. Caught off guard, I started to chuckle, but she was a serious businessperson, and I found myself stopped midchuck. She was all merchant. I should have said something clever or that I was an airman and we were a little different than soldiers.

But then she said, "I have one with just boys, if you like."

And I turned bright red, and my witty rejoinder came out as, "No, I like girls just fine."

The entire café erupted in waves of laughter again as brother translated for uncle as if it wasn't obvious.

"Well then . . ." she said, pushing the basket toward me with a grin. "Will it be three dollars or two for five?"

"I like girls, but I love my wife," I said, desperately pointing to the wedding ring I was holding up like a shield. "So, I'm sorry, I can't."

"Ah," she said, "love." She smiled, and her brown eyes brightened. "But a ring is a contract, not a guarantee, is it not? Love is different. It is, I think . . . rare. A very nice, rare thing."

I let out a sigh of relief and relaxed.

"Are you certain this is love?" she said, leaning in until we were inches apart.

"Yes," I said. "I love her very much."

"Hmm," she said, staring at me with the look of a predator that had caught the scent of better prey. Then, with the barest pause for a breath, she pushed the basket down the table, stared down my comrades, and said, "But you and you, I think, still look for love, do you not? And these are but three dollars." She had one hand on her hip and shook three fingers as she spoke to them in a very serious tone.

There was another burst of laughter in the café as each of my teammates, one after the other, hung their heads, admitted defeat, and contributed something to the local economy.

A policeman smoking at the table next to us offered me the mouth-piece of his *shisha* water pipe, and I took a long hit and signaled the wait-er for a couple of fresh teas. As we smoked and watched her collect her money, he said to me, "A Sunni, a Shi'ite, and a Kurd working together to sell such things. It's like a shameful joke."

"Is that really such a terrible thing?"

"A few years ago, I would have said yes, taken them somewhere, and punished them severely. But, perhaps today, I will just see children who don't know any better, who need to eat, and I will leave it at that. Better still, perhaps this tea and fine conversation has distracted me, and I did not notice them at all."

I tossed in a handful of MRE candy packs when she reached over to retrieve her basket. Then she cleared her throat, smiled broadly, and, look-ing at each of us, said, "Thank you. I do hope we will do business again."

It was a doubly momentous occasion. One, I'd never heard a little girl talk like that before, and two, it was the first and only time I was

255

ever thanked for the business I conducted in Iraq. When she walked away from us, the boys who arrived with her suddenly returned and circled around her. I expected them to harass her or take her money away, but even though they were bigger and older, she treated them like little brothers and gave them all the candy she'd collected. They ate it as they walked away, riffling through their pockets and passing her the crumpled dollars and dinars they'd collected.

I realized then that, while not related, they were a family. The need for family is hardwired into us—it's the structure that usually helps us survive adversity. If we're lucky, we either rise to the occasion, or the right people emerge and step up to help us with our shortcomings.

As they walked away, I thought that this was the girl who should run Iraq. Not us, not the CPA, not the graybeards jockeying for power . . . but a girl who could truly make something from nothing. Internet downloads that kept them fed and cheerful and in clean clothes despite the subject matter, dust, and rubble—a girl who could make a family out of the lost and discarded. Iraq needed more girls in yellow dresses who could make family from strangers and then keep them happy and alive. Once we got back into our Humvee and headed out to our next mission, I was struck by the idea that perhaps what we know as right just might not work in the different place and in the different context that was Iraq. After stopping for tea and talking to the local police, I left feeling more hopeful than I had in what felt like a very long time.

It got better. When I returned to Camp Victory, I found out that Saddam Hussein had been captured in a raid of his childhood homeland in the dusty rock outskirts of Tikrit. He had been extracted from a dirt hole, far removed from his presidential palace on the lush green banks of the Tigris River, by a task force from the 4 ID (Fourth Infantry Division).

It was a bad day for insurgents, but it was a great day for us and most of Iraq. When the CPA made the public announcement and aired pictures of his checkup, Iraqis cheered, and celebratory gunfire cracked away well into the night. In the distance, it sounded like microwave popcorn that didn't taper off until dawn, and burnt popcorn does smell a little like cordite.

New democracies are startups. Not every one of them survives. But one step at a time, and it's important to enjoy the good days. Saddam was in prison. History would show we'd turned a corner. Whether it was going to be better or worse, only time would tell.

CHAPTER 25

December 2003—Camp Victory, Baghdad

The big mystery I was trying to solve was: What happened to GPS?

We had a different clientele at night than we did during the day. By day, my work was divided between supporting military operations across Iraq, improving communications between our coalition partners, and helping rebuild Iraq's ability to control its national capabilities. At night, I supported special missions from different services, agencies, and countries. It didn't leave much time to sleep, but I did get to travel around Baghdad and help work out some postwar communications, surveillance, and urban reconnaissance kinks.

We lost GPS service in and around Baghdad, and no one could explain why. It was working fine, and then, suddenly, it was just gone one night. That happened the month before I arrived.

Losing GPS service degraded navigation, targeting, and force tracking, plus the million other things we use GPS to do that we don't think about until it's gone. It also meant we couldn't use some of our best and favorite toys.

The army blamed Saddam—they said he must have left booby traps embedded somewhere in the electrical grid, and, when we restored power, they'd come to life to jam us. I bought that answer at first, but something didn't seem right. As I got closer to the CPA comm advisors, my access to data improved, and it appeared that even when commercial

259

power went out, GPS remained unavailable. That didn't track with the story. So, I looked at unit arrivals and departures, and I had an idea. To prove it, I needed to bring in a specialist from one of our sister agencies. He showed up one night at 0200 while I was working through an issue plaguing a UK special operations team. Whenever they entered a target area, their comms and data dropped out. They had an important mission coming up, and we were trying to figure it out. When our meeting ended, the six of them left. The new late arrival came over after they were gone, and he offered me his hand.

"Hi, my name is Marcus. My boss said you wanted help triangulating a signal, and I've got some time to spare."

Marcus was like an MIT, summa cum laude engineer who also happened to play professional rugby. He was that kind of guy who made women, and a couple of the men, lose their composure when he came by or if he asked them question. It wasn't hard to see why—he was tall, handsome, and smart. It would have been easy to be a little jealous, or just hate him outright, if he weren't so self-effacing. He was hard not to like. He approached problems like a kid getting ready to open Christmas presents, and when I explained our problem and what I thought had happened, he got excited.

"We can find out where the signal is coming from by going old school. Everything is digital and hooked into a computer now, but for this, we'll go old school. It'll be fun."

He left and immediately started circling Baghdad with an oscilloscope, a sort of metal detector for frequencies and types of energy. After a two-week period of driving in ever-decreasing circles, he and I finally came to a stop in a parking lot with an army signals van, a row of tactical generators capable of powering most of Baghdad, and an impressive tower laden with antennae.

"So that's it?" I asked as I checked my gear.

"Yep. The signal originates at that horn-and-drum antenna. The power's off the charts. They're pumping so much energy through that link, it's kind of amazing the antenna hasn't melted."

"That's a point-to-point link. Any idea where it goes?"

"You were right. It belongs to an army brigade supporting their general at division."

"Spectacular. You are absolutely awesome. What can I do for you?"

"Nothing. No need to worry. I was never here," Marcus said with a smile. "But this is a good thing, right? You figured out how GPS got jammed; why don't you look happy about it?"

"These guys rode in like cowboys, disregarded the rules, and violated their orders so they could look good by finding a way to broadcast their general's video conference (VTC) so it was always perfect, reliable, and interference-free. Problem was, they took down GPS service for Baghdad and created a big horseshoe-shaped dead zone around it in the process. Once I knock on that door, minions who outrank me will deny everything, demand proof, make counter allegations, and then somehow blame me. That's why I needed ironclad evidence. Once they realize what they've done, most of the conversation will be about covering their asses and crucifying me. Don't get me wrong. I'll be happy when GPS is in the green again and we're drinking good coffee somewhere else, but this will suck," I said, getting out of the small SUV.

"You sure you don't want me to come for backup?"

"Nah. We have to keep this one in the family. But if you don't mind picking me up over there in about forty-five minutes, I'd be much obliged. I also need your technical report as soon as we get back to Victory. We have to make sure this never happens again."

"Copy that, sir."

"Thanks, Marcus. You did a really good thing tonight."

I took a deep breath, pulled a paper from my pocket, and walked up the three steps to the metal door of the signals van.

I took out my flashlight and pounded it into the door so hard the paint chipped off.

"This is Captain Riley, CJTF-7 FMO. Open this door immediately, and identify yourself."

After a moment, the door opened a crack. "Sir?"

"This is Captain Riley. Open the door now. Whom am I speaking with?"

The door slowly opened, revealing a young soldier who was trying to wipe the sleep from his eyes. "PFC Willard, sir."

The inside of the desert-sand-colored van was basically an olive-drab walkway between racks of equipment with two workstations on each side. It looked like the soldier was the only one on night duty. I reached into my pocket and pulled out a folded sheet of paper. "PFC Willard, I'm Captain Riley, chief of frequency management for this taskforce. You are broadcasting an overpowered signal on the wrong frequency. Show me your settings now."

"Sir—"

"*Now*, Private. As soon as you do, call your commander. He's going to want to know what's going on. Show me now." I pushed past him to the console.

He grudgingly showed me. No surprise. Both the frequency and power output were nowhere close to what they were supposed to be. I handed him the paper. "This is the FRAGO (army order) that shows your authorized settings. Apply these changes, then call your command post."

He took the paper and looked from it to me. "Sir, only our warrant officer is authorized to change those settings. He comes by every few days, and I'm sure—"

"So, if I did this," I said, powering down the link, "he'd come right away?"

"Oh my God, sir."

"Call now. I'll wait."

While he dialed his command post, I programmed in the authorized frequency settings and reset the link. Eventually, someone would have to make the same changes on the other side, but I had done what I could for the moment. After a few minutes, he handed me the phone.

"This is Captain Riley; who am I speaking with?"

"This is Major Davis; my soldier tells me there's a problem?"

"Yes, sir. I just restored GPS to the theater. Your equipment was operating out of spec and in violation of the FRAGO. The result was that you jammed GPS in and around Baghdad. I have to report this to the commanding general in the morning, so I need to talk to the signals commander or his boss at division, because I want to get the words right. Right now, I'm stuck on whether this was an equipment issue or criminal activity."

"I understand, Captain. What was the criminal activity?"

"I would characterize it as sabotage."

"Copy that. Stand by."

After he woke up the signals commander and connected me, their commander yelled nonstop, mostly, about things that revolved around my ass and what he was going to do to it. When I was able to get a word in, I said, "Sir, this is just a professional courtesy. It's a done deal. If you don't accept that, your ass is going to jail. My job is to fix this and make sure it never happens again. Stick to the plan, and everyone gets to talk

263

and do their job. Go rogue, and you destroy other ops. Simple as that. You need to order your other van at division to broadcast per the FRAGO now, and I'll write this up as an administrative error instead of sabotage. I'll stay on the line for your confirmation, but I have a call scheduled with your general in"—I looked down at my watch—"seventeen minutes."

Listening to someone curse you, your family, and your body parts makes time pass slow.

"Done," the signals commander eventually said. "We made your changes, Captain." He said *Captain* like it was a bad thing. Then there was a click, and the line went dead.

Unlike his signals commander, the division general understood immediately what had happened. After introductions and a short explanation of the situation, I ended with, "That's it, sir. You may have some issues on your VTC link now, but going cowboy hurts everyone, and this hurt force protection and every mission in theater."

"Did you explain all of this to my signals commander?"

"Yes, sir. He wasn't happy with my candor, but he said they made the changes on your end and they'd follow the plan now. I'm inclined to see this as an admin and equipment issue, so long as it never happens again."

"Understood. It will not happen again. File your report. I'll brief this to the commanding general in the morning."

"Thank you, sir."

"Two last things. Is GPS back up now?"

"Stand by, sir." I took the GPS terminal from my pocket, opened the door, and stuck the antenna out. It immediately began to track and update. "Yes, sir. I can confirm three satellites, one just barely, and we'll get an official confirmation back from external agencies in about an hour. Notices to airmen and other navigation restrictions should start getting lifted by early afternoon."

"Outstanding. Last thing. You're an air force captain?"

"Yes, General."

"Ha. I wouldn't have expected that. Good job, airman. Out."

I left a still-confused PFC Willard and met up with Marcus. He was parked under a street lamp, finishing his report. He looked up from his laptop. "You're seven minutes late."

"How do I even respond to that? Oh, yeah—fuck you."

Marcus smiled. "That's not very nice," he said, turning his laptop around so I could see it. There was a matrix of signal strengths, and everything I cared about at that moment was green. "GPS service is available again, so I guess no crucifixion?"

I showed him my hands. "Yeah. Better than expected. Please take me to coffee so we can wrap this up before anyone changes his mind."

"You got it, boss."

The next day, I got Marcus a letter of appreciation from General Sanchez, the commanding general. Then he melted away into his next mission. A few days after that, the army gave my guys medals for the outstanding achievement of restoring GPS service to Iraq.

It was a turning point for my team, but sometimes, a little early success makes things a whole lot harder at the end.

CHAPTER 26

Iraq was a lawless free-for-all, and too many Iraqis with weapons and a grudge used the opportunity to scratch people off their "you wronged me" list. Tribes took care of tribal business and tried to protect their own. There were a few organized insurgent groups, mostly terrorists, exintelligence, and military, who knew what they were doing; the rest were gangs, cleric-led armies, and criminals. In the south, Iran was killing government bureaucrats and militia leaders and replacing them with their own. Anarchy beyond military- and tribal-controlled areas drove the CPA to restore the Iraqi defense force and police and to create a first-responder system that worked.

British soldiers in Basra arrested eight young Iraqis and beat one of them to death in custody. He was the son of a prominent police colonel. The soldiers were charged and punished, and restitution was made to the Iraqi family. But this event had repercussions that soured the relationships among several key US and UK intelligence and operations leaders at the CPA and inside the taskforce. Protests grew more frequent and violent; suicide bombings and VBIED activity increased; and new Iraqi police force members were widely targeted and murdered.

The Iraqi Governing Council (IGC) released a decision to replace civil family law with Sharia law. The move reverted women's rights back to the Stone Age and effectively made them property. Feminist protests erupted across Iraq. After appeals to Mr. Bremer, the decision was repealed. That was probably the biggest success story of January.

I took our antiterrorism/force-protection (AT/FP) team out for lunch in the Green Zone, because I was feeling strung out and needed a break and because they were heading home and had done me and my guys a solid. I owed them more than I could repay. Those army sergeants and warrant officers had become my new best friends when they destroyed a nasty IED just before one of my convoys drove right past it.

We ate at the Al Rasheed Hotel, off real plates, using real silverware and cloth napkins, like real people. Stairs in the middle of the restaurant led up to the discothèque club that took up the entire floor above the restaurant. The club used to be open every Wednesday night, and it was, on occasion, a notorious party. It wasn't as grand as a vice buffet in Moscow or an orgy in the Hamptons, but they tried real hard. High-quality booze flowed for its mix of CPA political partyers, contractors, invitation-only military, and special Iraqi DVs, who packed the dance floor with wasted, eager-to-please pretty girls and boys.

The discothèque was finally ordered closed after an epic evening when a rumor floated around that a young embassy staffer had taken pictures of the fun and when, the next morning, a Humvee with a turret gun was found crashed into a pole in the hotel parking lot and no one knew what had happened.

I stopped by the CPA after lunch. They'd scheduled a mission, but their phone just rang, and I needed to confirm it was still a go. We were still looking for a fire station.

I found the advisor I reported to for that project wasted at his desk, surrounded by a backsplash of half-empty bottles of pretty good booze. Towers of emptying alcohol bottles seemed to be growing on desks across the CPA. It meant things really weren't going well across Iraq.

Lately, CPA briefings were peppered with statistics and metrics that showed how the CPA was beating every timeline the Marshal Plan had achieved to stabilize and rebuild Germany after WWII, but declaring that their success was faster didn't mean they were succeeding. Stopping all pay to the Iraqi army without having another force in place that could provide control was certainly making things worse for us. Rocket and mortar attacks were nonstop at night, and the Iraqis we needed to help us rebuild the country—a country where, by the way, we didn't even speak the language—were being killed off just for being seen with us. With the stroke of a pen, through the power of accounting, the CPA had turned the largest fighting force in Iraq—the one with the home-field advantage and access to vast weapon stores—against us.

CPA advisors and officers wouldn't show up for meetings sometimes, but finding one drunk and passed out at his desk was new. I offered to drag him to one of the couches in a back office. His staff was mortified that I would even suggest it, but they did confirm our mission was still on. Fortunately, aside from first-responder matters, I only needed his approval for national policy issues. As I drove back to Camp Victory to link up with the MPs providing security, I wondered if they should change CPA to mean Contractor Party Animals. Capitalist Police of America didn't seem to be working anymore.

A few days earlier, I'd come across a report from a soldier who had been going door to door on a weapons search when he saw an old-timey fire truck drive by his position and pull into a compound just past their regular patrol on Highway 6, not far from Sadr City. Jack thought it sounded promising, so he put together a team, and we were going to check it out.

I was tasked to help where I could. Most fire stations in Baghdad were annex facilities on big government compounds, and when Saddam's control slipped, they were pillaged and destroyed. So far, despite my efforts, I was zero for five in trying to find a surviving fire station. The only fully functioning fire stations I knew about were in the Green Zone, Camp Victory, and the airport. Some of the smaller military forward operating bases (FOBs) were starting to bring in firefighting equipment, but it still wasn't enough. This was the last lead I had, and if it didn't pan out, I'd have to shift gears. I had new orders to start working with the Iraqi police to help coordinate their initial communications and to participate in a Baghdad 911 plan that seemed to be more of a contractor-proposed wet dream than a possible way ahead. Getting the police basic radios, reliable phones, and network access was going to be challenging enough.

The MP compound on Camp Victory consisted of a main building, a few outbuildings, and a large motor pool secured behind easily defendable walls. Our convoy had two Humvees with turret gunners and two gun trucks with mounted weapons that made the turret machine guns on the Humvees look like toys.

"Hi, Jack," I said, shaking his hand. "I'm glad to see you, but I thought the CPA would send someone from civil defense or engineering for our field trip." Jack was wearing khakis, red Oakley sunglasses, and a Green Bay ball cap. His face was windburned, and he wore the scraggly blond beginnings of a moustache and beard.

"They're all too busy getting the new equipment for the Iraqi police organized so they can start issuing it," Jack said as he shimmied into beige body armor a little too tight for his frame. "This is Captain Delfina Green," he said, motioning to the woman next to him. She had high cheekbones, mocha skin, warm brown eyes, and a ready smile. "You two will be working together to support the main police station south of embassy row in the Babil district. It's essential we get it up and running. We have to counter the crime problem in south Baghdad."

"Captain Riley," she said, shaking my hand. Her hands were cool for the desert, but it was a good handshake.

"Call me Bill."

"Then call me Del. Jack's told me a lot about you."

I looked at Jack, but he just held his hands up and made that *I don't know what she's talking about* face.

"What did he say exactly, Del?"

"Only that you were short, ugly, and disagreeable. But he did mumble under his breath that you were a man who could get things done."

"I am short, and Jack works for the State Department, at the CPA. So, you should know that when his lips are moving, not much truth comes out his mouth hole. What's your take so far?" Then I looked at Jack, whose face was bright red, and I figured it out. "You guys are dating, aren't you?"

"Yes. But let me ask you a question. Is it true you got GPS working again in Baghdad?"

"I have a great team."

"Then I think ugly and disagreeable is just Jack's way of saying distinguished and interesting."

"Thank you, Del. You're a better woman than he deserves. I'm in your hands. Let's go find a fire station."

Our convoy was attacked en route. We took fire from a small, one-story building on a grassy rise. I saw muzzle flashes and heard rounds smack against the armored doors of our Humvee. Del made a call over the radio. There was an electric servo whine, and all the big guns on the convoy turned to target the building. I could hear the *thunk, thunk, thunk* of mortar and heavy machine-gun fire from the gun trucks and the throaty five-round bursts from our turret. By the time we rounded the corner, all hostile fire had ceased, and the building sheltering the insurgents firing on us was collapsed and burning.

Eventually, we found what we were looking for. There was a metal gate and a high stone wall that surrounded the fire station. The MPs took up positions in a semicircle across the street from the entrance, using their vehicles as cover. On either side of the gate, built into the wall, was a sandbagged guard position manned by what looked like ten-year-old boys with AKs. One pointed his weapon at us while his brother disappeared and shouted for their father.

A man appeared at the top of the roof from behind another sandbagged position with a heavy machine gun. After looking at us, he said something to the boys; they lowered their weapons, and Del gave the command for her team to lower theirs. The compound was in a relatively open space between warehouses and industrial buildings to the south and near the beginnings of the Sadr City slums a few blocks to the north. It looked like a fortress church from the Middle Ages that was part of a much bigger petroleum storage or refinery area where old chain-link security fences had torn-down sections. Garbage collected along the fence and walls, and even the street didn't look well used anymore.

Jack opened the door and stepped out with his hands up. He introduced himself and explained what we were looking for in Arabic. After a few exchanges, the front gate opened a couple of feet with a metallic squeal.

"That's our cue," Jack said, and I opened my door.

"Does it sound promising?" I asked.

"He says they have all the fire equipment, they used to work here, and they're willing to talk."

"I like the sound of that," I said, slinging my M-14 over my shoulder and grabbing a box of MREs. I fell in next to Jack as we walked over to the gate, and I heard Del on the radio reminding me that if anything even felt wrong, let her know, and they'd tear the gate down.

I appreciated that. I could hear gunfire in the distance and see columns of smoke rising from at least three areas in north Baghdad.

The gates were massive, rusty yellow-and-blue metal slabs at least two stories tall, and they closed behind us with a mournful metal-on-metal wail.

At least six other potential shooters were positioned in the high windows and along the roof with Kalashnikov rifles pointed at us. The one who seemed to be in charge, who acted like the father of the boys with guns, was an older man, maybe in his fifties, with a short, grizzled white-and-black beard and mustache and gray eyes. He wore a red-and-white headscarf wrapped like a turban, and he asked us a rapid series of questions I couldn't follow.

"Why did you come all the way out here?" Jack translated for me.

I pointed to the smoke columns to the north of us. "There's not a day Baghdad doesn't burn. We need more fire stations to protect more places."

"I told him," Jack said. "He said if we try to take the place, they'll fight. So, I offered to trade him for a big villa in a better neighborhood."

"I didn't know you could do that," I said to Jack. Then I said to the father, "*Tabarru'a*. This is a gift. For talking. See, MREs. *Ha'rel Lak'a*, this is for you."

The father pulled MREs out of the box and began tossing them to his people. Then he said to me, "You come. We wait, drink tea."

I smiled at the father, then looked at Jack and frowned. "So, I'm the hostage?"

"Looks like. It will take a little while to set up the deal for the villa, and they're going to want to see the new place before they move. Anyway, you're a resourceful guy; you'll figure something out if things go south."

"Yeah, yeah. And you always look so surprised when I call you a bastard."

I followed the father inside the station, drank tea, and showed the kids how to use the MRE meal heaters and where the candy packs were. Jack got on the radio and set up the deal to trade the fire station for a villa. After Jack finished arguing with the CPA property officer and left with two Iraqis from the fire station, Del was able to bring the rest of her convoy behind the gate. She found the boys and me with our long guns leaned up against the wall, making and flying paper airplanes while the dad smoked and watched. She came up behind me flanked by two of her sergeants.

"My guys are defending this position, and this is what the air force is doing?"

"It beats shooting people. Anyway, it's good for kids to play when they can."

"That's true."

"And it's never too early to motivate kids to reach for the sky. Flying is freedom, and now that the moon's in reach, we have to encourage the next generation to reach for the stars."

"And that's going to happen in Iraq?"

"Who knows," I said, throwing my last airplane. Three of them were still in the air, making lazy circles around the bay, and the kids were running around launching more. "I asked for the tour. Want to come along?"

"Sure."

"Aziz? Show. Fire station?" I asked, motioning all around.

"*Naa'am*, yes," he said as he motioned us to follow. His youngest made the universal noise kids make when playtime is over, grabbed on to my body armor, and looked at his dad. What followed was the stern speech dads give, and both children sighed, picked up the airplanes we'd made and their AKs, and went back to guarding the gate under the supervision of the remaining "uncles" in the windows. I retrieved my M-14, and, as I was slinging it across my shoulder, Del caught sight of it and laughed.

"I thought the air force was high tech. Why are you carrying around that relic?"

"You're right. I borrowed this from the army."

"Why?"

"It shoots straight and does what I need it to do. Anyway, if I actually have to fire this thing, it means your guys either aren't doing their job or something's gone wrong, and my basic shooting skills aren't going to make much of a difference anyway."

"Don't be a pessimist, it's bad for morale."

"I'm not a pessimist, I just know my limits," I said, lifting the M-14 up and passing it to Del. "She's a little heavy," I said. "But she can still kick ass, and that makes her a good backup. If I can't avoid fighting altogether."

She handed my M-14 back to me. "You're certainly not conventional. At least it'll make a better club than an M-16 when you run out of ammo."

"See. Another feature."

The fire station was a huge bay with garage doors at the front and back so vehicles could drive through the building, as well as upper floors with living, kitchen, and storage space. Inside was in pristine order. Gear was neatly stowed, and it still looked serviceable; water flowed from the spigots and hydrants; and the phones had dial tones. There was even a flush toilet on each floor that still worked.

Both fire trucks would have looked at home in a vintage parade. They were pumper trucks; one was short and red, the other long and yellow with ladders on the sides. Both were clean, waxed, and glowed in the fading rose-colored light. The CPA was putting together a contract for a fleet of new, European-style Mercedes Benz fire trucks for Baghdad, but that was the future.

The MPs insisted Aziz open the doors and enter each room first, and they followed at the ready. We walked through an upstairs dorm room to a single bedroom with a large window covered with iron bars, and Aziz showed me a gray uniform I had never seen before that had a badge on the sleeve with crossed fire trucks. He pointed from the uniform, to himself, to the building. I smiled, nodded, and patted him on the shoulder. I think it meant he was the former fire chief and had saved the building from being looted and burned because he loved it. There were pictures on the wall of the station being built and of him in front of different crews. From the back window, there was a commanding view of the abandoned refinery.

Then he took us to a sturdy, wood-plank french door. When he unlocked it, we were on a roof deck three or four stories up with a commanding view over the walls into the neighboring area. Past the deck was a tower, like a minaret, that reached another three or four stories high. Aziz began to climb. The MPs took up defensive positions, and I followed him, one hand against the smooth stone, the other hand on the still-hot iron rail. The narrow stairs corkscrewed around the tower until we reached a platform under a stone roof just big enough for two people. There was a 360-degree view, and I could see across the Tigris River to the Green Zone, to Sadr City north of us, and across the industrial wasteland into New Baghdad. The sun was setting, fires were still burning in places in the north and east, and I could see the two vehicles from our convoy heading toward us about six blocks away. Aziz and I sat there for a few minutes as he looked around and pointed to things. We spoke with what common words we knew.

To me, it seemed like he was saying goodbye.

It was dusk when Jack and the "uncles" returned to the fire station. After a brief discussion between Aziz and the uncles, the family surrendered the fire station and loaded their things into a pickup truck. Aziz and his sons took the front seats, and the six uncles sat in the back with their weapons ready. Jack took them to their new home, and Del arranged for two vehicles and more than half her team to stay and secure the fire station until reinforcements arrived in the morning.

It felt like we'd accomplished something important. We hadn't won a major battle or stopped a terrorist cell from blowing up a government building, but fire stations are an important part of a community. Maybe they wouldn't have pancake breakfasts, but over the next year, how many homes wouldn't burn down? How many people might that one station save?

You savor those moments. They don't last.

CHAPTER 27

January 2004—Camp Victory, Baghdad

CIA Chief Weapons Inspector David Kay announced that his team had failed to find evidence of stockpiled nuclear, biological, or chemical (NBC) weapons in Iraq. While there was evidence of Iraq's continued research in those areas, as well as evidence of a major period of NBC destruction in the midnineties, he was confident that 85 percent of Iraq had been examined and that finding significant WMDs was unlikely.[15] He stepped down from his post and called for an independent investigation into the intelligence gathered before the Iraq War, and we were unsure of how that would affect us. There were a lot of theories on where the WMDs had gone. Some said that they'd been shipped out to a neighboring country as we were invading. Others argued there were still secret caches hidden in the 15 percent of the country that remained unexplored.

I was inclined to believe we'd done our job too well during Desert Fox—that Saddam had cleaned up the mess, and either he'd lied to us about still having WMDs or his people had lied to him.

Only one thing was certain: the intelligence community was getting an enema.

As my convoy rolled through Camp Victory, en route to the CPA, it struck me that every building I looked at was a bunker. Windows and

---

15   Lauren Johnston, "Kay: 'We Were Almost All Wrong,'" CBS News, January 30, 2004, https://www.cbsnews.com/news/kay-we-were-almost-all-wrong.

doors were covered in decorative bars and hidden behind sandbag walls. The stonework across the compound had originally been white, but seasons of sandstorms had dulled and yellowed the walls. The architecture of Saddam's Al Faw Water Palace complex was predator-dental: administrative outbuildings resembled bicuspids, and villas looked like gold-capped molars. The guard towers inside the compound were designed to keep an eye on Saddam's "guests." They were positioned not only to keep intruders out but also to ensure that Saddam's guests, staff, and kin stayed in. Their rounded towers rose sharply above the other buildings. They flanked the mouth of each entry like fangs.

I got summoned to the CPA Ministry of Communications (MoC) to discuss the transition of Iraq from US control back to an Iraqi-ruled government. The transition would happen by the end of summer. They had less than thirty days to write a policy to transfer current projects and to secure formal agreements between the Iraqis who would take over the work from US forces and contractors. The delicate, but essential, part of the plan was the agreement on who would control what when Iraq was a sovereign nation again and how US military force communications would operate in Iraq from that point on. It was important, but I had other things on my mind.

My wife, Jodi, was very pregnant, I was in Iraq, and our landlord broke our lease to sell the house we were renting when the San Antonio real-estate market started heating up. He was a scumbag. We had a few options, but none of them were great. In the end, Jo thought the best thing to do was find a new place ASAP. Personnel from both our squadrons helped her, and the military even agreed to move us again because it wasn't our fault. But it was hard on her, and I was worried. She tried to be upbeat, but I knew it was taking a toll. When she did find a new place, the only thing she asked me for was a new bed.

She told me over the phone. "We wore out our bed."

"How is that possible?" I asked. "Our last mattress held up fine for like ten years."

"Well, congratulations, we did. It was mostly your fault anyway, so good job."

"Jo . . ."

"Plus, my back really hurts when I'm pregnant."

"So, just buy a new mattress."

"I did, but you're not going to like it, or the price."

"Why?"

"Have you ever heard of Tempur-Pedic memory foam?"

"No."

"Astronauts use it, and it's great for the back—in fact, it molds itself to you. I had them send you a factory sample . . ."

It cost almost as much as her wedding ring, and what arrived in Baghdad was a rectangular cross section of the mattress: a foot long, four inches wide, and two feet deep, wrapped in soft beige material. It was squishy, and Jo had pinned a note to it. *This one has a ten-year warranty. So, you can go all out.* That at least made me smile.

As I walked through the Republican Guard Palace barriers and up to the CPA entrance, it looked like all of Saddam's statues had been hauled away but one. It sat on its side, and Saddam's dour bronze face looked out at the parking lot like the head of a decapitated giant.

Three men in traditional white Arabic robes were clustered around the front of his face, and as I walked up, it looked like they were dancing.

As I got closer, I heard, "Oy, you bastards, get away from there."

The three Arab gentlemen hastily adjusted their robes and began to run away from the two British security NCOs who were now dashing after them.

There was a piece of paper duct-taped to Saddam's helmet, rustling in the breeze, a puddle at the base of Saddam's head, and the stench of a broken toilet at a summer ball game. As I got closer, I noticed the sign was handwritten in both English and Arabic. It said, *Please do not urinate on Saddam Hussein's face. It is NOT hygienic.*

Urine was still dripping off his nose.

I walked into the MoC meeting with the understanding that I was there as a military advisor. Ten minutes in, it became clear the CPA people hosting the meeting were under the impression that I worked for them and that I would do their job for them. I hate it when people think I work for them when I don't. Fifteen minutes into the meeting, I told them no, and it stunned the room to silence. "Here's what I get from this meeting so far," I said. "The CPA is going away. You need a game plan. It's important for future operations, economics, and diplomacy with Iraq. You don't have much time. You really don't have a plan, so you want me to write it for you, but you want total control."

"That's unfair, Captain. We do have a plan," said the man behind the podium holding the projector remote. "Give me a moment, and I'll show you what we'll be doing at the CPA."

I took my seat while he looked through the slides, and after a few minutes, he put one of them on the screen. Mostly, it involved getting documents into legal review and getting them signed.

"Is that it?" I asked.

"Yes," said the man running the briefing.

"So how many slides are in that briefing deck?"

"Just over a hundred."

"So, in round numbers, one task for you—the organization responsible for diplomacy and policy—and ninety-nine for the warfighter to write your policy for you. Let me offer you an alternative division of labor . . ."

Hours later, we concluded our business, but it was more "to be continued" than an ending.

I had one last thing I needed to prepare before I left the Green Zone.

IEDs had grown even more sophisticated. New insurgent tactics shifted bombing attacks from coalition forces to directly against the Iraqi people. The death toll of civilians spiked to record highs, and many Iraqis were maimed or badly injured. Gathering places had been specifically targeted to inflict the most terror possible. Multiple attacks destroyed my favorite café in Iraq. Sixteen people died in the first bombing. Eight more died two weeks later, and the area was finally abandoned as just another rubble pile in a Baghdad neighborhood.

Across the major cities in Iraq, the smoldering mood erupted. It became impossible to just sit and talk with Iraqis in the comfort of their own neighborhoods without recklessly risking our lives and marking any friendly Iraqis for death at the hands of their neighbors for the crime of drinking tea and trying to understand each other while having a smoke with their would-be liberators. For me, that was when everything changed.

Family can be familiar and frustrating—or as shocking and functional as resellers of porn in dusty, chaotic Ramadi in the heart of Baghdad. Eventually, we figured out a few things, made some changes, and killed a few talented bad guys, and the bombings slowed again.

It had been a while. Too many Iraqi civilians had died at the hands of Iraqi terrorists. I had one last thing to do before we returned to Camp Victory.

We came to a stop by what was left of the café. It was a hot, gray, cloudy day, and I waited for the call to prayer to stop before I left the air-conditioned comfort of my armored Humvee with its mounted weapon and cheerful gunner. I crunched over the gravel to where I had smoked and talked with Iraqis from that neighborhood just weeks before. The café that used to have people living in the apartments above and around it was reduced to three standing walls around a hill of debris that still smelled like scorched metal. The road wasn't deserted, and the soldiers I was with clearly thought I was nuts. So did the people I passed on the street, who stopped to stare. I was wearing layers of combat armor with a battle rifle over my shoulder and other weapons clipped to my hip and chest, walking alone with a huge bouquet of pretty flowers.

Regardless of where we come from and what we believe, no one wants to be the monster that pulls the trigger to kill someone who's come to honor the dead. Generally, if only for a moment, we set aside our differences out of respect and remembrance. However, there are real monsters out there who just see opportunity in a dropped guard; those are the people we need to stop. Idealists who don't let humanity get in their way. That's as good a definition of the scary creatures we call monsters as anything.

I'd asked the flower lady in the Green Zone for a bouquet as big as I could wrap my arms around. I didn't care what the flowers were so long as they were bright colors and smelled nice and she wrapped the whole thing with yellow ribbon. I had wanted to pay my respects sooner, but it was dangerous, and I had to wait for a lull. The florist and soldiers assumed I wanted the flowers for a girl. In retrospect, they were right.

When I walked through the shattered walls, even the sound of our chuffing Humvee was silenced. Crossing the threshold was like shutting a door. It was a somber place, so unlike what it had been before, when the old man ran the café. He made great tea, and his wife made tasty snacks from filo, nuts, and honey. His sons were still boys, but they were generous, especially when they packed *shisha* into the clay bowls of their water pipes and then fiddled with them and lit them so they smoked well with an easy draw. It had been a popular place, and people had come from all over to talk and argue and drink and smoke. In a pinch, Pops could make a decent cup of french press coffee out of truly awful grounds. They were good people who'd made a great place out of bits and pieces of nothing, and once I was there, standing in the muted rubble, I was angry that everyone and everything was gone.

I took off my helmet and set the flowers a few feet up into the side of the mound, knelt in the gravel, and realized I hadn't thought things through and didn't know what to say. My feelings were . . . complicated. I asked God to look after the souls who'd died there, and I prayed that the girl in the yellow dress had gotten somewhere far away to someplace safe, where she was OK with her patchwork family. Then, I didn't know what else to say. I looked at the destruction and flowers. I was hopeful for what we were trying to accomplish, and then I was filled with doubt. I was shocked by how easy hope fades. We'd done so many good things across Iraq, but none of them felt good anymore. Then the wind picked up, and the petals fluttered, but the bouquet stayed fixed to where I'd planted it.

After a few more minutes of taking it in, saying goodbyes, and trying to remember every detail of what the café and the people in it had looked and sounded like, I stood up and crunched back to my Humvee to return to base. As I secured my helmet to my head, I turned back for one last look at a place I knew I wouldn't ever return to. In that moment, the clouds broke, and the flowers blazed in a thin stream of light that cut through the shadows of the ruin. I stared. The people on the street stopped and turned to stare at the glow. It was beautiful. Then the clouds coalesced. The light was gone, and everyone turned slowly back to what they'd been doing.

The trip back to Camp Victory was uneventful. No one shot at us while we were at the ruin, or while I was out in the open, or on the way back to base. So that was progress.

One time, in Iraq, there was a little girl with a yellow dress who made a home for other children she found orphaned by the war. She took care of them and taught them how to work together, and they earned enough money for food, and to live, and for clean clothes. She made them into a family. I only saw her once, but she's someone we should never forget.

CHAPTER 28

We wound through traffic, crossed bridges over the wide, reedy Tigris River, and passed neighborhood buildings with shared walls and sections still made from brick and tile laid over sun-dried mud. The streets were overcrowded, and more cars drove on the wrong side of the road than on the side where they belonged. Children walked amid the traffic, and donkey-drawn wagons cut across the highway. It was morning rush hour in Baghdad, and getting traffic cops back on the payroll wasn't a priority.

Cars were more prevalent than they'd been when I first arrived. Iraq had no driver education or licensing, so if you could afford a car or truck, *Insha'Allah*, you drove it. Traffic jams on side streets were usually the result of an accident or something that began when two guys recognized each other and then stopped their cars in the middle of a major road for a talk that became a social event for the occupants of five or ten other cars. Sometimes there was honking. Sometimes there was singing. Occasionally, there was an exchange of gunfire, but that happened less than I expected, given that almost every male was armed with an old, Soviet-era assault rifle. Immediately after the liberation of Iraq, the biggest problem in the suburbs of Baghdad, aside from looting, was drunk drivers causing accidents every evening.

In key locations just off busy streets, Iraqis with containers and funnels gathered to sell gas. If you wanted to buy some, all you had to do was roll down a window and follow the gasoline smell to a cluster of people standing just off the roadside next to an odd collection of bottles, coolers, and drums leaking gasoline. Metal barrels mounted on wheels were popular. Collections of two-liter screw-top soda bottles and one-liter water bottles, drooping in the sun as the gas softened the plastic, were common sights. The "premium" bootleg fuel stands had funnels to guide gas into your tank and rags to wipe up anything spilled on a customer's car. Operators of budget-oriented stands poured gas into their buyer's tanks using their cupped hands to channel the gas in. It wasn't unusual to see older Iraqis smoking cigarettes while pouring gas through their hands into a car's tank, usually while arguing with a smoking driver revving up his engine to let the gas man know he was in a hurry.

Entrepreneurs walked up and down the gas-stand lines and hawked their wares. Refueling had begun to take a long time, and while Iraqis waited in their cars, they could buy tea, food, newspapers, and trinkets. The sudden fuel shortage that no one could explain created new classes of merchants and caused long lines to spring up everywhere. There were more roadside gas sales than I'd ever seen, and siphoning fuel from parked cars was big business. Some Iraqis would horde gas for the days when demand drove up the prices, and every Iraqi's car was filled with extra containers. If they could get gas, they could sell their excess later at a profit to other Iraqis too impatient to wait in line. Prices kept going up; it was unregulated and inconsistent.

Fortunately, we got all our fuel on base, but the last few weeks had been frustrating for the Iraqis and contractors in Baghdad. It wasn't uncommon to wait hours in line only to have the station run out of fuel just when you got to the pump. You didn't want to be the kid who posted the *No gas, come back tomorrow* sign. Drivers threw everything within reach at them, but those boys could run.

I left Camp Victory with Captain Delfina Green, US Army, and her team of MPs in a convoy of armored Humvees with heavy guns. We talked and drove for a while. We'd just finished a series of mission-essential errands, and we were en route to the Iraqi Ministry of Interior (MoI) to oversee the initial issue of gear for a new police station. She and Jack had been seeing more and more of each other since we found and negotiated the transfer of that fire station. We took pride in it finally getting back in service. The crew there had already put out two neighborhood fires.

"So how are things going with you guys?" I asked.

"I'm not ready to have his babies, but I might consider it, if he asked right."

"That's saying something."

"That boy's crazy, smart, and charming."

"That's not the Jack I know."

"Maybe he shows me a different side than he shows you."

"Thank God for that."

Del smiled. "How's your wife doing? Any progress naming that baby of yours that's coming soon?"

"She's stressing, but she'll be fine. Jo's tougher than she knows, but I seem to have a knack for picking all the baby names she hates."

"She's in a delicate state, and with her man being gone . . . It'll all work out when you see each other again."

"I do like the sound of that."

The convoy slowed as we turned down a side street and crossed what looked like a community market. Children were out in force, selling everything from candy to DVDs to fake Rolexes. I thought about buying a DVD for an instant, but we were pressed for time, and, outside of the "safe" zones, DVDs were still mostly porn and Adam Sandler movies.

I laughed every time I saw them side by side in some kid's sale basket. Maybe in Baghdad, *Little Nicky* was a special kind of kink.

The kids began to converge on us, and I couldn't get the face of that kid that looked like my son Xander out of my head. Never put a gun to a kid's head if you can help it. It fucks up the both of you. I flipped up the safety on my 9MM pistol. Then I took a deep breath and looked around. This was different. We were in armored vehicles with turret gunners, and these kids were randomly milling around, not locked arm in arm in a blocking line with some scumbag pimping them.

I realized I was sweating.

I didn't want to get pinned down again. I called up to our gunner, "Tell them not today. We've got to go, and I don't want the gravel to hit 'em."

He said something in Arabic too fast for me to follow, and the kids broke out laughing. They made a show of jumping to safety before we pulled out.

Our driver crept forward, and we were away.

I safetied my weapon and sighed.

Del looked at me, and her brown eyes narrowed. "Bad experience?"

"Yeah. My first time out. Insurgent scumbag used a bunch of kids to stop our Humvee so they could trigger IEDs. It had a happy ending, but groups of kids still . . . make me cautious."

"You OK?"

"Yeah, it took a while, but yeah. Funny story. The day after it happened, I met Jack. We had to work a miserable project for my commanding general and Ambassador Bremer, and we didn't quite hit it off."

"You're both stubborn, that's for sure."

The route to the Iraqi MoI is made up mostly of muddy roads that twist and turn for miles. We passed the national soccer stadium, then continued to wind our way through back roads and gates until we were let into an underground parking area massive enough to park an armor battalion with just over forty tanks and still have room to drive around. The roof was supported by a forest of concrete columns, and MoI was using the place to stage new equipment for the Iraqi police force.

Del left her guys with orders to get lunch and to make sure the vehicles were prepped to go in case we needed to leave fast. We walked over to a table, and the quartermaster had her sign a few documents before he handed her a folder full of paperwork and pointed us to the pallets of equipment set aside for our police station. The equipment was everything you'd expect to find in a police station. It included desks, chairs, lamps, weapon racks, computers, phones, new body armor, handcuffs, uniforms, filing cabinets, and assorted supplies. There was even a coffee maker.

I sat on a pallet, and Del paced as we waited for the police transport scheduled to pick up their station's equipment.

"You know this isn't actually their first issue of equipment," Del said as she stretched her arms over her head.

"So, the CPA decided to do it in stages? I guess that makes sense."

"Yes and no. The first issue was at the Iraq Police Academy. They were issued Glock 19 handguns, uniforms, basic equipment, and some body armor, but after they graduated, the cops that actually turned up for work only had a hodgepodge of their old equipment and weapons. And some of those weapons were rusted solid."

"What did they say happened?"

"Usually, they said they couldn't understand what we were saying. Even with a translator. Turns out, as soon as we'd issue them equipment, most of the new cops would sell it on the black market first chance they got. It took a while to sort out. Mostly because no one wanted to believe it was true."

"How'd you fix it?"

"We partly fixed it. Also turns out that too many of the new recruits were criminals and insurgents. The criminals tended to grab the money and run, so they disappeared fast. Insurgents tend to stay on, hiding in plain sight, so they're hard to sort from the good cops, at least for now. We got a lot of the weapons back, but it wasn't until we started docking their pay for losing their equipment that their weapons suddenly reappeared."

"So, are we wasting our time here or what?"

"I don't know yet, but I've seen our police chief with his troops, and I have to say he's pretty sharp. Despite being ordered not to trust anyone, he impressed me. He knows enforcement and how to do the job. He's a man of action. You'll like him."

"Is that him?" I asked, pointing to a guy hanging out the passenger-side window of a small white pickup truck and yelling at an MoI guard sleeping with his back against a column. The young guard jumped to his feet, stood at attention, and repeated, "Yes, sir," in Arabic. Then the police chief got out of the truck, and as he approached, the guard cowered in place.

"Weapon," the chief said, and the guard passed him what looked like a Bizon, a compact heavy submachine gun. They sprayed accurate bullets and could hold up to sixty-four rounds. The chief inspected it, then handed it back to the pale guard. Then he patted the kid on the shoulder, leaned in, and said something I couldn't hear. The guard turned red, snapped to attention, and saluted the chief. After the chief returned the salute, the young guard started walking the perimeter like he had a purpose.

That was interesting, but it wasn't what surprised me. I was surprised when the chief walked up to the MoI major smoking a cigarette with his feet up on a table and asked him, "Are you in charge of security?"

The guard major took a deep draw off his cigarette and replied, "Yes, I am."

"Good to know." The chief stepped around the desk and punched the major in the face so hard it knocked him and his chair to the ground. The major dropped his cigarette and scrambled for his sidearm, but the chief stood on his hand before he could pull it from its holster. Everyone in the huge parking garage stopped what they were doing and turned to see what was going on. I expected the major's men to come to his rescue, but not a single one moved to help.

The guard major spit out a torrent of gutter Arabic, at the core of which was, "Fuck. Fuck, fuck you, do you know who I am?"

"I need to bring something to your attention," the chief said, grinding out the major's still-burning cigarette butt with his free foot and then resting his knee on the major's chest as he leaned into his face. "Your security is shit, and we just had a firefight outside your compound. You should check on your men and make sure your perimeter is secure." He stood up and stepped away. "Now."

The major rolled over and crawled to his feet, grumbling, but he left without a single look back.

"Del, you were right," I said. "I like him a lot."

That was how I first met Iraqi police chief Mohammed Sawan— Chief Mo in private.

Del introduced me to the chief. He was a few inches taller than me, and he had the frame of a boxer. I assumed from the way he carried himself that he'd spent time in the military or secret police before moving to law enforcement. He had a well-trimmed black beard and mustache that were showing just a touch of gray. We exchanged greetings and talked together briefly before Del and the young Iraqi police officers left to inventory gear. I went over the communications kit with him. A radio base station and repeaters. Handheld radios with basic GPS location functions. Cell phones and chargers. Phone lines had already been installed, and there was a dish on the roof of the station that would let the computer connect to the Internet. He asked thoughtful questions about how to use different comm features to give his patrols an edge.

Del returned just as we were finishing. "Everything's good to go, and you can load up now, Chief Sawan."

The chief laughed. "You shall call me Mohammed, and I will call you Bill and Del. We work together and make neighborhoods safe again." Then he motioned to his men to start loading equipment. Before he left, he said, "Make no mistake. This is not like your police. This is another war where many good men and women will die before, *Insha'Allah*, we win."

Chief Mo took off his black leather jacket and began working with his men to stack all the gear, comm equipment, furniture, and supplies issued to him to outfit their police station into the smallest pickup truck I'd ever seen. He brought four other guys with him. They were cops of various ranks wearing light blue shirts and navy pants and vests. They took turns loading and smoking until they'd piled the small pickup truck almost three times higher than it was long with equipment. It was stacked so high they ran out of rope and needed to scrounge things to finish the job of holding the mess together. They tied the rope to a chair, looped a fan cord around that, then tied the cord off on the foot of a desk. A tarp was thrown over the top part of the pile and bound to the truck bed by extension cords. Finally, several turns of duct tape wrapped around the pile cinched everything together. Then, the chief made two of the guys climb onto each side of the crazy pile in the truck bed so they could hold everything together as they drove to their station over some of the worst roads in Baghdad. I watched them sit and smoke while their boss worked, and I thought it was disrespectful. However, when he told them to climb into that teetering pile and hold it together all the way home, his order, as crazy as it was, wasn't even questioned.

I was worried for them. Their chief was a man who took charge and got things done, but while they had their own way of doing things, it was like watching Cub Scouts on their first field exercise. Only they were armed, smoked more, and were responsible for public safety.

The chief and his driver climbed into the cab, and the last of his men were helped up to the roof of the truck, where they found a way to sit with their weapons at the ready. Everyone waved as they got underway. They represented hope and a fresh start.

I watched them bounce and sway as they made their way down the road. Then they turned the first corner, and I couldn't see them anymore. We followed them out at a respectful distance, just in case they got in trouble.

I gave them about one-in-three odds that they'd make it back to the station.

CHAPTER 29

February 2004—Camp Victory, Baghdad

It was the middle of midnight chow at the DFAC[16]—that magical military mealtime when you can get most of the leftovers from dinner cooked up with eggs and anything else on the breakfast menu. It was quiet, I was just about caught up, and except for me, a few AT/FP guys working in the back, and the two young soldiers manning the front desk, our communications suite was a dark, empty cave of a building. My stomach growled. Midnight chow sounded perfect.

Then I looked up, and there he was. I laughed and said, "I thought I recognized a familiar face in the crowd, and here you are."

He'd showed up unannounced, but I wasn't surprised. Before he even said a word, he handed me a hot coffee and held open a bag for me to inspect. It was full of fresh donuts. Normally, I wouldn't care. I only eat one type of donut—french crullers—but the bag was full of them.

"Hi, John." I realized as soon as I took the cup and said the words that the visit wasn't unexpected. His dark hair was longer than I remembered. The brush mustache was new to me, but it was full enough to have been there a while. Same piercing brown eyes, same goofy grin, same deft movements. A few new small scars on his face. "Welcome to the CJTF-7 FMO," I said. "But you knew that. What can I do for you?"

---

16   Dining facility.

"Come with me," he said. "Let's catch up. I have Cubans." He looked like a local businessman—except for the weapon he carried. On the way out of the building, we ran into a small group sporting Ranger tabs. Instead of an AK-47 slung over his shoulder, he had the kind of plastic Austrian weapon that made army guys excited; even in the yellow streetlights, they stopped him and asked if they could hold it. Then they clustered around to feel its weight, check the sight, and pet it.

We walked on for a while after that, because John always liked to walk awhile before he got around to talking. The coffee was good. Strong, black, fresh. Just how I always used to drink it. John was older than me and had always outranked me, probably by a lot now. The last time I'd seen him was Kuwait, and he'd been dating Lu.

"So, you're still a COMMO (communications officer). I thought by now you would have gone back to Intel or transferred to OSI.[17] You happy?"

"I am."

"You could make a lot more out of the military," he said after a while.

"I keep hearing that, but I like my life now."

"How much longer will you be here?" he asked as we passed over a small Romanesque bridge.

"In Baghdad, just over a month. What can I do to help?" I figured the reason for the visit would come out soon enough, but I was done with my coffee.

"So, you're still married. And that little boy of yours has got to be what, four?" he asked, apparently in no rush to get to business.

"Xander would say 'almost five,' and we have a new baby on the way, but I don't know if it's a boy or girl yet."

---

17   Office of Special Investigations.

"What is it about you having babies right when you get back from deployments?"

"Perfect timing. I make a point of being there for the conception."

John laughed. We ate donuts and eventually came to a villa on a small lake some distance from the Al Faw Palace and went inside. There was a covered roof deck. John offered me a chair, a cigar, and a drink. It would have been rude to refuse.

We caught up and traded stories as we smoked. John had just returned to Iraq after a long debrief, and after an hour, it was like we hadn't gone our separate ways almost five years earlier. One of the things that's hard to explain to someone who's never deployed, or had to put his life in someone else's hands, or been part of a crew where the stakes were high, is that time away is irrelevant. I could call up an old military buddy out of the blue after ten years, and our relationship would start up again right where it left off.

I listened and laughed. "One day, we have to catch up somewhere nice, like Vancouver or Reykjavik," I said, looking out at the lights around the pond. It had been gently raining for a couple of hours, and the sound of drops ringing the metal awning was relaxing.

"If you still want to meet somewhere after this job, I can probably make something happen. I'll leave it up to you."

John could have compelled me to do whatever job he had in mind, but orders leave a paper trail, and it was more civilized to talk about what might be possible. At dawn, he got around to it. They had a surveillance system and sensor that was important. A large VBIED had detonated close to it. Shrapnel had disrupted the sensor link, and he needed some equipment to bring his surveillance system back to life. He needed a small router, a few rolls of cat5 networking cable, a long run of optical fiber, and a few specialty tools.

"How long will it take you to get it all, Ringo?" he asked me.

"Ringo? Again? Does this mean we need a Paul and George?"

"Already taken care of," he replied, relighting his cigar. "All we need is the equipment and an extra set of hands." He poured us both another drink. "They'll take care of all the splicing, restoration, and upgrades. You're logistics and lookout. We just need it done right and fast."

"No Lucy in the sky with diamonds?"

"Not this time," John said as he looked away.

"Are you guys still together?"

"That's something we can discuss the next time we meet. I'll answer all of your questions when you bring the gear and supplies."

"John, I can get everything you need in a few hours, and I can head out with you on Friday."

"Perfect. Get on it. We'll meet at the CPA, Friday at 1000. Will transportation be a problem?"

"No, I already have a convoy set up for a regular 0900 meeting on that day. But I'd like to meet Paul and George today so they can go through the equipment and sync the plan."

"You can meet them here at 1900 hours. Now, what can I do for you?"

In the end, I agreed to help for a lot of reasons: because it was the right thing to do, because John promised it was going to be a repair job and not a raid, and because he promised me a favor if I ever needed one. Mostly it was because working with John always seemed to make a difference.

I cleared my schedule and started the Easter egg hunt for the equipment we needed.

I found the router right away. A small blue Cisco unit with more than enough ports. The soldier working equipment turn-in had a stack of them taller than he was. I took a good one off the top of the pile and told the soldier I was taking it. He just shrugged his shoulders and didn't even look up from his papers. It had twice as many ports as John needed, and when I tested it, they all came up green. It was small enough to fit in my helmet bag. The few rolls of cat5 wire were easy. They weighed in at about 120 pounds in three forty-pound boxes—we'd just gotten a shipment in and had two COMEX storage units packed full of them at the palace. The roll of optical fiber was a harder proposition. I was able to cut a deal and trade the fiber for a new secure phone because the Patriot missile battery's headquarters had broken theirs. It took three soldiers to lift the big roll of optical fiber into the back of my NTV, and it barely fit.

The parts that should have been easiest to get turned out to be the hardest. I had to call in a favor from a friend to borrow the tools and connectors I needed. He signed out two field repair bags to me with everything I needed, but he told me, in true army fashion, that if they weren't back in a week, it would be my ass. As we wrapped up negotiations, something exploded inside the perimeter. It shook our stone building, things fell and broke around us, and the windows shattered. It was strong enough to knock us down. After we were sure the attack was over and everyone was all right, we went out and checked for damage and unexploded ordinance.

When I opened the door, I caught a glimpse of a huge dog at the edge of the palm grove not far away. I stared at him, and he stared back. Then another dog came out of the woods, whispered something into his ear, and, with a yowl, they were both gone.

Overall, we were in good shape. Mortar, close hit, reduced our sandbag wall to a shallow hole and a splash of sand and debris. I called it in and left instructions to have the windows replaced and the wall rebuilt in the morning. I had to rush to meet the band.

CHAPTER 30

I knocked on the villa door at exactly 1900 hours. The shadows were just getting long. A large, shaggy man with thick glasses, board shorts, a red Hawaiian shirt, and a submachine gun opened the door. I'd never seen him before.

"Hi. I'm Ringo," I said, holding up equipment bags. "John sent me for takeout."

"Cool. I'm Paul. Come on in," he said, motioning with his weapon.

I dropped my 9MM pistol and the tools on the table by the door. I looked to my left, where another man I didn't recognize, wearing an orange Dragon Ball Z tank top, stood off to the side with his submachine gun in a ready position. It was always good to work with techno geeks; they were my people. "Hi, George," I said, holding up my hands. "Sweet shirt. Where's John?"

"He got called away," said Paul.

"OK, then. Either shoot me, or let's get the gear transferred and get down to business."

They exchanged glances, then slung their weapons.

"Nice to finally meet you, Ringo," said George when he came up to shake my hand. He had northern Italian features—blue eyes; dark, wavy hair.

"Good to meet you, too. It was a serious scavenger hunt. Let's get cracking."

First, we emptied the contents of my NTV into what was the villa's office. It was set up as a simple bench test lab for computer equipment. They tested the wire and fiber end to end, and after making faces and debating whether the tactical fiber with its thick, reinforced casing would work for what they intended, they bonded new connectors on the ends, and it tested fine. It was obvious they knew more about the equipment than I did as they scrutinized the router and subjected it to tests I'd never heard of. They seemed as relieved as I was when everything checked out.

Then we loaded all the gear and the bag with my extra weapons and ammo into their armored Suburban. It was black with thick, reinforced polycarbonate where the glass should have been.

"Talk about your stereotypes," I said, knocking on the window.

"Well, it works as long as the AC runs. We'll have other transportation from the CPA. You'll like it. We'll blend," said George.

After everything was stowed, we sat down to go over the plan. It was simple enough. All that was left was for me to meet them at the CPA in a specified place at a predetermined time. Knock on the door, and they'd be waiting.

Then we'd change clothes and vehicles and drop off the boxes at a building downtown. Once we were inside, we'd make repairs, give the system an upgrade, restore surveillance, clean up, and get out. Follow the plan, and the good guys get better resources to protect themselves and kill bad guys. What was not to like?

It was a simple plan. The guys seemed to know what they were doing. I was there to be their helper, extra shooter, and fresh set of eyes and to watch their backs while they worked. After we finished the basics, Paul grilled steaks on a hibachi.

It was a nice night. We talked and ate alfresco as we drilled in the plan.

I watched a car pull into the driveway, saw John get out, and watched him walk to the door on a monitor. A few minutes later, he was on the roof with us, putting together a plate and sitting down next to me.

"So . . . how did the concert rehearsal go?" John asked, looking at George and Paul across the table from us.

"Everything checks out," said Paul, opening a beer and handing it to John.

"He'll do," said George, looking at me.

"Then we're a go," said John, raising his bottle. "Liberty and justice for all."

"To liberty and justice for all," we repeated, with a clatter of glasses.

After dinner, we drank coffee and talked until it was late. I told stories about how we'd found a fire station, our work with different military forces, and our new partnership with the Iraqi police. But mostly I listened. They were good stories, and I was looking forward to working with the team. Then I turned to John and asked, "So how are things with you? How's Lucy doing? I haven't heard from her since Kuwait, and that's not like her."

As soon as I said it, a heavy silence fell around the table.

"John . . ." said Paul.

But John gave him a strange look and shook his head no. "Guys, give Ringo and me some space."

They pushed back from the table and got up.

Paul said, "It was good to meet you."

George said, "See you Friday."

Then it was just John and me, and I didn't like the look on his face.

"John," I said. "What?"

He stared at me for a long moment. "There's no good way to say this. Lucy died. It happened fast. She had a few bad days, but she didn't suffer."

I was stunned. I couldn't process it. Then I stood up over him, shouting. *"Who did it, John? Was it Fedyayeen, Al-Qaeda? Quds Force?"*

"Ringo . . ."

"Who did this, John? Who?"

"Ringo."

"Who. Did—"

"Bill," he said, standing up and grabbing my shoulders. "It wasn't anyone. It was cancer. Cancer in her pancreas killed her."

I staggered backward, and John stopped my fall.

"But she was young and healthy. She was so fit . . . How did it happen?"

"The doctors don't know. It was rare. It moved so fast. She went to the doctor because her stomach was bothering her. By the time the tests came back, it was inoperable, there was nothing anyone could do. She had less than a month left to live."

"Oh, John . . . I. Wait." I slapped his hands off of me, stepped back, and braced like I was fending off an attack. "When, John? When did she pass away?"

He straightened himself up and looked me in the eye. "It was almost five years ago, and she didn't want you to know. She made me promise."

"That was when we met up in Kuwait."

"Yes."

"And you both knew."

"Yes."

"And you didn't say a word."

"She made me promise, and you know how she was."

"I do know. I loved her. I loved everything about her. I owed her everything. Even my life. I wouldn't be here if she hadn't . . ."

"Christ, Bill!" John shouted. "I loved her, too. She knew she was going to die after Kuwait. She had a few good days left, and she wanted to spend them with the people she cared about. She didn't have any family. We were it. She wasn't going to die helpless. That wasn't who she was."

"After she was gone, you couldn't tell me, John? You could have found me. You know everything about me, and what do I know about you? John—no, Abdullah. No, Yakov. Or is it Grigori? I'm pretty sure it's Alex. Who the fuck are you, John?"

"I'm who I have to be," John said after a while. "She said we gave her the best days of her life, and she didn't want you to see her waste away when you had something important you had to do."

"Damn it, John . . ."

"She wanted you to meet your son and be a father with nothing but good memories. She said that was the best gift she could give you. 'We'll have great memories, then he'll be a great father.' That's what she said. It made her so happy. She wanted you to cherish that moment, not worry she was sick when you were having your first kid. She didn't want you to have to carry around the burden of her death on your son's birthday."

Tears streamed down my face. "I don't even know where the pancreas is, John. Can you at least tell me where she's buried?"

"She was cremated, Bill."

"That's unfair."

"Losing her was unfair. Cremating her was selfish. I wanted to call you. I needed to, bad. I held on to her until she was gone. I closed her eyes. I kissed her one last time. Then I drank for two straight days, sobered up, and had her cremated."

We stood staring at each other in silence. I was angry, and John was in front of me. I know it was wrong. I still had so much I wanted to say and do, but she was gone, and everyone knew but me. "You should have told me, John."

307

"I couldn't do it, Bill. Hate me if you need to. I can take it, but she was right, and you know it. You were so excited about being a father, and we weren't going to take that away from you.

"After she died, I took her ashes to a cay with a crescent beach and sand like sugar a short sail away from Key West. I cooked some of the things I thought she'd like to eat. I said everything I always wanted to tell her. The sunset was beautiful. Then I scattered her ashes there, because that was where we were going on our honeymoon. I have more to tell you. If you're up to it, you know where we'll be Friday."

CHAPTER 31

March 2004—Camp Victory, Baghdad

I was taking a group from the new signals brigade out to Abu Ghurayb. They had never been there, and we needed to repair a communications link at the prison complex. It hadn't worked right since the signals unit there swapped out with their replacement last month. There were reports of prisoner abuse at Abu Ghurayb[18]—commanders were fired and shuffled around, and the army locked down the prison during the investigation. It was still hard to get access approved, but I'd helped with a project there before, and our convoy was making good time.

We were near the end of the largest transition of combat troops since WWII. Army V Corps personnel had fought their way into Iraq and begun stability operations as the core of CJTF-7. They were being replaced by III Corps in stages, and a hundred thousand troops had already rotated out and in. The transfer of authority began with our new pharaohs chiseling all references to the old pharaohs from every visible obelisk, pyramid, and marker across their new empire. Signs for III Corps became bigger and better than the V Corps signs they replaced. Living and work areas moved around to better support the III Corps way of doing business. Warning placards hung from every fence to mark III Corps territory and trade routes. They eventually settled into the mission

---

18   In the US, most reporting spelled this as Abu Ghraib, but there were also other variations.

309

and did a great job, but it was their first time in Iraq, and some lessons have to be learned by doing.

There were two primary ways to get to the CPA prison complex. If you were coming from the CPA, it was only about twenty miles away and a straight shot down the highway. Depending on traffic and hostile activity, you could get there in under an hour from the time you left the Green Zone entry control point. There was a shortcut from the airport, but it took a little longer because travel was slow on the backcountry roads. The benefit was that most of the area was well patrolled by the Army, and the route was generally safer, with fewer IEDs.

I was riding shotgun in a Humvee with the doors stripped off to give us better long-gun coverage around our vehicle. Our down-armored, dedoored Humvees were the jalopies of armored vehicles, but they were maneuverable, reliable, and well ventilated. The M-16 combat rifle is just under forty inches long, and maneuvering it around in the confines of a closed vehicle is difficult, especially if you need to react quickly. If we'd had armored doors, it might have been different, but ours were made of canvas on an aluminum tube frame, so while they were a good place to rest your arm, they were otherwise useless. We sandbagged the floors of our vehicles to help minimize the blast of a mine or IED, drove fast, didn't stop for anything, and scanned assigned sectors with our weapons until we reached our destination or something went wrong.

The larger combat convoys were covered with so much firepower they looked like porcupines that belched dragon fire. Our convoys were for communications support, and we usually had only a 9MM semiautomatic for the driver and three M-16s sticking out the sides of each vehicle that rowed back and forth through Baghdad and her suburbs like oars.

We reached the edge of the town of Abu Ghurayb after snaking our way by dusty enclaves of one- and two-story yellow brick buildings, past warehouses and small settlements. Abu Ghurayb was more than a prison; it was a large town full of former military compounds, a half-abandoned ammunition production factory, postapocalyptic warehouses, two specialized regional airports, and an irregular grouping of ethnically divided residential areas. We had just looped through the central thoroughfare of the town, flanked by multistory buildings, en route to the highway and prison entrance when it began.

We passed through a narrow, cluttered stretch of road between two-story cracked stone buildings with barely legible signs and defaced murals of Saddam Hussein. We'd just cleared a debris field, and the smoke from a burning tire barrier made it hard to see. We were forced to slow as we wound single file through what looked more like a canyon than a neighborhood. Something glanced off my helmet.

It sounded like hail, but it hurt like hell.

Then, for a bright instant, we cleared the black, churning smoke, and it was raining rocks.

They bounced off us, our hoods, seats, and truck beds. There was a short, sharp intake of breath from the soldier next to me.

We were in the number-one position. "Floor it, and plow through anything in the road." Then I radioed the other vehicles, "Hadji's throwing stones—follow us through, and don't stop for anything." There was no shelter and nowhere to turn. All we could do was stay focused and minimize our exposure. For a long moment, big rocks, bricks, tiles, small stones, rebar, and, toward the end, something that looked like a toilet rained down on us. The Humvee kicked and bucked and dented.

My M-14 jerked and twisted in my hands when bricks bounced off its barrel. In the smoke, things I couldn't see careened off my helmet, shoulders, and arms.

Then we were through.

I looked back. There was gunfire behind us, but I couldn't tell through the smoke whether it was theirs, ours, or both.

My driver got a fat lip from a rock that bounced off the windshield rim and smacked him square in the face. If he'd flinched, it would have sent us into a wall or stalled the convoy. His teeth were red with his blood. He was lucky his nose wasn't broken.

When my last vehicle was clear, I got on the radio.

"Report status."

"Two. We're OK. My windshield is gone. So much for safety glass. Lowest fucking bidders."

"Three. That sucked. A few cuts, nothing major. Our glass is cracked, but it'll hold."

"Trail. We're fine. They used most of the big rocks on you guys. We were just pissed and emptied a few clips at them when they started pointing their AKs at us, but we had to stop because of the smoke."

"You guys did great. Copy all. We're two minutes out, stick close."

I let out a sigh of relief. When the road widened, I dropped back to check out two, three, and trail. The Humvees looked like they'd taken hail damage from bowling balls. Trail wasn't bad—a few dings. The engine hoods on two and three looked like chewing gum wads. They nodded and waived as we passed them to retake the lead.

My shoulder ached and was swelling up, but that was my only injury.

It could have been grenades, bullets, or boiling oil that rained down on us. We were damn lucky no one was hurt bad.

It looked like convertible season was ending early.

A few minutes later, we crossed the highway, dumped the rocks accumulated in our cabs, and navigated the serpentine gate into the coalition prison compound at Abu Ghurayb. The guards passed us through. I safetied my weapons and rested my M-14 against my leg, its scratched barrel targeting the now-empty sky. We circled around a few times until we found a place to park. After we stopped, I looked everyone over, and I sent my driver to the medic trailer in case his lip needed stitches. Our vehicles were beat up, but everyone was fine. That's all that mattered.

My driver met us a little later at the DFAC with an ice pack and a bottle of big orange eight-hundred-milligram Motrin ibuprofen tablets to share. It was the universal military cure-all. We called it "vitamin M." He passed them around, and we put a dent in his prescription. The hamburgers were pretty good, and after we finished lunch, we met with the army communications troops supporting the prison.

The CPA detention facility was a compound full of compounds. There was a detainee tent city made of long, beige tents surrounded by concertina wire. The old prison was made of bricks and cinder-block walls. It had been partially upgraded by the army and was used for high-value prisoners, but soldiers lived in the old section that looked like the shanty version of a Dark Ages keep. Camp Vigilant was a prominent part of the complex, as was a series of trailer parks. Fortunately, the problem they were having was easy to fix. We adjusted their broadcast frequencies and moved their vehicles to a different cantonment area away from their main antennas so their mobile jammers wouldn't also jam camp communications. Everything greened up and started working like it was supposed to. Their colonel was so happy he came by to shake everyone's hand. He offered me a tour, but I passed. They did have a few notorious terrorists and criminals there—supposedly even Saddam Hussein himself, if you believed the rumors.

Security was tighter than I remembered it being a few months earlier, but that could have been to stop firefights at their gate or to repel the jailbreak attempts that seemed to happen there every few weeks. It was late. Mortar attacks happened like clockwork just after dark at

Abu Ghurayb, and we weren't going to stay in case the fireworks started early.

My shoulder ached, our vehicles were damaged, and I just wanted to have my guys back safe before dinner. The MPs loaned us a broom, a dustpan, and the oldest, most tuberculosis-sounding Shop-Vac I had ever heard to clean out the shattered glass splinters and pebbles in vehicle two. We used clear packing tape to patch the crack on number three. The MPs said we weren't the first vehicles harassed on the way out to the prison, and we probably wouldn't be the last.

We took a slightly different route back. My Humvees stopped at Camp Victory, where we debriefed, and the signals team took a Blackhawk back to the CPA.

The motor pool NCO just shook his head when he saw his vehicles.

"Everyone make it back OK?" he asked as he filled out some papers.

"Yeah. Just cuts and bruises," I said.

"All right, air force. Better my vehicles than my soldiers. Keep it that way."

I nodded and made my way back to the FMO. There was still a lot of work to do, and there was something in the air that made it hard to breathe. Two things I won't miss about Iraq are driving through the clinging acrid soot of burning tires and getting stoned, in the Biblical sense.

I was finally able to work the timing out. I called Jodi at work, and she picked up on the first ring. I was happy, but that didn't last long. It was our first fight of the deployment. I caught her on a bad day, and she chewed off a good part of my face. She wasn't really mad at me; she just needed to vent. My tactical blunder was assuming I had a role in the conversation beyond making safe, sympathetic, noncommittal confirmations that I was still listening.

I didn't get to call home as often as I'd like, and Jo didn't understand how much the few words we got meant to me. Calls like that tore my heart out. It made it even harder because I knew she had so many responsibilities to juggle—work, Xander, being very pregnant—and it was her first week at home since I'd been deployed with no family in the house except Xander. Her sister had come out over Thanksgiving, and her mom to help for a while. But they were gone by then, and being worried and alone in an empty house can overwhelm even a strong heart.

I had a lot on my own mind I wanted to talk about. I'd seen and done some hard things. What I wanted, more than anything else, was for someone to listen and tell me everything would be all right, but I couldn't talk to her about any of that. She would only worry more.

I'd just lost one of my favorite people in the whole world. Even though I knew Lucy had died years earlier, for me, it had happened yesterday. I was still reeling from it. The only other person who understood how I felt . . . well, I couldn't even stand to look at him.

It hurt. I had only felt pain like that once before, when I was a kid—when I understood I'd never see my best friend Sarah again. When I knew I was truly alone.

It was the summer before high school, and it was almost over. I was playing pinball at Triple-P Pizza when Sarah came in with her girlfriends. The girls went to the counter and placed their order for italian ices and snow cones, and Sarah set down a shopping bag filled with wrapped presents on the table across from me and waved. I was on my last ball, racking up a

huge lead on Bobby Kaiser, but when I saw her, I froze. I completely forgot about the game because she was beautiful. Her blonde hair was divided over her shoulders and held in place by a flower-crocheted headband. She wore a white empire-waist dress, gathered at the bodice, that ended at a hem a few inches above her tan knees. She literally glowed in the light from the window, and I could see her silhouette through her white cotton dress. It was the first time it struck me hard that my best friend, Sarah, was a girl and that she had breasts. I had never felt so aware of her before.

The pinball machine made a sad noise when my game ball dropped down the hole. Bobby gave me crap about kicking my ass when we switched positions, but I didn't care about the game anymore. I went straight over to say hi. I knew my face was red. Sarah saw immediately that I had finally noticed, and her smile grew. Then her order was called, and she left to sit and eat with her girlfriends.

I lost to Bobby Kaiser, and there was a new high score that wasn't mine. Bobby was still doing his victory dance when Sarah said bye in that nice girl way as she gathered up her presents. I watched her walk down the street, and I had butterflies in my stomach.

I didn't really understand it. Sarah had always been there, and I'd never been nervous around her before. She was the first person to tell me that my mistakes were dumb but I wasn't too stupid to read. She was the reason I had finally been able to pick up that book and read about a yellow duck without making another mistake. We built forts and tree houses and had adventures. She scolded and encouraged me, and we honored pinky promises. We rushed to each other at every new victory or defeat. And I felt it all in that one instant. I wasn't just feeling butterflies; they were fireflies.

When I couldn't see Sarah through the pizza parlor window anymore, I finished my Coke, congratulated Bobby on his victory, and left. I still had time, but I had to go.

It was the end of a long summer day. It would still stay light for a while, but the shadows were growing. We knew for months before the "For Sale" sign was planted in her yard that Sarah and her family were leaving. Her dad was a nuclear scientist. His meetings in Switzerland had gone well, and they'd been holding a job open for him until Sarah graduated junior high. Rooms in her house were emptied and cleaned. The sign in her front yard changed to "Sold." Since early that morning, the movers had been loading box after box into a truck that blocked most of our street.

I had successfully managed to ignore that she was moving until the day Sarah had to leave. Neither of us knew what to say. I couldn't imagine a world without her.

An enormous lilac tree grew in the hollow past my grandfather's garden. It was two stories high and thick with boughs that draped down around it like a weeping willow. Our secret base was inside the tree, in the empty space between the dense flowering branches and wide gnarled trunk. Although we didn't specifically arrange to meet, we arrived at the same time. We were breathless when we slipped through the heavy purple blossoms. We didn't have a plan. We just knew we had to be there.

I wrapped my arms around her the minute she broke through the branches. We were the same age, but that year, she was a little taller than me. She pressed her body against mine and rested her head on my shoulder. We stayed that way for a while, holding on to each other and rocking gently inside walls that glowed green and lavender.

We wiped away each other's tears, and when we were finished sniffling, she grabbed both sides of my face, pulled me to her, and kissed me hard.

We met too quickly in the middle. There was a crack as our teeth hit, and we both pulled back, covering our mouths. Then it was hysterical, and in the middle of laughing, she kissed me again, and it was nice.

Then I kissed her. I wasn't sure exactly what to do, but Sarah and I worked at it until everything felt right. We grew breathless and bolder. Our tongues touched; it felt like electricity, and we both pulled away. Then we laughed again, and, slowly, we were pulled back together. Holding each other, a less tentative touching of lips and tongues, and the scent of lilac.

She felt good in my arms, and I didn't want that moment to end.

"I'll never forget you, Sarah. Every time I open a book or look at the ocean, you'll be there."

She smiled, and her soft lips kissed all over my face. "Every time I'm scared, I'll think about you, and it'll be all right."

We held on to each other and kissed until her father started blowing the car horn and calling her name. Then, I finally realized what I was feeling. It was what had been bothering me all day. It was why even though everything felt so good, my insides still hurt.

"Sarah, I love you. I've always loved you."

Then the horn blasts and shouts for Sarah grew louder. She let out a squeal and smiled. Then she kissed me one more time, turned away, and crashed away through the branches. Fat amethyst blossoms broke apart and fell around me. For a moment, all I could do was stare at all the shattered purple flowers strewn across the ground. Our secret base was never so empty.

At least I'd told her.

I'd kissed Sarah. It finally dawned on me, and I smiled a bittersweet smile.

I just stood there unsure of what to do next.

I looked around our secret base. I remembered where we'd found every item and how hard it had been to drag them in there. I was always at our base with Sarah, and now it felt empty. I knew once I walked out, I'd never visit that place again.

Then, there was a loud snapping of branches. I turned just in time for Sarah to crash into me at full speed. She hit me so hard she knocked me to the ground. I was having trouble catching my breath. When I opened my eyes, she was sitting on my chest.

"So heavy," I mumbled.

"Shut up. That's not something you say to a girl."

"Move, then, so I can breathe."

Sarah grabbed my shoulders and shimmied down until she was straddling my waist. I could breathe again, but she still had me pinned. "Welcome back. I thought—"

"Shut up. I had to tell my dad that I needed a little more time."

"What? Why?"

She bent down and kissed me. "Well, you said it so suddenly, I had to think about what to say."

"It wasn't sudden. It took me like seven years, but I love you."

"You can be a little slow," she said. We both laughed, then Sarah kissed me again.

"I love you, Billy. Always have, and I always will."

It was the happiest I had ever felt. I held Sarah and kissed her again, but then we both knew it was time to go.

She let me up, and we both wiped our mouths. I took her hand and led her out of our secret base, across the lawn we played on, and through the hedgerow to her car. I said goodbye to her parents and wished them luck and a safe flight. I shook her father's hand, and her mom gave me a big hug. I was always envious of Sarah's family, but they were kind to me, and I was sad to see them go. Then I opened the door for Sarah, and we kissed one last time before she got in.

Her dad's Plymouth rumbled to life, and I waved as she pulled away. I watched Sarah waving in the back window until the car turned the corner.

I wiped my tears on my sleeve. Then I took off running. I tore through my grandfather's hedges, dashed through a neighbor's yard, and launched myself over a small wall.

I caught up with them at the next stop sign, and I could see Sarah wiping her eyes and then laughing when she saw me. I chased her car for as long as I could. Waving and watching her wave back. I ran after her until I couldn't breathe anymore, and I had to stop at the side of the road, jumping and waving until I couldn't see her any longer. I couldn't stop watching until her car was a golden speck.

When I couldn't see them anymore, it hit me. She was really gone. I felt a kind of pain I'd never known before. I was alone. It hurt more than I could bear.

I felt hollow for a long time back then, and I felt hollow again now. But now, I wasn't alone. I wanted to talk to Jo about it because I hurt so bad I could barely stand. I listened to her and waited for my turn to talk, but she wasn't in *receive* mode. I listened to her complain for twenty minutes. It was one of the longest calls we ever had during a deployment, and all I could do was tell her that I understood and that everything would be OK. It made the distance even worse because her life was difficult. But she was home with our son in a safe place, doing things she knew how to do. Every word she said made me angrier. Everything she hated having to do was something I wanted to do again, desperately.

"I had a pretty tough week, too, Jo," I said. "But if you don't have anything else, I've got to go now. I know this is hard for you, but this is the first week you haven't had family there to help you out. I've been on my own in Iraq for a while now, and things aren't always great out here. I'm doing my best, and you don't have to worry about me, but I just can't listen to you complain anymore. This is our reality for a few more months, and I'd really like to hear about how Xander's doing, or the baby, or anything good that's going on. I can't listen anymore when a call is just you venting because you're angry I'm not there."

"I'm sorry," she replied after a long pause.

"I'm sorry, too," I said. "I hate it. I understand it, but I still hate it."

"I had my ultrasound yesterday, and the baby is a boy."

"Next time, lead with that. I—"

That was where the call dropped out. I was still frustrated and annoyed, but it was hard to stay mad. We were having a boy.

CHAPTER 32

March 2004—Baghdad and Camp Victory

Chief Mohammed Sawan and his crew made it from the MoI issue point to the new police station with all their gear. The only casualty was a broken lamp. The formerly empty shell of an ancient military outpost set behind a high wall was finally starting to look and run like a police station. Behind the sliding fortress gate was a police checkpoint where locals could report crimes. Past that was the main two-story building and the motor pool.

I was there to check in with our Iraqi police partners, ensure their radios still worked, and make sure they could use the features they needed. There was some initial confusion because the radio and GPS displays were only in English, but Mrs. Marjani Nassar and her team of Iraqi spectrum managers built a translation key for me that slid into a plastic sleeve glued under the display of each radio. They even drafted an Arabic user's guide.

I waved when I entered the station. Mohammed was in the back in his office, having a tense conversation on the phone about something that sounded like MoI business. The desk sergeant and a patrol officer gave me a quick tour. They walked me through the police blotter, and they were particularly proud that they already had criminals in their cells.

The CPA translator we brought was named Rocky. He was an Iraqi American taxi driver from New Jersey who came to Iraq because translators in country were in high demand and well compensated. He generally did a great job with regular conversations. He was a funny guy and a good translator, with one caveat: if there was a lot of technical military jargon, or if the conversation strayed from Arabic into Turkmen, Persian, or a dialect he didn't get, he made shit up because he wanted to be invaluable. I'd caught him in a lie the second time I worked with him. On my best day, my conversational Arabic is a sad, sorry mash-up of stock phrases, nouns, and verbs with a nasally accent. But I regularly see and hear Arabic military and technical words, many of which are adopted English and French words. And he lied anyway. I was in the middle of consultations with specialists from the new Iraqi army because some of their legacy equipment was interfering with coalition comms whenever their vehicles drove by and, strangely enough, randomly opening garage doors. I didn't even know there were garage door openers in Baghdad until the CPA started getting complaints from Iraqi VIPs.

I was at a point in our meeting where the Iraqi team leader said, "Our radio equipment for those vehicles operates in an encrypted frequency range of—"

Which was something I needed to know, because we both needed to change our radios slightly so we'd stop interfering with each other.

But Rocky translated it as, "Our drivers don't listen to the radio. How many times do I need to keep repeating myself?"

I asked him if he was sure and to ask our host if he could repeat it so he could translate it again.

He said he didn't need to. So, I had him escorted out of the room, and we were able to work out what we needed on our own. Then I made him take a cab back to the Green Zone. Rocky's rating as a translator dropped after that, but he still got paid because OK translators were better than no translators. He really shouldn't have been translating diplomatically sensitive matters anyway. So, I was surprised when I saw him in my Humvee. But Rocky was contrite, and this time, he was in his element, and he translated what the Iraqi police really said. In addition to starting community patrols, the police station crew had stopped a bank robbery. They'd also taken part in a joint operation with the MPs in which they freed a neighborhood from a group of thugs who'd taken the residents hostage. They were already making a difference.

On the wall were old pictures of Iraqi policemen and a banner in Chief Mo's handwriting that Rocky translated as, "Our goal is simple. We will protect and deter. However, that simple clarity is why our work will be difficult. May God watch over us."

If I had to describe Chief Mohammed in a word, it would be *samurai*.

After the tour, we were brought to a conference room, where Mohammed waited with glasses of tea. We exchanged greetings and shook hands. Then I reached into my helmet bag and pulled out twenty copies of the Arabic radio procedures and instructions booklet we had made to help the police, and I smacked them down on the table right in front of him.

He looked at them for a moment. Then he lunged out of his chair and hugged me.

"Yes. This will do, my friend."

I patted him on the back and then pointed to the map of Baghdad hanging on the wall with pins of different colors stuck in locations across the south.

He finally let go of me and started pointing and talking so fast Rocky had trouble keeping up.

The phrase that interested me the most was, "Today is a perfect day to start sharing intelligence. There is activity here," he said, zeroing in on a specific location, "that you must know about, now."

I took good notes for Del to review and pass along.

My part of the relationship was easy. He had the hard job, and his guys and the first female Iraqi police officer I had met were sweating and bleeding every day to establish order and security. At that point, just over forty Iraqi police (IP) worked at that station. Other stations had bigger numbers, but Mohammed had tough standards and turned a lot of IPs away. I helped wherever I could. I didn't have to go door to door like the army or participate with them on raids like the MPs, so anything my team could do to help them, we did. Every criminal or insurgent the police got off the street was one less bad guy the army would encounter kicking down doors and one less scumbag causing trouble for Iraqis where they lived. Everyone won, and that was something that didn't happen very often in Baghdad.

I traveled back to Camp Victory, debriefed, and caught up on my other duties until it was late and I was tired. I was shutting down my computers when a British Special Forces team stepped out from the dark hallway and surrounded my desk.

We tend to lump all Special Forces together, but there is a family hierarchy. It begins when certain specialists or combatants, based on aptitude, are vetted and then trained in special weapons, tactics, methods, and leadership. With experience, expanded skill sets, and maturity, some special operators become part of teams that provide unique capabilities to warfighters and governments. They run the gamut from combat advisor to assassin. Employed properly, special operators can provide the push that changes a battle. Some countries have used special operators to start conflicts; other countries, to deter war.

The six men standing in a semicircle in front of my desk were part of an elite group. UK SAS[19] operators. One of their jobs was to quietly snatch up or silence sophisticated insurgents. They stopped the kind of bad guys who were not only smart and capable of terrible things but also excelled at helping others do terrible things, too. The SAS team lead was a rugged man with a big toothy smile and cropped chestnut hair. I'd met him shortly after I arrived in Baghdad. His name was Reggie, and he had a problem.

We'd worked together before, and my team had been able to help his. His current problem had a thick wall of secrecy around it, and I don't know how to help someone if I don't understand what they need. Usually, we were able to find common ground, but lately our British and American intelligence leads had locked horns over sharing information, and that put us in a difficult position. Representatives of two great nations again separated by a common language.

People tend to imagine special operators as massive specimens who are part magician, part minotaur. It's true sometimes. There were two members of Reggie's team who looked like someone had slipped steroids into their bangers and mash since about middle school. I've always found special operators to be thoughtful problem solvers with an appreciation for strategy, an interesting skill set, and enormous endurance. Reggie couldn't have been more than five foot five, but put him in charge of a small group of like-minded specialists, and no one was unreachable.

"Hi, Bill. Mind if my mates put on a fresh pot of coffee?" Reggie said as he extended his hand and we shook. "We've got a lot of ground to cover."

I smiled. Reggie hated coffee. "No worries. There's a tin of tea there, too. Help yourself. No biscuits, but the cookies are good."

---

19   Special Air Service (SAS). SAS are elite UK special operators comparable to US Navy Seals.

While Reggie and I talked, his guys brewed pots of coffee and tea and ate through most of my stuff, but one of his mates brought me a cup of coffee before it was all gone.

"This is the problem," Reggie said. "Two days ago, we were on track to secure a high-value target. Assets were in place. We were poised to take a bomb maker off the board, shutter his lab, and destroy his inventory. Then it happened again."

"Your communications failed."

"Yes. No radio traffic. No data. Just static."

"Could you push or burn through it?"

"No way, mate, the signals were too strong. We were hard jammed. If I took a step back, all our comm kit revived. Another step forward, and it was gone again. It was like we hit an invisible wall. We had to scrub the mission."

"Where's the target?"

"I'm not at liberty to say."

"Why not?"

"It's time sensitive, and I'm not authorized to divulge details of ongoing operations."

"Reggie, then I can't help you. If I don't know where the problem is, I can't figure out why it's happening. I want to help, but you can't throw a rock without hitting a jammer in Baghdad right now. So, unless you can show me where your mission area is, there's nothing I can do, and you're going to have to start thinking about tactical communications in Iraq like a minefield."

A jammer is a device that denies the use of a bit of electronic spectrum in a certain place at a certain time. Some are sophisticated and can stop a specific device in a room full of similar devices from working. If you know what you're doing and have the right equipment, one computer, phone, or radio can be isolated from an entire network or blocked from the world. However, most jamming devices are primitive. What they lack in finesse, they make up for in blunt-force denial. They kill all comms and mobile devices within their range.

Electronic signals burn around us all the time like living electronic wildfires. Jammers act like wet blankets that put them out by smothering those signals.

Jammers can be offensive, to paralyze enemy communications during an operation, or defensive, to protect a position from enemy devices that might be used against us. The problem is that jammers don't care who or what they jam. The same device that stops a cell phone from detonating a bomb can also stop calls for fire support or requests to medevac injured troops.

"Thinking about Baghdad as a comms minefield isn't an acceptable solution," Reggie said.

"It is what it is, Reggie. Baghdad's a big place. I get the problem. But if you want my help, I need to know more."

"That's not possible."

"Look. I don't even know if I can help you. But this is put your cards on the table time. If there's nothing else, I'm going to bed."

Reggie made a complicated face I couldn't read. "Bill . . . let me use your phone."

I turned it around; he dialed, then put the phone on speaker. The line clicked and hummed as the call passed through different switchboards. It rang a few times, and the call was answered.

"Status?" said the ghostly voice on the line.

"Impasse, I'm afraid," said Reggie. "He can only help solve the problem if he has enough data and knows the variables."

"Go secure," said the voice on speakerphone.

I hit a button. Lights flashed and then changed colors when the call became encrypted.

"Secure," I said. "Go ahead."

"Captain Riley, tell me what you see as the problem?"

I caught Reggie's eye, and he nodded. "Look, we've been through this before," I said. "Your mission is near an area with powerful emitters. Your comms work fine. Then you pass a certain point en route to your target, and then they die. The radios in your kit don't tune to frequencies that will fix this. I can get you US radios, but they won't pass the types of information you need while you're on mission."

"That is the issue. The problem is time. Our window is closing. You have four hours," the voice said. "Reggie, brief him." There was a buzz, then a hum as the line disconnected.

"*We* have four hours," I said to the phone.

"Let me start from the beginning," Reggie said. "This bomb maker is a particularly nasty character who moves around a lot." Reggie showed me a folder with pictures and imagery of an industrial compound on the outskirts of Baghdad.

"I know this location. It's right in between two US Army bases. Why don't you let them handle it?" It was also the area of suspicious activity Mohammed had reported earlier.

"Tried that before, mate. Didn't work. We need him alive, and your army's a superb axe. But it's not the scalpel we need in the time we have left."

"How confident are you of your window?'

"Indications are he's already packing up and getting ready to move. We may not even get the whole"—Reggie paused to check his watch—"three hours and forty minutes."

"I'll need your boss to vouch, if one of my eagles or stars needs to hear the right words. Can you guarantee that?"

"Yes."

"And this will save a lot of lives, right? Who dares wins, right?"[20]

"Are you having a laugh, mate?" Reggie said, letting the frustration show in his voice for the first time. The other members of his team turned to look at us, and the side conversations stopped.

"'Fraid not, Reggie. I just figured out what we need to do to make this work for you. As problems go, it's huge." I motioned the SAS sergeant closest to what I needed. "Grab me a cup of coffee, while you're over there, would you, big guy? Everyone gather round. The only reason you can't grab the bomb maker and seize his IEDs is because the jammers put in place to protect us from IEDs are jamming your mission. Getting two army commanders to shut off devices they believe are keeping their soldiers alive has never been done before, but there might be a way. We're almost out of time. Indications confirm he's preparing to roll. So, I'm only going to say this once . . ."

We came up with a plan, and Reggie gave me the number to coordinate with Thomas at the UK command post. I finished all the preparations I could think of and rushed to the CJTF-7 Joint Operations Center (JOC). I was about to attempt to coordinate a mission between elements of the army, on behalf of UK special operators, so they could retire another nasty insurgent from the IED manufacture and distribution business, and I was feeling out of my depth. Success would deal a major blow to a terrorist who created advanced explosive designs used across Iraq. It could wipe out a cell of insurgents and eliminate a stockpile of death waiting to be used against us. If everything went half as well as expected, the mission would save many lives. It should have been an easy sell, right?

---

20   Motto associated with the British Special Air Service (SAS).

The problem was going to be finding someone with enough clout to wake up two army commanders and get them to make their guys flip two very important switches and shut down the jammers. Then they needed to lock them in the "off" position until the end of the mission. Since those jammers were in place for force protection, finding a commander willing to shut them down—even if it was just long enough for one mission to succeed—was going to be near impossible unless they were ordered to do it. Time and authority were my biggest problems. I didn't have much of either.

Reggie told me the bomb maker not only made IEDs but, more critically, also designed and built reliable remote detonators that made them even more deadly. With the bomb maker's detonators, IEDs were harder to find, attack timing was more precise, and there were fewer duds. If that weren't bad enough, his people were already busy loading bombs and instructions on how to make remote detonators into various cars and trucks inside their compound.

These terrorists moved fast. They trusted no one beyond a tight cell of family. They killed coalition soldiers and their own people in gruesome, public ways. They didn't discriminate between combatant and civilian, and they didn't spare women or children. No one was innocent in their eyes, unless it served their ends. If the bomb maker got away, he'd disappear again. Things would get worse for everyone, and more of us wouldn't make it home.

I entered the JOC out of breath and with less than an hour to spare.

The JOC was built like an amphitheater, in tiers of desks thick with computers and telephones, neatly arranged by functional area. Every coalition partner had a representative there, and every military specialty assigned to CJTF-7 had a watch officer assigned to field questions, maintain situational awareness for their organization, and show the progress of all major events. It was the nerve center for command and control of all military operations within Iraq. I looked for the UK representative. There was a seat, but it was empty.

The biggest display screens were against the far wall. They constantly rotated through maps, forces, operations, new intelligence, and items of interest. They provided focus and situational awareness for everyone in the operations center. The colonels and generals who advised the commanding general through regular meetings, reports, and battle updates sat at a long table below the displays. That table was the playing field around which the entire JOC stadium was built.

The gatekeeper for important combat-related issues was the battle major. I went straight to him, introduced myself, and explained the situation. We had everything already set up—people on the ground ready to lock down the jammer, a special operations team waiting for confirmation; all we needed was the division commander to agree—and give the order.

The battle major was a burly clearinghouse for all significant events that impacted operations, but he just didn't get it. After a lot of head nodding, he proclaimed, "This is an issue for C6, signals and communications," which referred me back to, well, me.

So, I told him again that in this instance, I was signals, and the problem was to wake up whoever had the authority to direct a division commander to temporarily shut off a device protecting a unit. I explained again that the situation required one of our units to assume a greater level of risk to attack by IEDs for a short time, for just an hour, so we could reduce the risk of IEDs for everyone in the area. Possibly for a long time.

The only effect I seemed to have on the battle major was to turn his eyes a shinier shade of glaze. "Well," he said, looking through a neatly bound sheaf of printouts, "I don't have a mission like that on the schedule."

"Do you coordinate and track special ops missions?"

"No, different task forces handle that. My sergeant can get you their numbers."

"I already have that. It's a UK team."

"Then try the UK representative," he said, losing his patience.

I pointed to the empty chair, and the battle major shrugged his shoulders. He clearly didn't want to get involved, and an army division commander certainly wasn't going to act on the sole recommendation of an air force signals captain he didn't know from Adam who worked on some staff in a Green Zone. The order had to come through proper channels.

If I were the commander, I wouldn't have either, but it had to be done.

I lost almost twenty minutes with the battle major.

After starting the story again, he waved his hands and dismissed me, grunting the words, "Well, that's too bad for you, but that's your problem, not mine, and I'm not making that call."

I shook my head in disbelief.

An entire special operations team was staged and ready to go into harm's way to take IEDs, detonators, and sophisticated bomb-making expertise off the streets of Baghdad. It would save soldiers' lives, maybe even the battle major's, if he ever left the safety of the compound, but he wasn't willing to put his ass on the line to even make a phone call to see what might be done.

"You're not even going to call someone in operations, or at the UK headquarters, or division to see what can be done?" I asked him.

"Nope. Not my problem." He sat back down in his starched army combat uniform, turned his back to me, and resumed typing an email to one of his buddies.

I couldn't restrain my disgust. "See," I said, "that's exactly the attitude that gets our guys killed." Then I left to find someone with the authority and balls to make a hard decision.

He stood up. I heard his chair slam into the desks behind him. Then he growled, "Captain. You get back here now," but I didn't stop or even look back. He was a big guy. If he was motivated enough, he could have easily caught me and beaten me down. But he wasn't that motivated. At least he was finally off his ass.

Time was ticking away, and I had to find someone in the JOC with enough authority to make the call—and, more importantly, someone who would.

I was making my way toward the commanding general's office, pissed off and probably about to commit career suicide, when I passed Colonel Raider in the hallway. Colonel Raider was the chief of operations for the CJTF-7, and as far as I could tell, when he was on duty, he was operations in Iraq. If any combat division needed anything for the war, he took care of it. If he needed anything from one of the divisions, he had a direct line.

Usually, his gatekeepers were the battle captains and majors, but the battle major hadn't hunted me down, and we were nearly out of time. We had less than forty minutes left, and terrorist departure schedules are more a best guess than something etched in stone. Colonel Raider was surrounded by action officers clamoring for his attention. He was a grizzly bear of a marine with a brush cut in a digitized desert combat uniform. He moved with a sense of purpose that made you very aware of the exits. He was the best chance I had, so I joined the queue, caught my breath, and organized my thoughts. I would only get one chance to convince him.

We were in a hardened building made of sandstone and marble surrounded by two perimeter walls. I could hear rockets exploding in the

335

distance over the hum of enough electronic and computer equipment to put a man on the moon.

I had one person left ahead of me. I could have jumped in, but as important as what I had to do was, there were a lot of important things vying for the colonel's attention. The officer in front of me was reviewing the casualties from the last attack with the colonel.

Time was tick, tick, ticking away. I was only going to get one shot. I had to get it right.

When Colonel Raider finished with his troops and turned to enter the JOC, I made my move. "Sir, we've got a problem. It's got a short fuse. We have less than thirty minutes left to make an important mission a go. I think you're the only person who can help."

He frowned, then said, "Talk to me while we walk, Captain."

I opened the door for him and began to explain the situation as quickly as my Long Island accent could carry me.

We walked fast.

As soon as we made it to his desk, he began making calls. At first to confirm my story, and then to squeeze a week's worth of coordination into less than twenty minutes.

When I finally caught my breath, I called the UK special ops control center, and I updated Thomas, the liaison Reggie had given me, on our status while Colonel Raider negotiated with the commanders of the jamming assets we needed to secure.

They went back and forth.

Additional commanders were called.

The situation was dissected and deconstructed from different angles.

From the sound of it, we'd stalled. The alarm on my wristwatch went off, and my countdown timer flashed nine zeros.

I listened to the update on the phone. It was time to go. Any further delay would scrub the mission. "I know, Thomas," I said. "Stand by one." I looked up, and Colonel Raider was scanning his boards and nodding. Finally, he looked at me and said, "The assets are secure."

"Sir, confirm hard down and locked until 0600."

"Confirmed down," said Colonel Raider. "The devices are hard locked until 0600."

"Thomas. The devices are secure," I said. "We're go on this end."

"Copy that. Confirm go."

"Go, go, go."

I listened as Thomas confirmed and repeated the information to the staff in his control center and then directly to his team. The echo of issued orders reverberated through the multiple lines.

Then they entered the dead zone.

"Thomas, how do they read?"

"They're in. Radios? Good. Data? Good. We're good, mate, we're good. Thanks."

"Then why are you wasting time with me?" I said through a haze of relief and adrenaline. "Get that bastard."

"Will do," he replied.

"CJTF-7 out," I said and hung up.

I was ready for a cigarette. I hate them, but I was suddenly tired and out of cigars.

I looked up at Colonel Raider. "They're in, sir, signals clear, send and receive all good. Thank you."

Colonel Raider said a few more things into the phone and confirmed a few things with the UK general before he hung up. Then he scowled and looked me up and down hard before saying, "Now that's done, remind me again who you are?"

"Sir. I'm Captain Bill Riley, chief of frequency management for the task force."

Then he narrowed his eyes and growled, "Explain to me why an air force signals officer is coordinating special operations."

"That, sir, is exactly the problem."

We talked for a while after that, and when the day shift chief of operations came on, I briefed him, too. I recommended CJTF-7 task the air force for a fully mission-ready electronic warfare officer (EWO) because there were more qualified people for the EWO job than me. But I was formally assigned electronic warfare duties and became the first US EWO for the task force, if only until a real one could be found.

We also talked about coordinating special operations missions and requirements across Iraq, but that was a series of talks operations would need to have, and I was out of my element. There was a combined joint special operations team that could represent the needs and capabilities of all the special operations units in Iraq, but back then, special operations were still handled like different tribes, and every country had their own special mix of teams and missions. Whether it was a matter of pride or policy, they generally didn't talk to each other.

In the middle of the conversations, we received word that the UK special operations team had successfully completed their mission and collected significant intelligence. EOD—explosive ordinance disposal— had begun destroying detonators, and they were preparing to destroy a large cache of IEDs.

By the end of the conversation with operations, I had an approved interim way to manage frequency issues that would otherwise scrub operations. It was a successful process, and we went on to pave the way for eleven more successful special missions.

I stood up to leave and noticed one of my NCOs walking across the JOC toward us.

"Morning, gentlemen," he said. "Just came by to see if Spike was still alive, or if the army was having him shot and I'd have to notify his family."

"Spike?" I asked.

"Yes, sir. Captain Riley. It's your new call sign. We've been talking about it for a while now."

"Spike, like a signal spike?" Colonel Raider asked.

"No, sir," my NCO said. "Respectfully, Spike like the name of a junkyard dog. Fierce, loyal, and territorial, a guard dog that doesn't know how to let something go once he grabs on to it. That's pretty much how my boss works."

"So, Spike the junkyard dog. I like that," one of the colonels said. Then they laughed and slapped me on the back—marine hard.

"Yes, sir, but if you colonels don't mind, can I get him back now? It's morning, he has a lot of work, and he probably hasn't slept in a couple of days."

Colonel Raider apparently told a funny story at the commanding general's stand-up meeting and credited the operation's coordination to Captain "Spike" Riley. After that, my call sign stuck.

CHAPTER 33

March 2004—En route to the CPA, Baghdad

I learned to hunt with an M-1 rifle one winter when I was little. The M-1 was the combat rifle that helped us win WWII, and in many ways, it gave birth to the M-14 battle rifle my father used in Vietnam. He was formally introduced to the M-14 in Marine Corps boot camp at Paris Island, and their relationship blossomed in Vietnam. He always spoke fondly of that weapon. It was the first combat rifle he ever fired, and it left an impression on him, which left an impression on me.

It was Father's first real love. Even though he eventually left her for an M-16, he would still talk about that M-14 nostalgically, as though it were a girl rendered more beautiful in spite of, and made more approachable because of, her flaws.

I never saw an M-14 until I was issued one by the army at Camp Victory in Baghdad. Since I'd learned to hunt with an M-1, firing and taking care of the M-14 was familiar and easy. I used an M-14 during most of my trips across Iraq, because it used armor-piercing rounds that packed a punch, and I was sentimental that my father had loved it.

But the M-1 was an unusual choice for a boy's first rabbit hunt.

January 1978—Catskill Mountains, Upstate New York

Father carried a Garand M-1 rifle across his shoulder on a sling. It was a heavy wood-and-steel weapon with a long barrel that was nearly as long as I was tall. It was the proud patriarch of the American combat rifle family, and it was the tool my father had selected to teach me how to hunt rabbits. While other kids learned how to hunt with a relatively benign .22-caliber rifle or shotgun, I would learn to hunt rabbits with a heavy 30.06-caliber combat rifle that kicked like a mule and killed things that looked like dots at more than five hundred yards away.

Rabbits were spread everywhere across the field. Cute, tiny heads with long, upright ears as far as I could see. Fluffy brown and gray coats. Soft cottontails. Some hopped together in clusters and stretched out in the morning sun. Most of them scratched at the snow for seeds and grass.

It was a Disney moment. I forgot all about my cold, tired self and why we were there.

The word that escaped my mouth was, "Bunnies!"

Father growled deep in his throat when I said it.

We watched together for a few minutes, then my father unslung his weapon and said, "Watch what I do. You stand like this, with your legs shoulder-width apart, so you can feel your weight divided between your front and back foot. Sight a rabbit; point your toe toward it; make sure you have tension between the sling, your shoulder, and your cheek. Take a breath, get a good sight picture, lead the rabbit if it's not stationary, and slowly let out your breath. Before your exhale is gone, gently squeeze the trigger, and kill the rabbit all in one smooth motion."

I was suddenly terrified. Everything had led to that moment. A day of shopping and packing gear. The car ride to the mountains. The wintry night spent in an ancient, snow-covered cabin that looked more like a troll's ice cave from a fairy tale than any place I ever expected to stay. The frigid march through a dark forest at a pace I could barely endure.

Shooting bunnies in a field. It was the culmination of events that began when my father sat down next to me on our one soft, plastic-cover-free sofa. I was curled up with a book, and he said, "This weekend, let's go away, just the two of us. It's time you learn to hunt rabbits."

I was excited about camping with my father, and I didn't give it much thought until it was real.

Kerpow! *I knew it would be loud, but my only other experience with long guns was firing .22-caliber rifles on the range at Boy Scout camp, where we wore hearing protectors, each shot was only as loud as a lawnmower hitting a rock, and the targets didn't bleed. The M-1 was different. Its report broke the bucolic quiet with deafening force. It was frightening standing next to my father as he pointed death at furry creatures I could barely see. Each shot unleashed a thunder that overwhelmed the field, raced away to berate the mountains, and then echoed back to brag.*

"Sight the next rabbit, pivot your weight, point your front foot toward the rabbit, adjust the tension you have on the weapon, lead the rabbit, exhale, gently squeeze the trigger, and fire."

Krackow!

"Find your next target, adjust your weight, point your toe, and check your tension. Inhale, and breathe out as you squeeze the trigger."

Kerpow! *As the shots were fired, frantic rabbits fled the field in erratic bounds like pachinko balls diving into snow-covered holes. It only took seconds before the field was almost empty.*

"Sight the next rabbit. As fast as he's moving, at this distance, lead him by about two body lengths. Confirm your footing and balance; hold your weapon firmly, but don't clench. Remember, a weapon is an extension of your will. Exhale; track your target by tightening or relaxing a muscle.

Don't try to move the barrel. Moving your weapon should feel like you're extending your arm, then shooting the next place the rabbit will be. Pick a place where the bullet will kill it instantly."

I unplugged my fingers from my ears and shouted, "How can I possibly know where a rabbit will be? They're random. They're running for their lives. All over the place."

"Really? Is that what it looks like to you?" he said, surprised. "Pick out three of them. Watch them for a while. Then tell me what you see."

Krackow! *More instruction.*

Kerpow! *More instruction.*

Krackow! *Then there was a metallic* pling *as the cartridge clip ejected from the top of the rifle and hit the snow.*

"With a little practice, you can do the same," Father said as he removed a new magazine clip from his pocket and reloaded the rifle. Despite hitting the snow, the top of the clip was still warm when I handed the empty one back to him.

I knew I had just witnessed an incredible thing. It wasn't an act I wanted to follow.

For the next hour, we followed blood sprays in the snow and gathered up dead rabbits.

Two rabbits died from gaping chest holes that mangled their bodies; four died with their heads blown clean off. It was amazing shooting, but when I looked at it, I almost threw up. I'd seen dead birds on the ground or fish washed up on shore. Occasionally, I'd found the crispy remains of some stupid squirrel that ran along a power line into a transformer and got electrocuted—but they were mostly intact, not disembodied. Not still bleeding.

My head started to clear after we gathered the six rabbits. I carried them in a bag over my shoulder, and even though it bounced against my leg with every step to remind me it was there, I pretended it wasn't. As we walked toward the river, the snow sparkled in the morning light, and the pine trees that weren't flocked with snow were encased in a thin layer of ice. As we passed by, animals slowly emerged back into their winter-silver world.

"You doing OK?" Father said, looking at the river. "You look a little green."

"I'm fine." But I was grateful for the cold breeze blowing on my face. "It's different than I expected." Then I had a thought. "Hey? How long have you been hunting? You're good at it."

He paused to think, and as he walked, the wavy auburn hair that stuck out from under his thick black watch cap curled in the wind. "Since I was younger that you are now. With a little practice, you'll be good, too."

"Right," I said, but I didn't believe it.

"Hand me the bag," Father said as he knelt alongside the water. He dumped it, laid out the rabbits side by side on the snow, and produced a knife with a hooked blade. "Pay attention. After I do the first one, you'll do the rest."

"I'll do what now?"

"After you shoot them, you have to dress and clean them quickly, or the meat will go bad."

"OK."

"First you take one rabbit and make a shallow cut through the skin from chin to anus along the belly. Don't cut into the organs, or it will ruin the meat. Then open it up, flip it over, and everything you don't need will fall out."

And with a spa-losh sound, it did, into a small, grayish pile.

"If the head's still on, start by twisting it off. Then flip it over again. Start at the neck, and peel the hide from the meat. You may have to slice around a few ligaments, but when you're done, the hide will peel off like a glove."

I stared at the scalped, gutted rabbit in my father's hand and the bag of skin on the ground, and I felt sick again.

"Then you just have to rinse it off," Father said. "Simple as that."

Father passed me the knife. It was still warm from his hand and sticky with blood from dressing the first rabbit. I gritted my teeth at the sensation and sighed as I reached for the next rabbit in line. It was one of the ones that still had a head, and I froze when I realized what I had to do next. I set down the knife, closed my eyes, said, "Sorry," and twisted the rabbit's head.

It came off with a wet snap.

I opened my eyes and looked at what I was holding. Head in one hand, body in the other. I put the rabbit's head gently down with its eyes facing away from me, picked up the knife, turned the rabbit over, and started to press the knife into the skin under its fur. But I couldn't move my hand to make the cut. "My weapon is an extension of my will." Bullshit. My hand was an extension of my will, and I couldn't make it work.

"It's all right," Father said. "Take your time."

My hand was shaking, and I pulled the knife away from the rabbit. I was cold from kneeling in the wet snow. I knew what I had to do, but I still hesitated.

"Start with a deep breath. Cut through the skin, and make one clean, shallow cut from top to bottom."

I looked up at my father with pleading eyes. He was watching me, weighing my actions, waiting for my choice, curious what I'd do next. He had pale, winter-sky blue eyes, and his gaze was as cold and sharp as the icicles hanging from the tree branches, but there was no disappointment in his eyes as he watched, and when I saw that, I felt better. I wasn't confident, but I was able to steady my hand, make knife touch skin, and, after a deep breath, I did it. I made one long, clean cut and unzipped that rabbit. Then I dumped its insides out in the snow.

The entrails steamed with a bitter iron stench. I gagged and was about to throw up when a strange thing happened: I realized it was the first time I'd ever noticed what was inside an animal, and I was surprised to find my curiosity trumped my disgust. I'd seen line drawings and pictures of organs in science class, but it surprised me that I knew what a lot of parts were. The ones I didn't know, Father explained to me.

After that, I skinned the rabbit. For some reason, that was easier. The next one went faster, and by the time I rinsed the last rabbit off and returned it to the bag, I felt satisfied. I didn't like how blood felt on my hands, and I didn't like the feeling of Velcro tearing when I peeled away a rabbit's hide. It scared me, but I could do it.

Father shouldered his pack. As he started to walk away, he turned back and said, "All the meat you eat starts out as a living, breathing animal that has to die so you can live. Remember that. After today, respect it."

When I stood up, the bag of rabbits was lighter.

I followed Father up a hill that was mostly a stack of windswept rocks. Right after I set down my pack and stretched, he handed me a cup of hot chocolate and hung a small pair of binoculars around my neck. The view from the hill stretched from the edge of the forest across most of the field, past a small stream, and all the way to the river. While I ate lunch, I watched rabbits. After a while, I was able to focus on what three of them were doing.

"Which rabbits are you tracking?" Father asked.

I pointed them out. "The one by the river next to the three stacked-up rocks. The grayish one closest to us by the hill with one tree. The brown-and-white one a little way away from the snowbank that looks like a caterpillar."

"I've got them," he said. "This time, I'm going to fire a shot near them. Watch what happens. Tell me what you see."

"Yes, sir."

"Three rocks. One shot only. Fire." After the long quiet, the rifle exploded next to me. The round hit the snow at the base of the rocks and punched a hole into it like a fist.

The rabbits scattered. Not just near where the bullet hit, but everywhere. I watched the rabbit leap away. Then I searched for the others. One was already gone, but the grayish one was zigzagging wildly down the hill. I watched him disappear.

"So, what did you notice?"

"Almost all of them ran for cover. All of them ran from high ground to low ground, and the ones that didn't run pressed themselves into the snow."

"So, some stand still, and the ones that run tend to move through the terrain from high to low."

"Yes."

"So, what does that mean if you're hunting one?"

"Hmm." I thought about it. "For the ones that don't run, if I miss my first shot, I should aim my second shot a little lower?"

"Are you asking me or telling me?"

"Telling you."

"What else?"

"If they do run, they'll probably run to lower ground. I should expect them to move that way."

"Those are good observations."

I continued to watch, and my father started melting snow in a small pot over a tiny single-burner stove. He smoked until the water boiled, and he made hot chocolate again.

After a quiet spell, the rabbits emerged and moved across the field once more.

"Now that your bunnies are back, notice anything?"

I scanned the field with the binoculars. "No way."

"What?"

"It looks like the three rabbits I was watching earlier are back. They're not in the exact same spots, but they're really close to where they were."

"Ever hear the expression 'creatures of habit'?"

"Yeah."

"What was that?"

"Yes, sir," I corrected.

He took a breath and exhaled slowly before he continued. "Now that your rabbits think they're safe, they'll mostly go back to what they were doing."

Looking around, I saw he was right. If I'd taken a picture before my father shot the rabbits and another one now, they would've looked nearly identical.

"Now. I'll fire another round near one of the other rabbits you're watching. Tell me if you notice anything else."

"The brown-and-white one back by that far snowbank that looks like a caterpillar," I said.

"Caterpillar. One shot only. Fire."

I looked through the binoculars and watched another fist slam into the snowbank inches above the rabbit's ears just as—krakow!—thunder echoed through the valley.

The rabbits scattered again. This time I noticed the rabbits that moved hopped all over the place, but their first leap was usually forward unless there was something blocking their way that they couldn't hide in or under.

"What did you see?" my father asked as he took my canteen, then lit up a fresh Marlboro.

"Rabbits run away from whatever scares them. Their first jump is straight away from it unless they have a place to hide close by; then they take the shortest path to it. But if there's something in their way, they try to take a path that still gives them cover."

"*Good observation. Next target. One shot only. Fire.*" Kerpow!

We spent the next few hours scaring rabbits to see what they would do. Eventually, I started to understand how they moved when threatened. It wasn't perfect, but patterns did emerge from rabbit chaos.

Father slung his weapon, lit another cigarette, and told me three things that he said I should never forget. "*Every living thing has a pattern,*" *he said.* "*Animals react based on what they know. Living things trace their patterns on their terrain, and most of them will follow the easiest path they can to survive.*" *He told me never to forget those things because it was important I understand how animals behave.*

"*Every animal?*" *I asked.* "*Even people?*"

"*Especially people,*" *he said, taking a last, long draw off his cigarette before pinching out the ember and putting the butt in his pocket.* "*Only people won't like you if you let them know you figured them out.*"

"*Even if it's true?*"

"*Especially if it's true.*"

I adjusted my gloves and watched the rabbits moving in the snow. The day was more than halfway over, and the sky was cobalt blue. "*Can't people change their patterns, though?*"

"*Yeah, but most don't, even if they know better.*"

"*But why?*"

"*Why?*" *Father thought about it as he topped off the canteens with the last of the boiled water.* "*Because it's hard and expensive. People always want to change themselves, but they always stop short when it gets hard or if they need to give up something they like. But enough talk. Get ready to shoot.*"

"*What do I need to do now?*" *I asked with more than a little apprehension.*

"*Your objective is to hit a rabbit.*"

"*That's it?*"

350

"Knowing where the rabbit will be and having the skill to hit it are two entirely different things. Both are important. Both are required to meet your objective."

"I've never fired a weapon like this."

"It sights like a .22 with iron sights, and you've fired that."

"Yes, but compared to a .22, this thing is a cannon."

"Works exactly the same way, only this kicks, so you'll have to brace yourself and lean into it. All your shots will fire above your target until you get used to it. If you don't pay attention, this weapon will hurt you and the people around you."

It was even heavier than I'd thought it would be, but I was finally able to get a decent firing position. The problem was I could only hold it for a three-Mississippi count before the weight was too much for me and I had to lower the weapon.

The M-1, like most firearms, has a basic sight comprising two parts: a single metal bar that looks like a capital I centered near the end of the barrel, and two bars with a gap between them, like a capital U, somewhere near the handgrip or stock.

One Mississippi. Try to line up my target with the front and rear sights. My sight picture looked like a Spirograph drawing.

Two Mississippi. Exhale, and try to put my M-1's I precisely in its U so it made a perfect, happy rectangle over the place I willed my bullet to go.

Fire. Hold the gun steady after the shot, and recover. Three Mississippi. That was the procedure.

"Your target is that dead and blackened tree trunk on the other side of the river at 150 yards."

"The one that looks like it was hit by lightning and burned?"

"Yes. Here," Father said, "put five shots in that tree, and we're done for the day. Before you start firing, you'll need these. They're going to feel cold

and clammy at first, but you'll be glad you have them." He produced the small bag filled with cotton balls coated in Vaseline that we used as tinder to start our fires. He rolled a couple between his thumb and finger, then stuffed them in my ears. Then he pointed out the target to confirm that I understood where to shoot. When he was satisfied I knew what to do, he handed me a round.

I rested the stock on my boot. Loaded the round. Took a deep breath, lifted the M-1, and got a good grip on it. One Mississippi—I aimed at the middle of the tree. Two Mississippi—leaned forward, exhaled, and fired.

Krakow! It was still loud with the cotton balls in my ears, but it was better. The gun bucked when I fired, I could feel the barrel rise and the M-1 push me back. Three Mississippi. I couldn't believe how much the stock driving into me hurt.

"Left. Your shot went wide to the left."

Then he handed me another round. I tried to adjust my aim to compensate.

Kapow!

"High and right."

Father handed me another round.

Krackow! Every shot was like being kicked in the chest.

It was nearly dark when I finally figured it out and put five rounds into that tree.

When my father said, "Hit," after the fifth round, I crumpled to the ground, exhausted. The weapon warmed my chest through my coat, and the walk back to the cabin was an uneventful blur.

I brought in wood from the cords stacked against the outside cabin wall and built a fire. After I finished layering the twigs and wood shavings inside a teepee of split wood, I remembered I still had the Vaseline-soaked cotton balls stuffed in my ears and pulled them out. Without giving it much *thought, I pulled them apart into tinder and, with one match, used them to get the fire going.*

Father was busy cutting up rabbit and onions. I went out back, broke through the ice in the water barrel, and filled a wash pail. The water was cold, but I stripped down and washed my parts before changing into my long johns for sleeping. I shivered, but it felt good to wash the sweat away. My chest, left arm, and part of my stomach were black and blue from firing the M-1, and my upper body stung in the cold air. In an instant, I was changed and back in the warm cabin.

Skewers of rabbit, onion, and what looked like mandarin oranges from a tin were cooking over the fire, and thin strips of rabbit hung on wires strung across the rafters where smoke exited through a hole in roof. I watched my father work, turning skewers, adding salt, cleaning his M-1. Not a motion was wasted. I sat on my sleeping bag with my back to the wall in the orange glow. I was warm, and it smelled good.

Father woke me for a dinner of rabbit-and-onion skewers with ketchup on the side and vienna sausages cooked on a stone near the embers until they deflated. My father used vienna sausages like camping condiments and worked them into almost every meal. I thought they were vile out of the can, but when he cooked them, they tasted like fried bologna.

I took a tentative bite of my rabbit skewer, and it wasn't what I was expecting. "It's good."

"You sound surprised."

"I am. It's really good."

"Good. It's what we caught. What were you expecting?"

"Something worse than vienna sausages," I said, looking away.

"You could do a lot worse than vienna sausages," he said, popping a couple of them into his mouth. Then he smiled when he saw me reach for another skewer.

"Aren't you going to shoot again?" I asked.

"I've already caught just about everything I can eat. The rest of our time here is for you."

I must have rolled my eyes.

"If you shoot straight tomorrow, you won't have to worry about them running all around."

"OK," I said. I could barely keep my eyes open.

"Now, get some sleep. Tomorrow's a long day."

I didn't sleep well. My dreams were full of snow swirling around giant, scorched pine trees that swayed and bucked in the wind. Thunder constantly echoed, and headless, gutless bunnies hopped and flashed their empty insides at me. Hundreds of them danced naked around fresh holes blasted in the snow, and they all laughed at me, even though they had no mouths.

March 2004—Republican Guard Palace, Baghdad

Meet, change, go, do, restore, return, change, forget. One job. Eight clear verbs, most of them one syllable. That was the mission. Like most plans, it only took us so far.

The trip to the CPA was uneventful. My morning spectrum-management presentation to the minister of communications went well, and if he approved the timeline I proposed, we'd be in good shape when the CPA transferred their authority to the Iraqi government over the summer.

The crowds thinned as I made my way to the basement level of the palace. It was a maze of marble-inlaid corridors, dead ends, and construction. After twenty minutes of searching, I found myself in an empty hallway in front of the right thick wooden door.

I had a lot to work through after John told me Lucy died. I was angry. I was hurt. I was left out, and now I was mourning the loss of a friend years after she was gone. I missed Lu. She'd saved my life. I owed her. Now, I'd never get to pay her back or hear her laugh again.

I knocked on the door, and almost immediately, there was the sharp snap of a lock disengaging. The door opened just a crack, and I pushed through. Inside was a small anteroom with a desk to my left and a man in a suit with a shotgun to my right. The room was bright compared to the corridor, and I had to blink a few times before my eyes adjusted. It was a simple stone room with another door in front of me. I stopped in the middle of the room in front of the empty desk. The door was closed and bolted behind me by another man I hadn't noticed when I entered the room.

No one said anything.

"I'm Captain—"

"Ringo," the man behind me interrupted. "Empty your pockets, and put everything into the box on the desk."

I did. I set my sidearm and clips on the table, then crammed the OD green helmet bag full of my stuff into the box. On top of that, I added my wallet, my only decent pen, line badges, two sticks of gum, a tin of Altoids, a lighter, and my last cigar.

As I turned to face the guards, one stopped me.

"Your watch and dog tags, too." That was a harder thing to do. But it made sense to sanitize, so I took them off. After lifting the chain from around my neck, I hesitated for a second. My plain gold wedding ring rode the chain with my dog tags. It was dull from the sweat, showers, and sand. Once I put it on top of the pile, I felt naked without it. I made a mental note to polish it up with a little toothpaste when I got back.

"Done," I said.

The guard to my right unbolted the other door and opened it for me. "We'll keep these safe," he said, "until you get back."

John was waiting in the next room with Paul and George, and as I approached them, the door was closed and bolted behind me. It was a proper operations center, with a briefing table, annotated maps, and analysts on computers busy reviewing intelligence and typing away in the corners.

The gang was all together, and our eight-word action plan was written across the white board. Another large board was draped with a sheet, and one of the presentation monitors facing us was turned off so I couldn't see the sensitive contents it displayed. More proof that, while I was a guest, I wasn't quite family.

We went over it again. Nothing new. Get in, make repairs and upgrades, get the sensors and transmitters back online, get out quietly, return to base.

Everyone was dressed for the concert but me. I got to sort through a box of assorted local clothes in sizes close to mine. I ultimately settled on relatively clean-looking underwear, a threadbare pair of grayish pants, and a faded green shirt with a worn-through collar that advertised something in Arabic script across the front. It was the best of what fit, and the clothes stunk of old sweat. My new scent choked me, but now we at least looked and smelled like the local laborers we were supposed to be. We looked more like *miskin*, the poorest of the poor, than the infidels we were. Since I was the only clean-shaven one of the group, I was given a scarf in addition to an embroidered skullcap that looked like a *kipot* but, once on, was more of a Moroccan fez. I have wide feet, and the only shoes that would fit were sandals.

John's clothes were negligibly nicer. He wore a headscarf and a blazer that would have been at home in a sixties sitcom, but he was the boss and the driver. Paul wore overalls. George wore a tunic of sorts with embroidery around the neck and a skullcap not so different from mine, only he looked more miserable in it. All my clothes, boots, uniform, socks—everything—went into a plastic garbage bag. John gave it to one of the techs as we left the room, and I followed him out with Paul and George flanking me. We had no weapons, and walking along unencumbered by firepower in Baghdad was another new sensation.

We left through another door, went down an empty hallway, and were let out of the building by another guard through a heavy metal door that opened into a courtyard garden. We walked a short distance past flowers and tropical fruit trees until we came to a locked door. John punched a code into a keypad, and with a *click*, we were in a motor pool. Some of the vehicles were standard issue. A few were special, and three were hidden under car covers. I couldn't make out what they were from their outlines. We stopped in front of a large white local van. We called them Shi'a vans, and they were everywhere in Baghdad. They usually transported workers or worshippers, and they were distinctive because they were unusually clean white vans with murals of a cheerful religious figure on each side. I couldn't tell who it was. I should have asked, but I didn't. I know it couldn't have been Allah because locals would shoot you for that. Whoever he was, he was a popular wrap on vans, and he always looked happy.

Our gear was already loaded in the back. John did a quick inventory. We function checked the weapons we found in the van, and then Paul and George climbed aboard. John slid the door shut and looked at me. "Are you up for this?"

"I promised I'd help. I wouldn't be here if I couldn't do it."

"Is that a yes?"

"Yes, it is."

"Are we good?"

"We are. I understand what happened. I miss her, though."

"You and me both. Lucy said there was nothing left to say. We parted in Kuwait in the best possible way, and anything after that would have been too sad."

"She saved me in Yugoslavia, John."

"I know. Funny thing is, I've heard both sides of what happened during that riot, but the way Lucy told the story, it was always you who saved her."

"What does that mean?"

"It means you did more for her than you realize. You and I are probably the last two people left in the world who still know her name and who she was. After this, let's take the time to remember her right. Deal?" he asked, holding out his hand.

After I shook it, there was a gold necklace left in my palm. "What's this?" I said, turning it over in my hand.

"It's a Saint Christopher medal. Look at the back. She engraved it."

I turned it over. It said, *Bill, still watching over you. Lu.*

I could feel my eyes tearing up.

"He's the saint who watches over travelers. Lu made me promise to put it in your hand personally before you went into harm's way again. I'm sorry I'm late."

"It makes sense now. The last thing she said was she would be my guardian angel."

"All right then. Put it on, and get your ass in the van. We've got work to do."

After I slid into the front passenger seat, George leaned forward and patted me on the head.

"Did you guys make up?"

"Yeah . . . shut up, George."

CHAPTER 34

January 1978—Catskill Mountains, Upstate New York

It snowed hard, and the roof groaned all night. By morning, my body ached so much I couldn't stand it. I could barely sit up when I heard Father getting breakfast ready. Gusts slammed against the cabin and everything inside rattled.

"Why are you making that face? It's just a little wind."

"I'm sore from yesterday."

"Humph. Pain is nature's way of letting you know you're still alive."

"Do you have anything that'll help?"

"I do, but you won't like it."

"I'll try anything."

"OK." He rummaged through his pack and handed me two tablets and a warm canteen cup of what looked like hot chocolate in the dim light. "Chew these, and wash it down with this."

"Thanks." So, I popped the tablets in my mouth and started chewing, then almost spit it out. It was the worst thing I ever tasted.

"Swallow it and empty that cup." It wasn't a request. The bitter taste got worse the longer it stayed in my mouth. So I gulped down the contents of the cup, but it didn't get better.

"What is this? It's disgusting, and this drink is worse. What is it?"

"It's the taste of adulthood. Aspirin and black coffee. Get used to it."

"It's awful."

"You'll thank me in twenty minutes."

I groaned.

"Here's breakfast," Father said as he passed me a plate of rabbit and eggs he'd fried in bacon fat with a slice of brown bread from a can. After I dug in, he poured me a cup of Tang.

"You had Tang? Couldn't I have just swallowed the aspirin with the Tang?"

"Sure. But they work faster and better if you chew them with coffee."

After eating, I was still sore, but I did feel better. I'd learned two things few twelve-year-olds knew: that chewing aspirin with coffee was good for quick pain relief and that the combination also melts and jump-starts your bowels. After a dash through deep snow to the outhouse, I finished breakfast and sat with my father by the fire until the blizzard tapered off. When the sun was bright enough to look like moonlight through the clouds, we doused the fire and left.

We made our way back to the hill that looked like it was made of stacked, windswept blocks and circled around the middle row until we were mostly out of the wind behind a rockfall the snow had missed. It took a while; there were deep snow drifts. I was shaking cold when we stopped, and Father started a small fire against the stone cliff to our back. We had a commanding view of a white section of field. When my teeth finally stopped clattering, he handed me a cup of hot Tang, and we waited for a break in the weather. It looked like we were the only living things out in the field. "I'm not seeing any rabbits."

"Give it time. They'll come out after this blows out. Now's the time to get ready."

Father handed me the M-1 with a five-round clip loaded. There was no bullet in the chamber, so I checked the safety and slid forward the action. Now it would fire once every time I pulled the trigger until my five rounds *were gone. Now I could find a place where I could rest the weapon so I could focus on aiming and shooting and not bearing all that weight.*

I looked around and found a good spot just past the fire where I could straddle my pack and rest the M-1 on a flat rock I could use like a bipod. Not long after we settled in, there was a lull in the storm, and about thirty yards away, a rabbit emerged.

I was excited. "There," I said, pointing it out to Father. Now I could fire the M-1 as intended.

"That's off limits."

"What do you mean off limits?" I shouted.

"With a weapon like the M-1. What are you going to learn, taking cheap shots like that?"

"It's snowing, and I don't have a scope."

"See that stream? You can shoot any rabbit you see on the other side of that stream."

"But I can barely see the stream in the storm."

"Then you'll have to look for holes in the storm."

"That's more than a hundred yards away."

"I'll spot for you," Father said.

The worst thing about trying to hit a moving target is the target moves. What's worse than trying to hit a moving target? No target at all.

Then there was an opening in the storm, and I could see the stream again.

"Rabbit," Father called out. "Two o'clock, one hundred yards. Moving away from the stream."

"Two o'clock?" I looked back at my father. "What does that mean?"

"I know you're not that stupid." Then I felt his big hand grab my head. "Twelve o'clock is straight forward." Then he twisted my head to the right a little and stopped. "One o'clock." Then he twisted right some more. "Two

o'clock." When my head was to my shoulder, he said, "Three o'clock." Then he twisted my head forward again. "Twelve o'clock, get it?"

"I get it."

Then he snapped my head left in increments. "Eleven o'clock, ten o'clock, nine o'clock," and my head was turned all the way to my left shoulder. Then he snapped my head forward again and said, "Twelve o'clock, get it?"

"Yes, I get it," I said, and he slapped me in the back of the head.

"Don't be stupid. You're better than that. If you think about things, you can figure them out." Then he lit a cigarette. "Get ready to fire."

"OK," I said, taking my position, finding my grip on the M-1, and pivoting the weapon on the rock toward some space on the other side of the stream. I sniffled, and my eyes were blurry. I blamed the snow and dumb rabbits and stupid rules. I sniffled again.

"You going to cry now?"

"No. I'm not going to cry," I said, as I was crying. Stupid Dad. How could you be so smart and so dumb—idiot. Idiot. IDIOT. Jarhead. Jerk. How about you think about things and figure them out? Stupid clocks. Stupid patterns.

"Asshole," I whispered.

"What did you say?"

"Nothing. I'm better than that."

"OK. Then let's get something straight. I love you, but I will never, ever be your friend."

"Maybe I don't see as well as you or I'm not strong enough or my hands aren't steady—"

"That's not it. You're soft and a little too sensitive, and if you don't toughen up, the real world is going to eat you alive."

"You could be a little nicer."

"Nice won't make you strong."

"I love you, but you can be a real jerk. I'm twelve, you know. I'm a kid."

"Well, you got to grow up sometime. I'm here to teach you something, and you're out here to learn. I guess we'll both be making some hard choices."

"I guess we will," I said. Only my father was confident enough to hand someone a loaded combat rifle and then pick a fight with him. The wind was quieting down, but swirls and eddies kept stirring up the snow, and visibility didn't much improve.

"Rabbit," Father called out. *"Eleven o'clock, 120 yards. To the right of the tree."*

I wiped my tears on my sleeve, blew my nose, then rolled up two of the cotton balls we used to start fires between thumb and forefinger and stuffed them in my ears. They were freezing cold. Then I lifted my M-1, made a few adjustments, moved the safety to fire, and tried to find the rabbit.

"Got him. First shot."

Kerpow!

"Miss. Right and high."

"Second shot. Fire." Exhale, and squeeze the trigger.

Krackow!

"Miss. Right. Close. Rabbit lost."

Three shots, two, one. Then there was a metallic *spling* sound as the clip ejected and rang off the rocky ground like a bell. Over the next hour, I fired five clips, twenty-five shots. I got close, but there weren't a lot of rabbits in the snowstorm, and the ones I spooked faded like ghosts.

I took a break to warm my hands by the fire. My father handed me a hot chocolate.

I said, *"Thanks."*

He grunted.

After a while, the wind died down, and the snowfall dwindled. When my fingers were thawed, I went back to my perch, and Father spotted.

"Rabbit. One o'clock, 150 yards. Climbing a small hill," he called out.

I loaded a fresh clip. Selected fire. Adjusted my grip and tension on the weapon, took a deep breath, and as I lined up the shot, I tried to relax as I squeezed the trigger.

Krackow! *At 150 yards, a rabbit looked like a bug to me, and the snow didn't help.*

"Miss. Close. Low. Left."

Four shots, three, two . . .

With every failure, my resolve increased. It wasn't about pride or to please my father. I just wanted to kill a rabbit and be done. I was a gang member initiate, and my task was to cap a critter to prove my loyalty and secure my place in the food chain. No more, no less.

"Miss." "Long." "Short." "High." "Low." "Left." "Right."

I got closer, but all I heard after each shot was you suck.

Suddenly, the field grew dead still. A tear opened in the sky, and through its ragged edges, long rays of sunshine hit the field like spotlights. Little rabbit heads started popping up to taunt me all across the no-bunny-kill zone while I waited for my father to call out a legitimate target.

It didn't take long.

"Rabbit. One o'clock, 110 yards. Moving toward a small pile of rocks."

"Ready to fire. First shot." I only had one shot left, and the clip would eject. The rabbit was moving down a drift toward a clear open space. It would probably try to stay close to the rocks. I lined up the shot. I pulled the trigger.

Kerpow!

For the first time, I felt good about the shot.

"Miss."

Spling. *The clip ejected, and I loaded another one, slapped the action forward, and targeted the other side of the rocks in case he exited there.*

"Correction. Hit."

"What?" I said. "I hit?"

"Yes and no. It looked like the shot hit the rocks the rabbit passed behind. But the shot must have gotten through. Look, there's blood."

I looked through the binoculars, and there was blood, but I didn't see the rabbit.

"Yes!" I made the weapon safe and handed it to my father. My father seemed perplexed but cheerful, so we stomped out our embers and left. It took us twenty minutes to find the spot. There was a hole in the loose stone where my shot had hit the rock pile. Around back, there was a softball-sized crater where my shot had exited, and just past that, drops of blood and splinters of rock were embedded in the ice and snow. I realized what I'd done when I saw the blood trail along the ground, and I didn't know what I felt. I wasn't happy.

We followed blood drops and paw prints at intervals in the snow until we reached a small hollow in the rock. Curled up with its back against the wall was my rabbit. It was brown and white, and stone fragments had penetrated its blood-soaked neck, chest, and flank like flint arrowheads.

"Congratulations on your first kill."

"Thanks. Can we still eat him with all this damage?"

Father knelt and looked the rabbit over. "Yes. It'll be fine." As he examined it, his fingers felt around inside one of its chest wounds.

"I can't say I feel great about this. But I did it, right?"

"That's right," he said as he stood up. Then he turned around, grabbed me by the coat, and smeared a handprint of blood across my face and mouth.

I tried to stop him, but it was already too late. He wound up holding me up off the ground by my coat with one hand while I screamed and shouted. He seemed to be having a good time.

Eventually, I hung limp. "Can you just put me down now?"

He laughed as he did.

"What's wrong with you?"

"Me? Nothing," Father said. "That's the tradition after your first kill. Normally we'd also eat its still-beating heart, but . . ."

"It's disgusting. I really hate being small enough to pick up."

"The good thing is, you'll grow."

I knelt, and Father handed me the knife with the curved blade. I pulled out the rock splinters, lined them up in the snow, and said, "Sorry," before I gutted and skinned the rabbit.

As we carefully walked over the rocks to cross the stream, Father lit a fresh smoke. "How does it feel now that you got one?"

"I don't know," I said, stopping to clean some of the blood off my face in the water. "I feel good and bad. I don't know if that shot actually counts as my kill."

I had taken one of the most important firearms of the twentieth century and used it to kill a rabbit by stoning it to death. I hadn't shot it directly, and the rabbit looked like it had been hit with a shotgun. Even after that, it had still been able to hop far enough away to hide until it died from blood loss. The only worse kill would be if a rabbit hopped into me by accident and I clubbed it to death with the M-1's stock. But I couldn't have done that. It would violate the "no hunting closer than a hundred yards" rule.

"You, without a doubt, killed that rabbit."

"I didn't hit what I was aiming at, though," I said, still feeling guilty.

"Your objective was to hit a rabbit, and you hit your target. A hit's a hit, and a kill's a kill. The proof is in that bag."

"OK."

"Good. Now let's get some of his friends."

"Dad," I said after a little thought, "I think I'm more of a fisherman."

March 2004—Baghdad

We navigated parts of Baghdad I had never seen. Past scarred colleges, lonely monuments, shopping districts, an electric substation, and young men playing cricket in a field. After running a few errands, we circled the Sadr City slums, turned back toward downtown, and arrived for work.

It was a tall two-story warehouse behind a broken wall, with boarded-up windows and a central tower section that climbed at least four stories above the warehouse roof. John did a quick drive by, like we were looking for an address to make a delivery, but the place was quiet. We got there in the middle of the afternoon on a hot day, and it was like a ghost town.

We stopped at a loading ramp in front of a metal roll-up door. Paul and George entered through the side door, one after the other, and swept the building. A few minutes later, the garage door opened, and we drove in.

The building was vast, hot, and damaged. Piles of debris formed small hills and berms in the middle of the warehouse where big sections of the roof had come down. Streams of sunlight cut through the dust, and pigeons took flight when we disturbed them. A bus plugged the hole the explosion had made in the brick wall where the VBIED had detonated.

A web of metal stairs and lofts covered the inner walls. Metal hooks hung in a row along one wall. Metal mesh security cages, some with their doors ripped off, were bolted into the floor across from the hooks. Drains were regularly spaced in the floor, and a desk and chairs were set up in a cleared space across from the loading dock we entered through. It could have been a factory, a prison, an interrogation or research facility, or some combination.

It took us about fifteen minutes to unload the van. We put on headsets and did one last radio check, and John left to take care of other business. It must have been more than 120 degrees in the building, and after we organized the equipment, we guzzled water and began to assess the damage.

It was substantial. Shrapnel from the explosion had blown through and shredded parts of the surveillance system. Sensors, components, and wiring needed to be replaced on almost every floor, and almost all the optical fiber needed to be rerun up to an antenna tower. Fortunately, the central controls and power were mostly intact in the tower section. Our task would be replacing parts, rerouting cables, and adding armor to the important bits to shield them from further battle damage.

Even though the building was sealed and deserted now, prior attacks from rocket-propelled grenades (RPGs), mortars, and rockets had weakened large parts of the structure. Damage from the last explosion had not only taken out the surveillance system but also knocked down several of the brick columns that supported the large metal loft that made up a huge section of the second story.

As I wound my way through debris taller than me, I noticed some of the columns were so badly spiderwebbed with floor-to-ceiling cracks that I could see light shining through them from the other side. Rubble blocked two of the stairs, the sky was visible through the roof, and in places, the metal stairs had broken loose from the walls. I gave the brick column supporting the loft a hard push, and the loft and stairs climbing the wall to my right shuddered.

The tower was in good shape, but the sections of scaffolding over the warehouse we had to use to get there were dicey. It took hours to get all the gear where it needed to go. In places where the stairs had fallen and there were gaps, we had to use rope to climb and hoist the equipment.

It took a few more hours to run all the cable. While Paul and I finished up, George positioned CCTV cameras embedded in fiberglass bricks around the exterior perimeter of the building and epoxied them in place. When I looked at a cross section of one of them, in addition to the camera, there was also an antenna that looked like a tiny aircraft transponder. It seemed out of place for the type of surveillance we were setting up, but it was the upgrade John said we needed to get up and running as soon as possible.

After we finished the grunt work of lifting stuff and pulling cable, I left Paul and George to the task of bringing the system back online while I found a covered spot with a good view of the stairs and main floor to keep watch with my M-14 and George's submachine gun.

Paul hummed while he worked, George cursed, and I prompted them for updates, which I passed along to John. I was surprised by how fast they got the system running again once all the new cable and equipment was in. They packed a few spares in security cabinets, locked the heavy upstairs doors, and began to work their way back down.

"John, this is Ringo. Stage lights are on, please confirm."

"Stand by, Ringo." There was a pause for a few minutes, then John came back on the radio. "Lights confirmed, show's a go. Ready for pickup?"

"Stand by." We checked the area around the building from the upstairs windows; the surrounding area was empty.

"All clear. Ready for pickup."

"Copy all, Ringo. See you in fifteen."

I hit the transmit button twice to acknowledge and switched over to the egress frequency.

"Gentlemen," I said over the radio, "the band's getting back together. Rally in the lobby. Next show starts at 1600."

I heard four hits of static to acknowledge. I tossed George his weapon when he passed my position and headed down the stairs after him.

We took one last look and rallied where we came in a few minutes ahead of schedule. Overall, a good run. We had a new tool in our arsenal to fight bad guys, and I'd made my peace with John.

I touched the Saint Christopher medal hanging around my neck, and—contact. The snap and crack of AK-47 fire erupted through the front of the warehouse. The only thing that saved us was a pile of roof debris. We hit the ground and took cover behind the support columns. The wall between the windows started to crash inward, and rounds started ricocheting around the building. Chips of brick and plaster shot everywhere, and the room filled with white dust.

"John, change of plan. We're under attack. How far out are you?"

"One minute."

"Avoid the front of the building, we're taking fire."

"What do you need?"

"Short of an air strike, how about you show up at the back door and we all go home?"

"Copy that," John said. "See you there in three."

"George, Paul," I called out, gesturing wildly behind us, "change of plan. We're going out the back door."

They nodded and started to work their way to the rear.

I muttered under my breath, "Don't worry. It's just a little repair. It'll be easy."

One of the support columns buckled under the constant fire. I was knocked back by a hail of stones and heavy dust into a shaft of light and went blind. It was a whiteout. I kept backing up, trying to get my bearings, trying to get the hell out of the light. My feet ached from stones bouncing off them. Fucking sandals. I was getting too old for reunion tours. I found cover behind another column, out of the light, and I could see again.

Three minutes under fire is forever. Incoming rounds shattered all the windows, destroying the few remaining pieces of furniture, and the middle of the front wall collapsed.

Whoever they were, they pushed into the warehouse, and they were still firing. I emptied another clip at them and kept moving back. The roof over our position was supported by parallel columns of plain dressed stone and concrete, and it was coming apart.

"George, Paul, status."

"Still alive. Falling back."

We finally got close enough to see each other. We were about halfway through the warehouse, winding around piles, leap-frogging away from the light and behind whatever cover we could find.

Fire. Fall back to the next column behind your buddies; add distance from the commotion. George is clear. Fire again. Paul passed behind me. Fire again.

Stay low. Get clear. Keep moving back.

I realized I was humming something every time I fired. I couldn't hear it so much as I knew I was doing it. An old M-14 isn't as smooth as an M-16. It used big, heavy 7.62 NATO rounds that kicked every time I pulled the trigger and punched holes through whatever I pointed at.

During a lull, when the incoming rounds had stopped and we were busy reloading and scrambling back, the only sounds were our labored breaths and the slither of small, unseen stones falling.

I realized I was humming "Pop Goes the Weasel."

We reached the last row of columns. Then it was just a short open space to the back of the room, John's arrival, and our escape.

Grenades exploded, and the concussion made the building shudder. More chunks fell from the ceiling and walls. The stairs above the opening in the wall twisted, and the huge metal scaffold that made up the second-floor loft swayed back and forth. It felt like my ears were bleeding.

George was crawling the last few feet to open the back door when the *thwacka, thwacka, thwacka* of a heavy machine gun opened up from the top of the first mound of debris, and the columns three rows up from us vaporized into shards of hot concrete that sliced everywhere.

Paul and I fired back, but I couldn't hit them.

Thwack, thwacka. Thrwack. The building shuddered again, and the choking dust got even worse. The moment George got the back door open, the heavy machine gun took notice of him, and I lost George in a fog of debris.

"George, status. George. George."

"I'm pinned down behind a pile of crap next to the door. My arm is cut up, but I'll be fine."

I looked over at Paul. We were OK, but we couldn't move.

What could we do? They controlled the area with their machine gun and kept us pinned down. Then shooters would work their way down the sides of the building to get an angle on us. We were outnumbered, outgunned, and I was almost out of ammo.

Thwack, thwacka. Thrwack. Thwack. Machine-gun fire tore apart another column, ripped apart the back door, and tore through the debris in front of us reducing the metal, wood, and stone to splinters and confetti.

I lobbed a smoke grenade across the warehouse and rolled away, wishing it was the real thing.

It formed a bright purple, roiling snake of a cloud between us and the bad guys, and machine-gun fire savaged the spot where I'd just been.

I knew where they were and what they'd likely do, but I didn't have a shot. If we could stop them for just a moment, we could get out, but the smoke wasn't enough. Then I looked up.

I felt the weight of the M-14 and rested it on top of a pile of stones next to the column that sheltered me. I adjusted my position one last time and fired at the last column supporting the edge of the metal second-story loft by the entrance, and one of the bricks moved. I fired again, and it blew a chunk from the column. Shot after shot knocked out brick after brick. It reminded me of the old Atari game *Breakout*, but I felt like I was trying to chop down a tree. Finally, the column shifted and collapsed. I got ready to move. The loft twisted, but it didn't fall. It still hung from a metal support in the ceiling. Bolted to a place I could barely see. Fuck.

Thwack, thwack, wacka, thwacka, twack, and more splinters cut my face and opened up the back wall.

I had one mag left. Twenty shots. I was bleeding and half-deaf. I shouted into the radio, "On my mark. Make for the door."

Paul looked at me like I was nuts. I pointed up. His eyes followed. After a moment, he nodded. "Draw their fire," I said, and Paul fired at the machine gunner's position as he moved away.

I was strangely calm, despite the building coming down around me.

I took a breath as I looked down the barrel. The dust and smoke thinned. The last bolt supporting the loft was less than thirty yards away, a metal bar no thicker than my wrist. The weight on it had to be tremendous. It was closer than the tree or the rabbits my father had made me shoot in the bitter cold when I was a kid.

Thwack, thwacka. Thrwack. Rounds slammed into the column I was behind, ripping out chunks of stone that shattered around me.

I knew exactly where the gunners were, and I had the skill to hit them. I was back at the point of convergence my father had described when we hunted when I was a kid.

I took another deep breath, adjusted my grip on the M-14, added tension between my cheek and arms to make sure the barrel wouldn't buck and ruin the shot. I relaxed my arm slightly, and the sight moved to rest comfortably centered at the top of the twisted metal ceiling support.

My left index finger applied gentle tension to the trigger.

The M-14 was an extension of my body.

I was afraid, but I knew what to do.

I exhaled, and my finger moved. My weapon was an extension of my will, and I fired one shot. It hit, and a vibration went through the metal scaffolding. I fired again, and one side of the loft seemed lower than it was before. I aimed higher, where the support connected to the roof, and took a deep breath. I felt the tension on my weapon and relaxed my body as I slowly exhaled. My world was the sight picture of a bolt behind the capital letter *I* at the end of my barrel and the *U*-shaped sight inches from my left eye.

When they were lined up perfectly, I gently squeezed the trigger. A new hole punched through the ceiling. There was a *snap*, and the steel-mesh loft crashed down on the debris mound with the shooters like a fly swatter.

Enemy fire stopped. I shouted, "Go, go, go!" over the radio. And we ran from the warehouse and into the brightest light I'd ever seen. They started firing again, but we were gone.

Jack was there with the van, and we clambered in.

I slammed the door and popped smoke. Jack floored the throttle, and the alley boiled orange. I tossed my last smoke grenade out the window to cover our exit where the alley dumped into the main road. It was supposed to be red, but a bright pink cloud covered our retreat.

It was the finale of our psychedelic tour.

I vaguely remember John asking if anyone was hit as we raced away through the Technicolor smoke in our Shi'a mystery machine, but everything was a blur. Once the gunfire was gone, all I could hear was my throbbing heart.

Paul bandaged George's arm, and except for needing a couple of stiches, everyone seemed all right. Maybe someone was watching over us. I felt wired, tired, and lucky.

I was covered in dirt and debris, and my sinuses ached.

Someone tossed me a roll of toilet paper, and we passed around a plastic container of Huggies baby wipes. No matter how much I blew my nose, all that came out was a paste like Elmer's glue and an occasional pebble. I twisted a wipe into a rope and corkscrewed it up into one of my nostrils as far as it would go. It felt cool, but when I pulled it out, so much cement and mucous drained from that side of my nose that it made me gag and cough. Then I did the other side. It was disgusting, but I could finally breathe. As a bonus, everything smelled just a little baby fresh.

I turned to the driver. "John," I croaked, "is it working?"

"Everything still looks good."

"Groovy." It was all I could say. I slumped in my seat. I didn't have the energy to elaborate.

Paul passed me a bottle of water and said, "Not bad for an air force puke."

George was already tearing into an MRE. We looked like scorched flour dumplings. I just nodded. The static in my head made conversation hurt.

We entered the CPA complex through a back way I didn't know existed. The civilian guard looked like he wanted to say something when he looked us over, but he didn't. A dog checked the van for explosives. Then they waved us through. We left the van in a different place, and instead of walking through the gardens, we followed a service tunnel back into the palace.

It was surreal. Someone I'd never seen before handed me my uniform on a hanger wrapped in plastic, along with a bag with new packs of underwear, socks, and T-shirts. It was like clothing issue in basic training, except they got my size right.

I said goodbye to the band in a cloud of dusty hugs and pats on the back. Then John led me over to a man I didn't know who thanked me and shook my hand even though I was filthy. He wore an expensive watch. He also wore a pair of polished Berluti shoes that cost about a month of my salary. I smiled. He was someone important, but I was coming down from the adrenaline, and everything was starting to feel too real. It made me less chatty.

John said, "You did good, Ringo. I'll see you again soon."

Then Mr. Watch & Shoes led me down an empty corridor and through a progressively smaller series of rooms until I was in a nice marble bathroom with a big shower, comfortable chair, and real towels. He asked me if I was going to be OK. I told him I'd be fine. I meant it, and he left.

But I didn't think I'd go on tour with the band ever again.

I turned on the shower, hung my uniform, and set the rest on the chair. It took a while to strip off my tattered civilian clothes. My hands wouldn't stop shaking, and it was like the rags were Velcroed to me. But, with a little effort, they made it into a plastic-lined trashcan next to the sink.

My sinuses were so screwed up I had no sense of smell. I knew I still stank like a camel's ass, but it didn't even register. At least we'd gotten through five of our eight mission verbs: *meet, change, go, do, restore*. We'd finished the job, but I was keen on getting to the *return, change,* and particularly *forget* parts. I could see where my uniform was hanging in the mirror. It was in a dry-cleaning bag. I hadn't seen one of those since I left home.

My mottled sand, olive, and brown camouflage-patterned uniform looked like a bag full of dry Halloween cornstalks inside the dry-cleaner bag. Before I left for Iraq, Jo and I had driven to Hondo, Texas, to take our four-year-old son Xander through the huge cornfield maze they have there every year. The sun was warm, but not Texas hot. It wasn't anything a four-dollar lemonade or iced tea couldn't take the edge off. I thought it would be hokey, but Xander and Jo wanted to go.

It turned out to be hokey and fun.

I remembered holding Jo's hand as we watched Xander play with scores of kids running and sliding in huge bins of dried corn. He fired air guns that shot corn ears thirty feet away and knocked down metal targets of cartoon farmers and animals to win prizes. I remembered how she laughed and squeezed my hand and how beautiful she looked in that white cotton summer dress covered in little flowers. I could almost feel how her hand felt in mine, and I missed them.

Those were the things I pondered as I stared at the laser-straight creases starched down the arms of my desert camouflage uniform. I don't know how long I stood there. The mirror fogged over. I didn't think about where I'd been or what just happened at all.

I thought that I hadn't worn shoes in a long time or used soft towels, just boots and the towels that came back stiff from the base laundry. Towels barely large enough to do the job, but thin enough to fit in a travel bag without taking up too much space.

The water was still hot when I finally got into the shower. My hair was stiff like it was caked in plaster. The first thing I did was check that everything important was still there: head, heart, penis, both testicles, ten fingers, ten toes. There were no new holes, so I was fine. I could even just make out the sound of water running.

The dirt ground into my skin turned dark when the water hit it, and with a little scrubbing, it slowly washed away. I was covered in a thin layer of caked-on blood. That surprised me. I had a few big nicks, but nothing major. I expected to see blood here and there, but not everywhere. After a minute, the blood gave way. The stains in my skin got smaller and smaller until only little marks remained, everywhere I could see. The soap stung, but there was almost no more bleeding.

I looked closely at my arm, and it was covered with tiny block-letter L's and I's and bigger cursive J's all about a fingernail width apart. They were the initials of stone fragments. They were carved into me, everywhere.

I was stiff and sore, but otherwise, I felt fine. The hot water never ran cold. No one pounded on the door for me to finish. The towels felt like they were the softest I'd ever used in my life. They were burgundy. It seemed like a funny towel color for an airman playing soldier in Baghdad.

My sense of smell was returning, but all I could smell was some kind of dust. It had a distinctive, familiar smell, but it took me a while to place. I laughed when I finally figured it out. It was a smell from a long time ago. It was the same smell and taste as the burnt dirt in that schoolyard the day my father made me go back after losing a fight, to return and fight again.

It was bitter, like washing down chewed aspirin with black coffee, but it didn't hurt anymore.

Except for the fact that my face looked like I'd had a seizure in the middle of shaving, I looked OK. Nothing out of the ordinary, nothing to worry about. Nothing to see here.

My feet were swollen, and my legs and back were bruised, but once I laced up my boots, I could move around OK. The Saint Christopher medal Lu had left for me already had deep scratches. I smiled when I saw them. When we were training, Lu used to say, "A scar you learn to never get again is a conversation starter." I learned that day I wanted to live a quiet life. There would be no more scratches on my Saint Christopher medal.

I almost didn't keep the promise I'd made to Jo at the airport when I left for Iraq. The marks carved all over my body spoke to me. They said I still had a lot to learn.

I had left San Antonio what seemed like forever ago. My wife, Jo, was an air force officer with significant responsibilities of her own, a boy to raise, and a baby on the way. I was headed into a combat zone, and she was going to be left on her own again.

Airports are lousy places to say goodbye.

I stacked the four overstuffed green bags, the sum of my belongings for the next five or six months, along with my backpack and weapon case on the curb next to her blue minivan.

"I love you, Jo," I said.

"I love you," she replied. It was a brave farewell.

We kissed an amethyst kiss goodbye. Flowers didn't explode all around like fireworks the way they had when I was a kid, but she smelled like summer, and it was nice.

Afterward, I wanted to say a thousand things, but all I got out was, "I . . ." before she put her hand over my mouth.

"Don't worry about us. Just come home safe." Then she took her hand from my mouth.

"I will," I said.

"You better," she snapped like it was an order.

"I will," I said.

Then we kissed again.

She turned away quickly, slowly pulled herself into our minivan, com-posed herself for a moment, then drove away. She was gone, and I had a plane to catch.

Simple as that, but simple isn't always easy.

I was heading back home to her soon, and I still had a promise to keep.

Mr. Watch & Shoes met me outside the bathroom door with my weapons and helmet bag and escorted me out of the suite. "You did good, Ringo. Really good."

"What did you expect?" I said with a smile. "I'm the drummer in a kick-ass band." It came out more like a conversation with a dentist after he packs your mouth.

Mr. Watch & Shoes smiled and gave me a card. "If you ever need anything, just call."

CHAPTER 35

January 1978—Catskill Mountains, Upstate New York

We climbed back to our perch, and Dad got a fire going just before the next wave of the storm hit us and visibility went from worse to zero. Father finally called it, shouting over the wind. "Snow's getting bad. We head back. I'll get the gear."

"OK," I said. "Be there in a sec." I was stiff from the cold and waiting for targets. My adrenaline was gone, and I was ready to go. Hunting lessons were over. Soon, even the freezing cold would be a memory. It was hard. Parts were awful, and it was amazing.

I needed a moment to say goodbye.

I felt the weight of the M-1 again, adjusted my position one last time, and checked the different clock positions. I got mad again, then let it go and looked down the sights one last time. I was calm and, despite the monstrous storm bearing down on us, serene.

I took a deep breath as I looked down the barrel. The snow cleared for a moment, and I saw a rabbit stopped a hundred yards away, right where I was aiming. It was a perfect shot. An easy shot. Right along the path we would take to the cabin.

All I had to do was pull the trigger, and Father would be proud of me. I wanted that, and I knew I could hit that rabbit with certainty. It was the same conviction I'd felt when I figured out how to hit the tree. I knew I could finally do it, and it was a powerful feeling.

I knew exactly where the rabbit would be, and I had the skill to hit it. It was the point of convergence Father had described when we arrived. It seemed like weeks ago, but it was just days.

As the rabbit stood on that small rise, sniffing at scents, adjusting its ears, and listening for threats—I held its life in my hands.

I took a deep breath, adjusted my grip on the M-1, added tension between my cheek and arms to make sure the barrel wouldn't buck and ruin the shot. I relaxed my arm slightly, and the sight moved to rest comfortably centered at the bottom of the rabbit's chest.

My left index and middle fingers applied gentle tension to the big trigger.

The M-1 was an extension of my body.

I felt no fear. Only an electric confidence I never felt before.

I exhaled, and my finger moved.

I slid my M-1's safety—to safe.

It was my shot. The weapon was an extension of my will, and I chose life.

Just because I could do a thing didn't mean I always had to do that thing.

Animals, even humans, trace patterns on their terrain, and most follow the easiest path they can to survive. Most, not all. That's what Father said.

I was just beginning the pattern I would trace. My choices, my pattern.

I watched that rabbit for another moment, in perfectly lined-up sights, and tracked him when he turned to hop down a drift. He followed the path I thought he'd take, and he stopped where I expected he would. "Bye-bye, bunny," I said to myself. Then the wind resumed and drove the snowfall hard again, obscuring the rabbit, then the hills, and finally the stream from my view. It was as though white curtains had been drawn.

March 2004—Camp Victory, Baghdad

Sound carried, but so far, the explosions rattling the trailers and echoing across Camp Victory came from our EOD[21] teams destroying ordinance and IEDs captured on raids. It was the sound of progress. The day was bright and brisk with good visibility and nearly unlimited blue sky. When the wind shifted, there was just a whiff of burnt chemicals, cordite, and scorched metal in the air.

Camp Victory was in the final stage of building a radio room in the Al Faw Palace to better handle and control radio traffic for the task force. I was at the highest point on the roof with the engineer in charge, looking at antennas and going over the ops plan for all the new devices they'd installed. The weather was cool, and I was sitting in a sunbeam when the breeze picked up. It felt perfect.

The roof of the Al Faw Palace was a canyon of irregular shapes, covered areas, and small rooms that were like caves embedded in the metal and stone. It was the second-highest point on Camp Victory: The first was a manmade communications hill that was often the target of rocket attacks. From the top of either one, I could see Baghdad, the airport, and almost to the Euphrates River.

We were just wrapping up when there was a noise that was more of a vibration than a sound.

The engineer and I climbed over to the far side of the palace roof for a better look. By the time we got there, a thick, seething column of

---

21   Explosive ordinance disposal. EOD teams are the military experts who handle, defuse, and destroy explosives.

smoke had already formed over southern Baghdad. We watched it for a few minutes, and I tried to get the bearings of where it was. The signals engineer offered me a small pair of binoculars, and as I looked for points of reference, my heart sank.

It was the new Iraqi police station. Chief Mohammed and his guys.

I gave the binoculars back and made a beeline to the JOC.

Initial reporting was in. A car had smashed through the gate, crashed into the station, and detonated. There had been a firefight, and RPGs had been launched from the compound walls into the station.

The last update described small-arms fire in the area, and the army and CPA were both responding. The compound and vehicles burned for a long time before the fires were contained.

After the area was secured, Del took a group out to look for survivors. Jack was already there with an army infantry detail and a handful of rescue workers. I stopped in my tracks two steps out of my Humvee. I could smell iron over the smoke, and everywhere I looked was charred, pitted, and splattered with blood. It was terrible. If I hadn't known where I was, I wouldn't have recognized it. It was a massacre.

I found my friend Jack between a fire truck and an ambulance, getting an update from the first responders. He had a hard look on his soot-stained face.

"How you holding up, Jack?"

"About how you think."

"Any word on survivors?"

"It'll take days to work that out, but this was an assassination and a message to the CPA. Chief Sawan was the target. We have confirmed reports he's dead."

"He was a good man," I said, taking it all in. "It's a sad day for Iraq."

"He was the best. They were a good crew," Jack said. "Del's going to take this hard. Let's see if there's anyone or anything else to find."

"You got it."

We searched until nearly sunset. We found a few more survivors: some were Iraqi police; others were civilians there to report crimes; one was a prisoner. All of them were shredded and burned. They were evacuated to a nearby hospital, but it was a long shot that any of them would make it. The last witness who'd seen Chief Mohammed Sawan was the prisoner. He said the chief had released him and pushed him out a window after the bomb went off, but then the rockets came and reduced the rest of the station to rubble.

We looked until there was nowhere left to look, and we turned over every stone we could lift.

Rubble was still burning when we drove out.

Their station had been taking Iraq back. Chief Mohammed and his crew had been doing what he promised he'd do. The area was stabilizing again, and people were finally starting to breathe easier. I could see it on their faces. In Baghdad, it had been a long time since people smiled when they saw a police patrol.

Del reported to the MP building and filed a report before she asked her commander for twenty-four hours off. It was the first, and only, day she ever took off the whole year she was in Iraq.

Jack and I walked with her to her room. She was composed until the moment the door closed. I'd never heard Del complain or express discomfort once. I never even heard her say an unkind or negative thing. But when the door clicked shut, she wailed and sobbed.

It was heartbreaking and contagious.

Jack went to comfort her. I wiped my eyes, said goodbye, and turned to leave. But she reached out and grabbed me from behind and held on to me.

"Why does it always have to be the good ones?" Del asked.

"Because they *are* the good guys," I said. "They make a difference, but doing the right thing is hard, and there are always consequences."

CHAPTER 36

Insurgents assaulted the CPA checkpoint. There were at least eight of them. They grabbed random women crossing the street and used them as human shields. They shot from behind the women as they pushed into the checkpoint. People fled past me. I got there as the quick-reaction force surged in with armor, closed on the insurgents, and blocked the road. People screamed and cried. Soldiers enforcing the cordon pushed us behind a wall for cover until they got the all clear. There was a firefight. The insurgents killed the guards and fired RPGs into the adjacent building.

The building burned, the insurgents disappeared into the smoke, and five of the women were left dead—executed in the middle of the road. There was another firefight; men cried out as they were hit and knocked down. They bled as they crawled to cover. Blood pooled around the dead women in the street, but the terrorists were gone. They made it to an alleyway two streets down and bled to death. The three-story building they'd attacked burned out of control. Sirens wailed. Burning clothes and debris littered the previously well-maintained street.

Ambulances and fire trucks came through after the explosions, and half an hour later, we were queued up and directed to a new checkpoint if we absolutely had to get to the CPA.

It was the second time in my life I had to step around puddles of blood in a street while people screamed and cried in a language I didn't understand. The scene was horrific. The guy behind me fell to his knees in the middle of the road and threw up, repeating, "Oh my God."

I pulled him up and dragged him out of the middle of the carnage.

The bodies of the dead were carried into the shade of an alleyway and lined up. Iraqi women on one side, CPA guards on the other. No one could get close to the bombed building yet because of the flames and the firemen trying to put them out. Inside the checkpoint, I set the guy down in the shade and asked the guards for a couple of bottles of water so he could wash himself up. It looked like it was just the two of us crossing the street for a little while, and the guards opened a cooler and tossed the bottles over.

"What's your name?" I asked as I cracked open the first bottle of water and handed it to him.

"Aaron. It's horrible. They're all dead."

"Aaron, you're going to be OK. Rinse out your mouth, and run some water over your head. You'll feel better."

He had emptied everything in his belly, but he was still heaving.

"Th . . . thanks," he said and gave it a shot.

"You're in shock, Aaron. Take a deep breath, hold it, then let it out slow. Do that a few times, and you should be able to keep down some water. Hold a breath, and breathe out slow. Keep down some water, and your head will clear. When your head clears, you'll be able to move again. You understand? Nod your head, and let me hear you say it."

"OK," he said, nodding his head in the affirmative. "I got it. Thanks."

The guards who responded first were chain smoking and talking about pulling cowering bystanders from the street and getting some of them to the hospital. I talked to the guards for a few minutes until Aaron got his legs back under him. They were talking fast and still coming down from the engagement. One of them had blood streaks running down his body armor. When I asked him how he was holding up, he told me the blood wasn't his, but he showed me where a round had hit him in the chest. There was an elongated mark on the ballistic nylon and Kevlar outer shell of his body armor. He showed us how the round had cracked his SAPI—ceramic armor plate—but he was fine. "Hurt like a bitch, though," he said. Still chain smoking, but fine. They looked so young. I didn't know what else to say, so I gave them the cigars I had on me.

"Thanks, sir," the NCO with the broken armor said. "Three weeks to go, and I'm out of this godforsaken place."

"Where you heading?"

"Back home to Alabama."

Aaron groaned as he hauled himself to his feet.

That was my cue. "Take care, soldiers, have a safe trip to Alabama. Keep your heads down."

There was a chorus of, "Hooah," and I crossed into the CPA compound.

I would have left after the attack and gone back to Camp Victory if I didn't need to be somewhere in the CPA. I walked past trailers and through a dusty orange grove as security and medical teams ran back and forth. The CPA would be gone in about ninety days, when government control transferred back to the Iraqis. The atmosphere was already tense, and recent attacks had driven security to lockdown mode. The pool area was empty. I could see people peeking out of bunkers, waiting for the compound to sound the all-clear signal. Then the silence was broken again by the tearing sound of rockets launching and explosions reverberating from all over the other side of the Green Zone. It took a while, but I finally got into the palace.

I'd spent my morning driving through some of the more "transitional" neighborhoods in Baghdad, getting shot at so I could get Iraqi ministers to sign copies of what needed to become the basis of a treaty, because the CPA copies they were waiting for somehow never arrived.

One Iraqi businessman I used to see frequently after losing a big contract told me the walls around the CPA were nothing more than the teeth of a hungry dog sinking its fangs deep into the throat of Iraq. He'd sung a different song a few weeks earlier, praising American capitalism, because he was making money hand over fist. He would have kept his contract—and cash flow—if he had provided even some of the services he was paid to deliver. I had a lot of reasons, especially that morning, not to like the CPA, but the truth was if an Iraqi or US contractor just tried his best and delivered something the CPA needed, it was hard not to make a million dollars. They were pouring millions of dollars a day, sometimes an hour, back into the local economy, and there was still a ridiculous amount of work left to do. Anyone who could do anything, and do it reliably, got paid handsomely. And with the clock ticking down, the CPA was having a fire sale.

I made it to an office suite with an ornately carved and painted ceiling and searched for the executive I needed. It pissed me off that I was becoming a CPA apologist. They had a tough job, and they were expected to do the impossible in a short timeline. After all, we needed decades to stabilize Germany and Japan after WWII, and they were relatively homogenous societies characterized by ridiculously strong nationalism and work ethics. Iraq's culture, by comparison, was like a shattered ruby we were trying to reassemble to its original beauty while denying that Saddam had already plundered the best stones. It was a welfare state that required real fear and control to make work, but the CPA kept dismantling the controls that were already in place because they were distasteful. After WWII, to rebuild the world, we had to keep certain Nazi and Japanese imperialists in place because they understood how things worked and because they had the clout we needed to be successful. We focused on rebuilding those nations and prosecuting the true villains of the war because life is full of shitty compromises. Sometimes we have no choice but to deal with devils so good people don't have to, so we can protect who and what we love.

I'd heard someone say the CPA "couldn't provide air." I felt like that at times, but it wasn't quite right. The CPA reestablished infrastructure that was neglected because Saddam had shifted resources from the economy to the military since the 1980s. After two decades of bombardment and neglect, most of Iraq's infrastructure barely worked outside of Baghdad or the major military- and secret-police-controlled areas. Now, water distribution had been restored. Electricity and sanitation improved. Schools were reopened, and telephone, rail service, roads, and other lines of communication reached new people every day.

Don't get me wrong; they fucked up a lot. But give the devil his due.

I finally found the man I was looking for at the end of a long trail of empty gin bottles. He was passed out at his desk, and even from a distance, he stank like old booze and sweat.

"Hello, sir," I said. "How are you doing?"

I got no response, but I didn't really expect one. I dug through his inbox; buried in the bottom were my papers. He hadn't even looked at them, so I retrieved them and shuffled them behind the Iraqi ministers' signed papers in the folder in my bag.

I sighed. I had even splurged on nice paper, with a high cotton content and watermark, because we'd worked so hard with the army, coalition forces, and the Iraqis to write this transition of authorities plan. It was going to be international policy. His jacket hung from a stand across from his desk between two large, sandbagged windows. It was Brooks Brothers, and it smelled better than he did, so I took it and folded it into a rectangle that

I set in the chair next to his desk. I always liked Brooks Brothers suits, but they always seemed to be cut a bit too slim for my frame.

He had a beautiful Parker pen on his desk next to the stack of papers he was supposed to sign. I took it, unscrewed the top, and set the pen and top back down. I paused a moment to look around. Then I slid all the remaining papers on his desk out of the way.

I thought a lot of bad thoughts. I was in one of the most secure locations in Iraq, in a room with a government executive who directed a large staff, and he was drunk off his ass while his staff was still cowering in a bunker. He was probably the civilian equivalent of a colonel or one-star general, and it disgusted me. He was trying to find his courage in the bottom of a bottle.

Bad place to look.

It was so quiet I could hear the fans shuffling air around the room. The postattack "all clear" sounded in the distance. I figured I had about five minutes before his staff shuffled back.

Sometimes, you just have to do things you'd rather not.

I wrapped my hand around the executive's tie, dragged him back into his chair like a hangman maneuvering a body by a noose, and dumped the entire contents of the water bottle I'd been carrying over his head and lap. He was so wasted I was even able to toss the empty bottle into his trashcan before I got a response. It was a shame. He'd been a good man once.

He woke with a start, no idea where he was as he flailed around. Unfortunately, the water didn't wash away the stench, and wet garbage smells worse than dry garbage.

"What the fuck? Riley, is that you? I'm going to have your ass for whatever it is you think you're doing," he slurred. So, I let go of his tie, and his face slammed down into his desk.

"Yeah, that's not going to happen," I said.

"Fuck . . . Do you have any idea who I am?" he groaned as he started to pass out again.

I pulled him up by his collar and slapped his face, hard. A couple of times. He looked at me again with livid anger, but he just hung there like a wet doll.

"I know who you used to be, sir. Hopefully, you'll be that guy again, but for now, I need you to sign some documents."

"Fuck you," came out clear, but the rest fell apart. "I'll. Your ass. Mine."

I could never figure out why, whether it was the army or CPA, they always wanted my ass.

"I'll save you the time, sir. Let's go to Ambassador Bremer's office now. Walk him through how you've been drunk off your ass at work for the last three weeks and why nothing's got done in the meantime. I'll need to get a cart for you, but I don't mind pushing. It's not like he's busy or has Congress crawling up his ass to show results, right?"

"What do you want?" he asked as he partially pushed himself up to almost a sitting position.

"Here," I said, drying his head with his jacket. "I need six signatures from you, and then I'm going to drag you to your quarters. After you sleep it off, you're going to get some professional help, because everyone here needs you, and right now you can't even stand on your own. What I *want* is for you to do your fucking job. You're a smart, accomplished man. Be smart. Be that guy again. These people need you, and right now, all you do is reek."

"Asshole," he mumbled.

"Yeah, that makes two of us. I'll steady your hand. Now sign here and here and . . ."

After that, I had my signatures, and one of our leaders was back in his quarters because he was feeling a bit unwell. I let his secretary know. Then

I went in search of Jack. He was the only person I trusted at the CPA to get the documents to all the right places before time ran out.

I found Jack in a conference room with the team of Iraqis who would form their version of the FCC,[22] a team from electric production, and a small group from the oil ministry. It was a joint meeting about infrastructure problems, and everyone was unhappy and looking for someone else to blame. I nodded to Jack, then slipped into an open seat in the back of the room. It was a CPA meeting, so there was no tea. I wished I had thought to grab a third bottle of water.

The gist of the meeting was that after a year of rebuilding, Iraqis still didn't feel safe or secure, and they had a lot of good reasons. It was a cold March, but the Iraqis felt the power situation was tolerable. Electricity came on for three hours, then off for three hours, during the daylight and would stay mostly on from midnight to six in the morning. The situation was better than before the war, even though the Americans at the table found it unacceptable. While electricity, even with outages, was comfortably predictable as we rolled into spring, no one thought it would be adequate once the summer heat came. In summer, the sun can bake Baghdad to 120 degrees in the shade. Touch any exposed metal on the brightest, hottest days, and your hand comes away blistered. Attempts to cool homes and buildings would be frustrated by clever people stealing electricity, and the already overburdened, fragile system would fail. Air conditioners would stop cooling, fans would stop turning, food would spoil, and people would die. That was the ninety-day forecast.

Creating infrastructure wasn't the big problem. There were legitimate challenges, but we were good at building and fielding things that worked.

---

22   Federal Communications Commission (FCC). They became part of the Iraqi Ministry of Communications (MoC) to govern Iraq's communications across the country and to operate within the international community.

The problem was securing the infrastructure once it was in. Wholesale theft of infrastructure in the sparsely populated areas of Iraq was common. Bandit groups almost the size of small private armies roved the vast, empty spaces between the cities of Iraq. They tapped into pipelines, filled tanker trucks with stolen oil and gas, and raced to the friendly havens to fuel the black market that existed at every border to buy and sell plunder.

Raping Iraqi infrastructure was a thriving business. It looked like scenes from a road warrior movie, but the business hadn't changed much since Ali Baba and his forty thieves. However, the recent policy decision to disband Iraqi security forces had virtually ensured there was no one around to slow the bandits down. Contractors were put in place to guard critical points in Iraq's infrastructure, but the contractors were expensive and outgunned.

By the time the CPA figured out what went wrong, the criminals were long gone. Regional communications and power disruptions across Iraq were due largely to neglected, failing infrastructure and cable wire theft.

Metal harvesters became so adept they could knock down towers for miles, cut and pull the cable, strip the casings, and even have time to smelt their reapings into copper, steel, and aluminum ingots in just a day or two. It left the bad guys plenty of time to move out, avoid most authorities, and pass through the porous border surrounding Iraq. Stripped line casings littered the desert like the black shed skins of giant snakes. No one asked questions, and everyone made money.

It was easy to blame the dark and disconnected calls on America.

No one looked happy at the end of the meeting. After the attendees filed out, Jack waved me over, and I sat with him and the Iraqi communications engineers and frequency managers. After an exchange of greetings, I slid the folder across the table to Jack and explained what I needed.

He chuckled when he saw the papers. "How'd you get him to sign them?"

"I simply appealed to his better nature."

"You always say that. What happens when they don't have a better nature?"

"I appeal hard," I said, smiling. "By the way, I kept signed copies for the task force. We'll continue to operate as we have until the status of forces agreement is ratified and published."

"Fine by me. If you're happy with it and the Iraqis are happy, I'm good. I'll get these to the right people. It's all in the lawyer's hands now, anyway. God help us all."

"If we're done here, buy me food. I'm hungry."

"Aren't you the one who owes me?"

"Yes. Thanks. I really mean it. We couldn't have made this work without you walking those through. I brought you a couple of Cuban cigars, Montecristo No. 2s, to celebrate the signing, but things were awful outside earlier, and I gave them to some soldiers in the thick of it."

"I do know a joint with a discrete back room that makes the best grilled chicken in Iraq."

"You fly, I'll buy."

"We can actually walk there, but you can still buy."

"Done." I looked around the table. "Come to lunch. This might be the last time we're all together before I head out. Come on. Best grilled chicken in Iraq, on me."

Jack dropped off the treaty papers. It was a twenty-minute walk.

Smoke columns were still billowing up at the edges of the Green Zone, and armored vehicles and tanks usually kept in reserve were dug in at each checkpoint. A military tow truck was still dragging the carcasses of blown-up cars away, and the streets were otherwise empty.

Our destination was deep in an alley, a couple of streets back from the main vehicle entrance to the compound. I could smell the smoked meat a block away, and my stomach growled. White resin café tables and chairs lined the left side of the alley. There was a large, hand-painted menu sign and a door to the right. We weren't five steps into the brick-and-wood building built into the alley when the huge, round Iraqi man sharpening a cleaver behind the counter set it down, smiled, and rushed over, wiping his hands on his apron.

"Mr. Jack, I'm glad to see you're all right. The attacks were bad today," he said, hugging him. He was wearing a red-and-white-striped rugby shirt and sweatpants under his apron, and his hair and beard were black.

"I'm happy to see you, too, Za'id. You can let me go now, big guy."

"And here I thought you were still with Del?"

"Screw you. Za'id's awesome," Jack said, then he introduced us one by one.

We sat on the chairs and sofas in the back room, and two boys brought us water and tea with mint and sugar. I ordered grilled chicken meals, sides, and desserts for everyone, plus a couple of dishes of the lamb special of the day to share.

While we waited for lunch, Za'id set out trays of assorted dried fruits and pickled vegetables. They were the best pickles I'd had since I left Turkey.

There were eight of us. Six Iraqi engineers, Jack, and me. The engineers were all female, in their twenties with dark hair. They dressed conservatively, but their shirts and scarves usually had a splash of color. They were communications experts, and the speed at which they learned impressed me. It was different than my experience in Saudi Arabia, where women existed behind walls, or in Kuwait, where there was a protective formality that had to be observed in public. The professional women in Iraq were, for lack of a better word, more Western. They were led by Mrs. Marjani Nassar, who seemed to have reached the point where she trusted me even though she still didn't like me. If one of her engineers smiled or laughed at one of my jokes, she still scowled them into submission, but they took it in stride. They acted how little sisters act when their big sister brings a boy home for dinner for the first time: they were curious, initially timid, sarcastic, and then cute and a little annoying.

Mrs. Marjani Nassar was smart and brutally honest. I didn't always like it, but I appreciated it, and I respected that she could get difficult things done. When she talked about the mood in Baghdad, it was more accurate than most of the intelligence reports I read. I returned the favor by trying to address any local problems she brought me and by being truthful with her. When she took the tone of voice that I was responsible for all the coalition's failings, a tone she knew I hated, my response was to call her "Marj," which I knew she hated. It was how we both knew we'd reached ground truth in our many discussions. It made observers both uncomfortable and amused. In another place, we might have been described as an old married couple.

"How's Sami doing?" I asked. "I've only seen him a few times since the new techs were hired. Urban services are better than they've ever been, but he seems to still have a lot on his shoulders."

"Mr. Bishara is doing well. I will let him know you asked after him. He is slated to hold a high position in the Ministry of Communications after the CPA is gone."

"I'm glad to hear that. Sami's a man who gets things done. I respect him."

She grimaced and nodded her head. "Security hasn't improved, though. If anything, your people continue to make things worse."

"Mrs. Nassar, Bill isn't—"

"It's OK, Jack. Marj is upset. Let her get it off her chest."

One of her engineers started to chuckle, but Mrs. Marjani Nassar squelched it with a look. "Idiomatic expressions certainly do reflect a culture's character," she said, then paused before she continued. "Aeni's son was kidnapped last week just after school let out. Neither your coalition nor the local police were able to do a thing about it. No one would even investigate."

I set my glass down, and Naylaa, the youngest engineer, refilled my tea.

"*Khr'iye*, sister," Aeni said in an upset voice.

"I am very sorry to hear that," I said to Aeni. "Can you tell me what happened?"

"*Na'qib*, this is uncomfortable, but it is as Mrs. Nassar says. My boy was hostage. It was terrible. They ask for $200,000, but no one help. Authorities say just pay, but no one has that much. After many threats, they return my boy for $1,500 US. He was scared but not hurt, thank God."

She was on the verge of tears. "You were very brave, Aeni. I'm very happy to hear your son is safe and home again."

It was hard to see her like that. It was a sad but common story. Kidnapping and hostage taking are frequent elements of negotiation or extortion in the Middle East. The coalition doesn't get involved, and the police are still mostly ineffective. They have little real authority, and currently there aren't many laws they can enforce. Most laws on the books still pertain to crimes against Saddam, and retooling the country's legal structure has been difficult and slow.

Za'id and the boys began setting out plates of food, and we settled in to eat.

The room filled with the scent of sweet smoke, coriander, cumin, peppers, cardamom, ginger, garlic, and rose. My stomach growled again, and after a bilingual, "Thanks for the food," everyone dug in. Jack was right: it was the best grilled chicken in Iraq. There was a happy silence as plates were passed and bread was torn and shared. The chicken glistened with perfectly rendered fat, and the meat fell off the bone in bites of crunchy, juicy goodness. Spices I didn't recognize kissed my tongue in a way that was almost erotic.

The Iraqi engineers used the flatbread like napkins to wipe the juices from their fingers and mouths before they ate it. I thought that was brilliant and followed suit. When I finally pushed myself back from the table, there was still a lot of food left.

When conversation resumed, we joked and laughed. Naylaa wanted to hear stories about where I grew up. She was fascinated that I lived by an ocean she'd only seen in pictures. Somewhere between stories, Za'id brought coffee and sweets, and his boys packed up all the leftovers to go.

Naylaa had grown up near Nasiriya and told us stories of playing as a little girl in the ruins just outside of the great ziggurat pyramid of the ancient Sumerian city of Ur.

"They built the pyramid in steps," she said, "so that the priestesses of Nanna, the god of the moon, could climb into the sky and tend to their god when his crescent appeared in the sky. In the desert there, the stars were big and bright. My mother always used to say the stars were the children of the moon and sun watching over us."

Lunch took more than two hours, but there was a lot that needed to be said, and I still had more than an hour left before I had to meet my convoy back to Camp Victory. Marj and Naylaa were sitting next to each other on the sofa across from us drinking coffee. The others had gone to arrange for the car to take them home. I suspected they were all gone because Marj still had something she wanted to talk about. Marj fiddles with her hair while she talks when she's nervous, but once she realizes it, she stops. Her hair was long, almost black, and wavy. She usually kept it subdued under a scarf, but she was busy drinking coffee, glaring at me, and twirling it around her finger.

She finally put the coffee and her hair down and asked me, "When I leave here, am I a target? Are we targets even with you?" She had dark, piercing eyes.

I had to think that through. My first thought was, "No, absolutely not, you're the good guys," but when she left, she'd be watched by security. And when she left the building, soldiers in unseen positions would track her in case she acted suspicious or tried to enter a restricted area. The bad Iraqis had new tactics. Once they suspected that she worked for the government, she was at risk. Terrorists killed public servants wherever it was convenient. Her neighbors would watch her movements; the jealous ones would threaten her and her family. The opportunistic ones would turn her in for cash or to protect their families. That was her world. That was the reality of all the Iraqis I worked with.

I looked into her dark eyes and told her the truth.

"I'm sorry. You are a target, probably more than I am."

She wasn't surprised. Even though it was more of a rhetorical question.

"I expected you to lie so we would continue to cooperate."

"I'm glad, after all this time, I can still surprise you. I respect you and your team. I think it's better I tell you a hard truth than an easy lie. You can protect yourself if you know the truth."

"Do you finally understand now?" she said, topping off my coffee. "This is what the occupation is for us. No one is safe, and if you stand out or try to make a difference, it's worse."

"My hope, Mrs. Marjani Nassar, is that Iraq will find her own way, and there will be peace and prosperity again."

"You are a strange man, *Na'qib* Bill Riley."

"Why do you say that?"

"Because you appear to really believe that it's true."

"I do."

"Then I will have faith, but I do not believe it will happen soon. Thank you for the excellent meal. I hope the future you talk about has many more like it."

When the rest of the engineers returned, we stood and said goodbye. They came up to me one by one, shook my hand, and offered me a safe trip back in Arabic. It was a rare thing, and I considered it an honor. Iraqi women do not normally shake hands with men. I thanked them and, with my hand over my heart, wished them well.

Jack and I walked Marj's engineers out to the MoC van waiting at the entrance of the alley to take them home. We waved as they drove off, and I hoped they'd be OK.

Traffic was flowing again as we walked back to the Republican Guard Palace. It was sparse, but people were on the sidewalks, and there were only a few columns of smoke still burning on the perimeter. It was late afternoon in March, and it was chilly.

"So, I'm leaving in a week," I said to Jack. "What's your exit strategy?"

"Transition the CPA, stay on to train the new guys at the new embassy for six months. After that, a month of debriefing and reeducation at Foggy Bottom, then a senior posting in Barbados."

"Barbados. That's awesome. You might actually get tan. Can Vikings tan?"

"Del is leaving the army after this tour is over, and we started making plans."

"She's a better woman than you deserve."

"Yeah. Ain't that the way it ought to be, though?"

"Congratulations, Jack. I'm really happy for you guys. I wish you all the best, my friend."

"Hey. You be careful," Jack said sternly.

"I'm always careful."

"Well, that's bullshit."

"I only have one mission left, and then I'm done."

"Be extra careful, then," Jack said. "The worst accidents always happen closest to home."

We talked until we were stopped in front of my convoy.

"Looks like your ride's here," Jack said. Then we shook hands, and the big goof actually got a little teary eyed. "When you get settled into your new job at Langley, come visit us in Barbados."

"I will, if I get invited to the wedding."

"We'll be living in sin, but even if we don't have a spare room, I can probably pull some strings."

"Deal," I said, shaking his hand.

At least nine soldiers in three vehicles were put at risk every time I needed to move between the CPA and Camp Victory in an army convoy to do my job. It wasn't something I took lightly. I had to make sure that each of those trips was worthwhile and made a difference.

They were good troops. I got in the lead Humvee, and a young NCO said, "Sir, everything's ready."

I waved to Jack one last time, then said, "Take us home."

"Hooah!"

Traffic still moved slowly after the morning attacks, and there were detours. I don't remember the snap of weapons charging or the engines starting up. I remember putting my seat belt on, flipping the safety off my Beretta, setting it in my lap, and placing my old M-14 down between me and the driver. I wanted to sleep, but I had too much on my mind, so I watched the scenery change through the cutout where the door used to go.

That day, "CPA" meant "can't protect anyone." My biggest accomplishment was slapping around a drunk so I could get the Iraqi version of a bill made into a law. It wasn't something that watching *Schoolhouse Rock!* as a kid prepared me for. Infrastructure was still being stolen. I could be happy if I were sure we were still taking two steps forward for every step back, but children were still getting snatched and held for ransom on top of that. Then there was the huge attack in the morning where women, a lot like my colleague communications engineers, were grabbed, used as shields, and then executed.

I sighed and hung my head. I was lost in my thoughts for a moment. Then I noticed them. There were blood splatters on the sides of my beige-suede desert combat boots, and the blood was turning black. I had fewer than ten days left in Iraq and more than a hundred days' worth of work left to do. I missed Jo and Xander, and I had a new son on the way who still needed a name.

Looking at someone else's blood on my boots didn't make me sick or sad—it made me angry. It was such a waste. Women going to work were killed so terrorists could slaughter the guards at a CPA checkpoint and then blow up what turned out to be a laundry.

It was a tragic waste of life. I had one mission left, and I could go home.

CHAPTER 37

March 2004—Taji, Iraq

My last mission required a translator, and Rocky was my draw. We were at Taji, eighteen miles northwest of Baghdad. Taji had been bombed during Operation Desert Fox because it was a hub for chemical weapons, and there were still scars and damaged infrastructure from those attacks. It was another connection between what I did in Kuwait and what I found in Iraq.

Taji was slated to be an important base for what would become the Iraqi National Guard, but there were logistical and communications problems that still needed to be worked out. When Rocky started to ad lib his translations, I only needed to ask one question to keep him honest.

"Do you really want to find your own way home, from all the way out here?"

"Let me ask him to repeat what he said again, sir. And we'll see if we can figure it out."

"Thank you, Rocky. Please do."

When the translations made sense again, we were able to finish. At that point, the Iraqis didn't have a reliable way to protect and share classified information, so it limited some of what we could do, but we were able to get their radio command and control network up and running again.

We sat with our backs against a thick concrete Texas barrier wall that blocked the rotor wash, and our pilot stuck his head around the corner to tell us our Blackhawk would be done loading and refueling shortly. We could head back to Camp Victory in twenty minutes.

I thanked him, and Rocky pulled out an Arabic newspaper.

"Is that today's news?"

"Yes, I picked it up before we left."

"Anything interesting?"

"The police chief we met with who was assassinated has been officially declared dead even though the Ministry of Interior was unable to recover his body."

"Chief Mohammed Sawan was a good man, Rocky. Several groups claimed responsibility for killing him, but no one really knows yet."

"His death is a loss for all of Iraq," said Rocky. "They also say the final death toll is twenty-six, including the police chief."

We sat in silence until we boarded the Blackhawk and flew back to Camp Victory.

What was the point of doing good things if they didn't make a difference? What was the point of making good things if they were so easily swept away? Twenty-six good cops were dead. We still didn't know how many civilians had gotten caught in the crossfire. They'd died so a few criminals could prosper, so a group of terrorists could make a point.

I came to Iraq to improve our force's ability to communicate and access information and intelligence. I was confident I'd done that. But I was also tasked to help rebuild Iraqi lines of communications so they could better protect and govern themselves. I knew that I was just a small, squeaky cog in the great machine. Iraq was broken, and we were helping put it back together. We were just there for structure, and maybe to make sure no one disturbed Iraq until the glue was set. Maybe I'd been arrogant when I arrived. I really believed that even one person could make a difference, but it was hard to watch so many people who had made a difference disappear and die.

I was losing faith, and I was tired. I had two days left in country. My last missions were over. My replacement was in, and my handoff was complete. I had a wife and son and a boy on the way.

I loved them. I was done. Getting home to my life was my last objective left.

It was a short flight to Camp Victory. The door slid open. I hung up my headset, shook hands with Rocky, and stepped out with my bag. I walked to the edge of the helipad, the rotor wash increased, and the Blackhawk flew away. I could have called for a lift, but the weather was nice. I had a lot on my mind, and I needed to walk.

I wound up in a familiar place I'd only been to once before. Last time I'd been there, it had been the massive ruin of a fountain, still half-full of brackish water, where my face was harshly reflected in its oily bottom under the blue-green light of an ornate lamp that could have come from Paris.

It had only been five months, but it seemed longer.

When I'd stood there before, I'd felt like I was looking into a mirror and a corpse was looking back. Now, it looked like someone had driven a tank through the middle of the fountain. The white marble basin with blue veins was pulverized at the front and back. The statues that had been pulled down were broken and crushed. The only recognizable remains were the dismembered stone hands, feet, and heads that protruded from the weeds.

I wondered: What would I have seen in the water if it were still there?

The lamp that had been there was gone, but across from the fountain husk was a set of carved, high-back stone benches. Next to one of them, the long, slender arm of a female statue eerily reached three feet out from the ground. I opened my bag, took out a cigar, and smoked until moonrise.

The night was quiet, the moon was full, and palm trees rustled at the edge of the field. I stretched back against the warm stone, enjoyed the cool breeze, and felt the nicotine start to unwind my knots. The statue's open palm was the perfect height for an ashtray.

The path back was lined with trees. On one side were date palms; on the other, elm-like trees with long, yellow-gray seed pods. The wind tugged at them, and the seedpods shook and tapped. They made a distinctive sound, like maracas. I called them clickety trees.

I reached the maze of tall concrete barriers that marked the more civilized parts of camp, rounded the last corner to my tent, popped through an opening in one of the walls, and stepped right into a pack of wild dogs. They were as surprised as I was. I saw six dark shadows with reflective eyes and teeth in growling mouths. Five of them leapt back and flattened their ears. One of them walked right up to me. He was just the outline of a big dog in the dark. He put his muzzle against my chest and sniffed.

I reached out and patted his head. He stiffened but didn't move. It was foolish. I've seen dogs hunt in packs and maul people. I've even seen the size of the needle they give you for rabies, but I just reacted. I scratched his ears. He wagged his tail; I felt better afterward. It was a fair exchange. The wild dogs loped away to the top of a berm and began to howl.

I washed up, dropped my gear, and went to bed. I looked at the picture of my wife on the footlocker I was using as my nightstand and suddenly realized that the tent that had slept twelve of us when I got to Camp Victory was now empty except for me. My replacement, and everyone else I knew, had gotten a billet in one of the new trailers. They were insulated, near real showers and toilets, and only two people had to share a room. But I was used to living in a tent. I was already settled in, and I was too stubborn to move. There was something relaxing about how a tent flexed in a breeze, and the smell of sunbaked canvas was comforting after a long day.

I didn't have to set an alarm. I could sleep in. I had nowhere left to go but home.

I embraced the deepest, darkest sleep. Then I had a dream that Del was yelling at me.

"Good morning, sunshine," she said when I opened my eyes. Del was sitting in the chair across from my cot. I looked around. The lights were on, but it still looked dark outside. I checked, and I was wearing boxers and a faded orange sweatshirt from OTS. So, I sat up and stretched.

"What time is it, and why are you here?"

"So, you're grumpy in the morning."

I checked my watch. "Not that I mind a pretty girl waking me up at 0400, but when they come for me in the dead of night, usually there's gunfire, explosions, or an evacuation."

"Maybe I just missed your smiling face?"

"I'm pretty sure General Order No. 1 lets me shoot you right now."

"So, this is how the air force lives," Del said, looking around. "You get a whole tent to yourself, and I get two roommates."

"There are only three female officers in your MP brigade, and it's a huge room . . . Why am I even arguing? Is that coffee I smell?"

Del smiled and handed me a cup. "It's clean, at least. I like the Persian carpets and furniture. It looks like Napoleon's campaign tent."

"Everything stays. Take what you want. This isn't chow hall coffee. This is good."

"Today's a special day."

"Did Jack propose?"

"Nah. I'm pretty sure he told you we'd be living in sin."

"So, it's not that. You're in a great mood, and I know you're not here for my charms. What gives?"

Del grinned ear to ear. "Iraqi police chief Mohammed Sawan is alive and well."

I paused for a moment to process that. "No way. We know he was there. We saw what was left of the station."

"He called, and I sat with him at the hospital until just a little while ago. I figured you'd want to know."

"How's that possible? I flew over what was left of the police station yesterday. It looked like the cold, turned-out remains of a charcoal grill."

"You know when he let that prisoner out of the cell, right?"

"Yeah. Right after Mohammed got him out of the building, they pounded what was left of the station with RPGs."

"Mohammed says his leg was already hurt, and he couldn't follow the prisoner out. When he saw the line of RPGs pointing at him on the wall, he dove down the basement stairs and got the door open just before the explosions."

"What happened then?" I asked as I drank my coffee.

"He doesn't exactly know. He woke up in pain in the dark. He said the light on his watch was enough to show him his leg was in bad shape, and the corridor he came through was collapsed. He said he called out for help, but no one came. So, after he picked some shrapnel out of his leg, he looked around, but the only rooms he could access were the armory and the storage room under the old part of the building."

"He's one tough old bastard."

"I know, right? He says he would have died if he hadn't found a half pack of cigarettes and a book of matches."

"What happened next?"

"In the old supply room, he found water, a box of MREs, candles, rope, and a flashlight that worked."

"What about the armory?"

"Mohammed said he had all the firepower he could use, but machine guns and RPGs weren't of much use. He did say he took a pistol, a bayonet, and a shotgun to use as a cane."

"So how did he get out?"

"He said it was slow going. He explored every inch of the place, and there was no way out."

"But the story doesn't end there."

"No. He said after that, he passed out from the pain."

"You really suck at storytelling."

"Want me to stop?"

"No. I want to know how he got out."

"You know that station was a former military compound, but did you know that compound was built on top of an old Ottoman stronghold?"

"Cool, but why is that important?"

"The Ottomans had extensive experience with siege warfare," she said, watching me while she sipped her coffee.

"So, there was a well or an escape tunnel."

"Very good, air force."

"So that's how he got out?"

"Not exactly. He searched until he passed out again, but he didn't find any escape. When he woke up, he was convinced he was going to die there."

"But he didn't."

"No, but he was down to his last cigarette. So, he did what people do when they lose it: He screamed, yelled, cried, prayed, broke things.

Eventually, he found a comfortable spot in the storage room, propped his leg up, lit every candle, made sure his pistol was loaded, and enjoyed his last cigarette."

"So, he was going to check himself out?"

"He said as soon as he felt the heat from the ember on his lips, he was going to pull the trigger."

"But he didn't."

"No, he didn't. He was sitting back taking deep draws off the cigarette. When he exhaled, he watched the smoke dance around him . . . then it got sucked down into a crack in the floor."

"Down?"

"That's what he said. So, he followed the smoke to the tiles in the floor, and when he looked close, they had holes in them. When he pried the stones up, he found the mouth of the old well. He lowered the flashlight down with the rope and hit the bottom thirty feet down. The cavity was large. There was water at the bottom. It was shallow, but as he swung the flashlight around, it looked like the well wall opened up on one side, and he thought he saw a passage."

"That's hard to believe. Did he think he was hallucinating?"

"He wasn't sure. Looking at it, he had enough strength to make it down, but he didn't think he could make it back up. He still thought it was a one-way trip, but he said in his mind it beat doing nothing. So, he lowered himself down and found the opening in the wall did lead to a passage. He followed it to a chamber with old stone stairs going up. Did you know that Baghdad used to have canals everywhere for commerce, and some were just covered up and not filled in?"

"No, I had no idea. So, he climbed the stairs and escaped?"

"Pretty much. But he hit another snag. When he got to the top, he figured he was near the surface, but the passage had collapsed there too.

He was pissed off, but then he felt a breeze. He found a small opening and dug a hole wide enough to squeeze through. He emerged in the old park just across the street from the Greek embassy. He was free—broken, exhausted, and dirty, but finally free."

"Then you met him at the hospital?"

"Not quite. There was still one last unexpected indignity waiting for him. He dragged himself home, and just when he thought it was finally over, his wife opened the door."

"But that's a good thing."

"If she had cried and hugged on him, it would have been. Instead, when she saw him, she screamed and tried to put two bullets in him with his old service revolver before he was able to wrestle it away. She thought he was a ghost or zombie that had returned from the grave. She was hysterical, screaming. Fortunately, the commotion woke the neighbors. They brought him to the hospital after they were sure he was the real Chief Mohammed and not some demon."

"That's an incredible story."

"The Iraqi police, the rest of his station crew, and the MPs are guarding him while he recovers, but that's not the most amazing thing."

"How can all that not be the most amazing thing?"

"Because this is," Del said. She handed me a roll of paper.

"What's so amazing about this?" I asked, unrolling a rough architectural drawing.

Del smiled. "These are the plans he drew up for his new and improved police station."

I was so happy, I couldn't stop laughing. The unstoppable Chief Mohammed Sawan of the new Iraqi police. He not only cheated death; he restored my faith in what we were doing.

CHAPTER 38

March 2004—Camp Victory, Baghdad

Paul and George got takeout for dinner on their way back from the Mansour district. It looked like they'd snagged four of everything from the menu of a restaurant and pastry shop. It was a bewildering array of mezes and salads, game, lamb and rice, platters of assorted kabobs, oval-shaped *samoon* flat bread, dates, and olives. It covered a big table.

I didn't have dinner plans. I was taking a walk down the road, and they literally cut me off with a van and snatched me off the street. John was driving; he looked back at me, sandwiched in between Paul and George, and said, "You didn't think we were going to let you leave without saying goodbye? You're going to like this. Tonight, everything is two for one at the villa."

After dinner from two restaurants, where we had to eat at least two helpings, John broke out the Little Boy Blue and declared everyone's glass had to be at least two fingers full at all times.

"Ringo, you get first toast."

I stood up. "To the president of the United States and the guardians who hold the line, to the friends with us," I said, looking around the table, "and the friends who watch over us."

"To the president, the guardians, and our friends," was the response as we clinked glasses.

We drank and laughed and told stories.

After coffee and dessert, John asked, "Remember when you told me no one knew who was really responsible for the attack on the police station?"

"I do."

"That isn't entirely true," he said with a smile.

"What are you saying, John?"

"We figured it out. Welcome to the 'kill two birds with one stone' portion of the evening. Take a look at this." John handed me a device like a personal data assistant that was bigger than a Blackberry, heavy for its size, and sported a short, thick antenna. The video that played on the gray-green screen looked down from the sky from a wide view before it tightened on idling trucks and people walking around what looked like a factory or maintenance building.

The screen was small, but the resolution was good. There was targeting information and a time stamp and coordinates crawling across the bottom of the screen. "What is this?" I asked John.

"The future," he replied with a smile. Then he leaned over the back of my chair, reached over, and held down a button on the side. "Smaug, this is Ashur. Pan left twenty degrees."

"Copy that, Ashur, panning left twenty." The view on the display changed to a road with a patch of desert to the left.

"Pretty sweet, right?"

"Remoting the feed to a mobile device is cool, but I've seen imagery like this on the big screen at Nellis."

"Really? Well, I was impressed. You're a tough customer. We'll just have to do better, then." John keyed the mic on the PDA again. "Smaug, this is Ashur. Resume mission profile."

"Copy that, Ashur. Resuming mission."

The screen changed again as the camera came back to center and focused on activity around a group of buildings behind a wall. I offered the PDA to George and Paul, but they declined.

"I had elements of the group that attacked you followed. They all converged at the same place. The compound you see now is their base of operations. It's their lair. Because of how we use the building you were attacked in, we initially assumed they were elements directed by a foreign nation, and that concerned us because we thought the attack meant someone was on to our surveillance project."

"Who was it, then?" I asked. "They shot us up pretty good."

"Appears that we were caught between rival gangs trying to control that area. They may not have even been aware that you were there."

"They acted aware. It seemed pretty personal at the time," I replied.

"Well, it was. So, upon further investigation, it seems they were providing arms and money to the actual insurgents. Also, they were the group responsible for the attack on your police station. Most of the terrorists from the attack are garrisoned at that center building on your screen." John flashed a grim smile.

"Two birds?"

"Exactly," he said. Then John made a phone call. "This is Ashur. Confirm status. Copy. Confirm vehicles. Copy. Confirm weapon signatures. Copy. Confirm task force containment. Copy. Execute authorized. Engage, engage, engage."

"What are you doing, John?"

"Watch the screen. There are four buildings inside the wall. A main building, a motor building, a support building, and a weapons storage facility. Over one hundred criminals, terrorists, and insurgents. People who tried to kill the three of you. Bad guys who destroyed a police station and tried to assassinate Chief Sawan. Scum turning their own neighborhoods inside out."

The clock clicked to 0300; the picture went out of focus, as though the camera had been hit; then the screen went solid chartreuse green.

"Wait for it," John said. "They had a hand in everything. They tried to kill you and your friends, and it's estimated they've killed hundreds, if not thousands, of Iraqis."

When the screen rebooted, the wall was still there, but the main building had collapsed in the middle, and the three other buildings were flattened. Everything in the compound was burning.

There were flashes. Weapons were fired by the forces surrounding the compound. A vehicle moved forward, and the soldiers fired on it until it veered off, crashed into the wall, and burned. There were secondary explosions, but the UAV continued its lazy orbit, unfazed.

"Did you see that at Nellis?" John asked.

The green, digitized glow still danced on the screen. I held death in my hand, and I felt the weight of it one last time before I handed it back to John.

"I've never seen anything like that," was all I could muster. Part of me was happy. It was exciting, but it was hard to watch. Justice was served. More than a hundred terrorists died. They couldn't hurt anyone else anymore.

I couldn't see who was shooting at us, and I couldn't see who died. Only that people *did* shoot and people *did* die. It was unreal. It was vengeance and retribution. They'd tried to kill me, they'd destroyed a successful police station, they'd bombed cafés, and now they were dead. All of them.

Baghdad would be safer for a while.

It was a lot to take in. It was thrilling, and it was terrifying.

"Payback's a bitch," was what I said out loud. "We should raise our glasses to a successful mission and to the spirits of our comrades."

"Now that's a fine idea."

After one more drink together, I said my goodbyes to George and Paul. Then it was just the two of us. There was John, and there was me, and it was finally time to talk. It was time for Lucy's long overdue wake.

John said she had more good days than bad days. Lucy said, even at the end, the pain was nothing compared to a bad mission or John's cooking.

"You should have told me sooner."

"Maybe . . . you're right, but I couldn't figure out how, and the timing was always wrong. She left me with a lot of rules, and you know that's not my strong suit. More than anything else, she wanted to make sure we were going to be OK after she was gone. She seemed to think we'd be lost without her."

"She was always bossy."

"Yeah, right. I married her in the hospital, and she insisted on her wedding night despite being on an IV and hooked up to a monitor."

"Now that's an image I'll never forget. Thanks for that."

"Fuck you, it gets better. The nurses I paid off had a shift change, and in our enthusiasm, we knocked her monitor leads off, so these nurses come bursting in with a crash cart, and there we are in the middle of it, and Lu turns to them and says, 'Just a little more, I'm almost there!'"

"Now I have to get therapy."

"Good thing for all of us, they shut off the monitor, backed out, and left."

"I don't know if congratulations is the right thing to say, John, but I know she loved you. She always wanted to get married one day. I know that marrying you made her really happy."

"Aside from the obvious, she said she had only three regrets: that we all didn't get to spend more time together, that we didn't get to go on our honeymoon, and that she never got to hold your baby." He paused; we wept. "She passed away three days after we were married. With a smile on her face. Who gets that after the kind of life she had?"

We talked until the sun came up. It was something we both needed to do. We weren't alone, and part of Lucy would always be with us. I touched my Saint Christopher medal under my shirt, and I knew everything would be all right.

"Thanks again, John. I'm sure you have my number."

"Have a good flight, Spike. I'll see you around."

"No more Ringo?"

"Nah. Spike is better."

"Are you staying John, then?"

"To the best of your knowledge," he replied.

I smiled, hugged him, and said, "Stay well, my friend."

"I owe you," said John, holding me by the shoulders and locking eyes. "I don't think my guys would have made it out if you hadn't been there. They feel the same way. You should get off your lazy ass, learn another language, and come work for me. I'd make it worth your while, and you'd make a whole lot more."

"I love what I do."

"Not too smart, though," he said.

"Well, your job interview sucked."

We laughed and shook hands, and he was gone. I walked back to my tent alone with my thoughts. I had mixed feelings, but no regrets. I was ready. It was time to go home.

CHAPTER 39

April 2004—Camp Victory, Baghdad

President George W. Bush said, "We still face thugs and terrorists in Iraq who would rather go on killing the innocent than accept the advance of liberty. And there's a reason why. They know that a free Iraq will be a major defeat for the cause of terror. This collection of killers is trying to shake the will of the United States. America will never be intimidated by a bunch of thugs and assassins. We are aggressively striking the terrorists in Iraq. We will defeat them there, so we do not have to face them in our own country."[23] The president gave this speech at a fundraiser in Washington as I prepared to leave Iraq. Based on my experience, every word was true.

A huge dog howled on a small hill next to a date palm tree. He was as big as a wolf and covered in grizzly black fur. As we cleared the checkpoint, other dogs began to howl responsively. That was the last thing I saw as I left Camp Victory, and the convoy rolled on to the ballad of the wild dogs of war. It was the perfect sendoff for my April Fools' Day travel home.

I was surrounded by good guys on that convoy: almost my whole FMO team, a few new guys from the AT/FP team, and a bunch of other

---

23   The White House, Office of the Press Secretary, "Remarks by the President at National Republican Congressional Committee Dinner," news release, April 1, 2004, https://georgewbush-whitehouse.archives.gov/news/releases/2004/04/20040401-7.html.

officers and NCOs I'd come to rely on and respect. Together, we represented every service—the US, the UK, and the Netherlands. We'd been through a lot together. We'd made a difference in missions across Iraq, and we'd helped rebuild the infrastructure of an entire nation. I was so proud of each of them it was hard to find the right words to say goodbye. Relinquishing command of my team to another officer was as much of a regret as it was a relief, but it meant I was going home. We'd shared an experience where we stretched our skills to the limit, righted wrongs, and did good things in a perilous place where many nights were a storm of incoming mortar, rocket, and machine-gun fire.

It was a place where counting Mississippis didn't help.

We had a happy exchange of goodbyes, handshakes, slaps on the back, and, eventually, salutes. I watched their convoy drive off until they were out of sight. The first leg of my long trip home was complete. I sat on a great green pile of my gear and wondered what April Fools' Day still had in store for me. I swapped stories with the other airmen and soldiers. We joked about heading home from a combat zone on April Fools' Day, but no one really laughed.

It started out as a quiet night.

Our C-130 transport lined up on the runway for final approach two hours after sunset. Just as its landing gear went down, it suddenly jinked left, then right. Its four massive turboprop engines roared as the pilot pushed the throttle to the firewall, and then the transport aggressively corkscrewed its way back into the sky. Change of plan. It left in its wake an orange pyrotechnic display of popped flares to distract heat-seeking missiles. In the dark sky, the afterimage that burned into my eyes fluttered like an angel's wings.

I held my breath, but nothing rose from the ground to chase after our C-130. There were no explosions, and once the aircraft was gone, it was eerily silent except for the distant buzz of tactical generators. I grabbed a cup of coffee at base operations, but the boards were clear for the rest of the night. The passenger terminal NCO said they had to wave off all the remaining flights due to surface-to-air missile (SAM) activity near the airport.

It was a long, cold night camped out in the open. There were concrete pads with cots, but there were no roofs or real shelter. It would have been a night spent under the stars if the air hadn't been so still. There was dense fog starting at three feet up. Being on a cot, I could reach up, touch the cloud, and, in the damp, thick parts, watch my hand fade away. The cloud hovered like that for most of the night. After reading the same page in my book several times, I fell asleep content, dreaming of boy names I knew Jodi would hate. I'd just dozed off when the attack came.

I rolled to the ground when the explosion woke me and, after a moment, got my bearings and crawled to a low wall. I couldn't see the flash from the explosion, so it was on the other side of the building from me. The other soldiers and airmen around me had taken up similar positions.

Then there was silence again.

Just when I started to get up, there was a series of sounds like paper tearing. *Chew, chew, chew.* It was the distinctive sound of rockets launching from tubes. Their corresponding explosions echoed along the fence line. They were loud, and flashes danced through the fog that looked like chain lightning strikes in the distance.

Then the mortars came. They stepped through the compound, explosion after explosion, closer, then farther away, and just when they'd seem to be fading into the distance, a round would hit close by again. Loud enough to be deafening and hard enough to rattle the buildings in front of us. The ground quivered in little earthquakes, and then it was silent again. Just buzzing in the ears. I got up and walked around. Everyone was all right.

"How's everyone doing over here?" I asked.

"Fine, sir. Hooah. It would suck to make it this far and not get home."

"You're gonna make it home. Flight's coming in the morning. Hole up, get some sleep, and we'll be in Qatar by lunch."

"Copy that, sir. We're good to go. Fuck Iraq."

Three minutes after the attack stopped, the warning siren finally sounded, and an announcement was repeated over the PA system called the "giant voice."

"Incoming attack, take shelter."

I rolled over to try to get some sleep. There was nothing to do but laugh. If they could shave another four minutes off their timing, it would be a real warning instead of insult to injury. But Iraq was consistent to the end. Even trying to leave could be made harder.

Dawn came, and a light breeze shredded the fog. There were gaps in the perimeter where Texas-sized barriers had been knocked over on their sides. The mortars had dug pits in the ground surrounding the runways and destroyed a handful of vehicles, but the runway was still intact.

A C-130 is an old tactical transport aircraft with four propellers in the front and a drop ramp in the back for loading people and cargo. It was designed in the early fifties, and it's still a great workhorse. It isn't sexy like an SR-71 or an F-22, but a C-130 is, without a doubt, the most beautiful bird in the world when it drops out of the sky and lands to take you home.

I think the aircraft was still moving when we climbed up the back ramp, loaded our gear, and strapped in. We taxied down the runway and clawed our way into the air as we bucked and jumped and explosively flapped our angel wings as hard as we could to fly away from Iraq.

It was a wild ride. I don't know if a SAM[24] ever targeted us, but our pilot wasn't taking chances. The loadmasters manned the porthole windows in the cargo area. They scanned for threats, and the pilot maneuvered hard and bounced us through the sky, just to be safe.

Flying sideways in an aluminum can, with no horizon to see and little ventilation, screws with your sense of balance. Light turbulence can cause nausea and vertigo. It gets worse when someone shakes the can. By the time we landed, about a third of our company had puked, and streams of vomit snaked through the aisles.

Across from me, a marine captain removed his shirt and rolled it up as a pillow to comfort the young airman sitting next to him, who'd emptied everything from his belly and was past the dry heaves, with nothing stopping him from passing out but the shakes. The marine reassured him over the protesting engines that it was OK and everything would be all right. He was covered in that kid's puke, and all he cared about was taking care of him. It was an impressive thing to see.

We landed hard, and when we finally stopped, we were counting the seconds for the crew to drop the loading ramp so we could breathe fresh air.

I was used to flying in bad conditions, and even though I didn't spew, I still had the sweats and came close a couple of times. Looking around, everyone was ragged as the loadmaster began to make his way to a control panel, taking care not to step in any of the puddles.

There was a cheer when they dropped the cargo ramp. A hot blast from the desert cleared the air, and I could finally breathe a little easier. I unbelted, stood up, and stretched. I felt like I'd been beaten with a stick. Rivulets of puke flowed down the ramp, and a pair of ground crewmen

---

24   Surface-to-air missile.

who were joking as they walked up froze when they saw us. One said, "Damn." His partner put his hand to his mouth, jumped off the ramp, and threw up on the flight line. Our pilot's Texas accent crackled through the cargo-area speakers. "Welcome to Qatar. Congratulations. Hard part's over. Please gather your gear, deplane, and follow the ground crew's instructions."

I shouldered my pack, pulled a few airmen to their feet, and had the ground crew call the medics for our sickest airmen and soldiers. A few looked like they were going to need IVs. The medics appeared almost immediately, carrying stretchers, but the passengers didn't want to be carried out. That was fine by me. "If you can walk, that's outstanding," I said. "Follow these sergeants. They'll take good care of you." The people next to them lent them a shoulder, and they filed out behind the medics. The rest of us fell in line and followed them out.

Except for the faded bits of color stubbornly clinging to a few of the buildings that made up the airbase, the dull ground and pale dust hanging in the air cast everything in a crisp, empty white light. As far as I could see, we were in a place the exact shade of a blank sheet of notebook paper if you deleted all the lines. Past the high chain-link fence was a tabula rasa. In the middle of the Qatari desert, the airbase looked like it was built on the surface of the moon.

The flight-line staff had the instincts of border collies, and they expertly herded us to a large beige Quonset hut, where we were divided up for briefings and follow-on flights. There was even coffee and a shower. My hair was still wet when they sealed the door on my flight to Germany.

The closer I got to home, the more colors there were. Qatar was pure white. Then the sky was blue again. After living in the muted white, brown, and beige of Iraq, it was like the sand had scoured hues from my memory. Along the way home, it felt like my empty crayon box was starting to fill back up again, and the colors startled me, like they were fresh and new.

Shocks of color erupted everywhere. The first greens to jump out at me were in the muted camouflage patterns worn by the airmen who greeted us at Rhein Mein Air Base, Germany.

The terminal was festooned with all the colors of children's art. Banners from many schools were hung from wall to wall to support and inspire the soldiers, sailors, airmen, and marines fighting the war on terrorism. Messages underneath in German and English block letters encouraged us with "You are our heroes"; "We're proud of you"; "Come back home"; "Be all right." In the terminal, a German kindergarten class had traced their hands on a massive canvas to offer us a symbolic pat on the back. A third-grade class had drawn pictures of themselves and thanked us for fighting all the bad guys, for being brave, and for keeping them safe.

At Baltimore International Airport, we cleared customs, and I pushed a cart laden with gear alongside one of my former tent mates from Camp Victory. When we rounded a corner, a big band started to play "The Stars and Stripes Forever." A crowd cheered. Then they threw confetti and welcomed us home. They were waiting for someone else, but every time a group in desert camouflage uniforms walked by, they struck up the band and cheered.

I was too wired to sleep on my flight back home. I had a lot on my mind. There was still a baby to name. I missed my son, Xander, and my wife, Jo, and I was tired from being away. I began to feel a real longing for home. I could finally feel the feelings I didn't have to set aside any longer. I'd done things and made decisions in Iraq that I was going to have to live with for a long time.

For better or worse, Iraq was a part of me now. I will never forget the look in that boy's eyes when I pried him off my Humvee with my pistol in his face or the relief I felt when those children finally scattered. I shot insurgents trying to kill me. I saw blood spray out of their bodies, and, later, I calmly watched them all die with no regret, as terrible as that is. I learned how to slay monsters.

I saw a little girl in a yellow dress make a family out of orphans and do more than just survive. She gave me hope for Iraq when I was in a dark place trying to make sense of it all. Sometimes, I still say a prayer for her. I never saw her again, but if an assassinated Iraqi police chief can survive a bombing and RPG attack, claw his way out of a building's worth of rubble, and still walk home . . . I have room for a little faith.

For various reasons I don't always understand, women have mostly been generous with me. In fact, every great thing I ever did, I did to impress a girl. I learned to read for Sarah, and she taught me how wonderful life could be with a friend to share the adventure. I learned how to accomplish a mission and stand up for myself for Isabel. I took my finals and graduated high school because I didn't want to let Patty and Adriana down. I learned how to have real faith and went back to school because Lucy saved me and then showed me how big the world really was. She taught me how to be a better man, to fight harder, to know when to stop, and how to really eat with chopsticks. I miss her. It took a long time, but I finally learned how to be brave when I had to, when all I ever wanted to do was run away.

I became a father and tried to be the best dad I could because it was important to Jodi, and I really wanted to be the man she saw when she looked at me.

I wondered what Jo would see when she saw me now.

Jodi picked me up from the airport in San Antonio. We hugged and held on to each other for a long time. It's hard to describe how it feels to touch someone for the first time in months. I've heard it described before as the feeling of a dam bursting. For me, it wasn't that; it was the floating sensation just at the top of a roller coaster. It was that weightless pause full of anxiety and anticipation, excitement and fear. That place just before the rush of speed that marks the point where the real ride finally begins.

Her pregnant belly pressed against me, and I could feel the baby inside her move. I held on for a long time. She smelled like home.

Xander was sleeping when we arrived at the house. Jodi stayed downstairs to get something ready. He had grown so much. He was wrapped in his blankets like he was curled up in a nest. His soft brown hair had a couple of cowlick curls, and his pajamas were covered in characters from a new cartoon I didn't know.

I gave him a kiss on his forehead, but he didn't even stir. I looked around to make sure no one was watching. Then, I checked to make sure he was breathing.

I sat on the floor with my back against the bed and listened to him breathe for a long while. With every one of his breaths, I could feel another muscle I didn't realize was tense relax.

Our old, blind cat Fairfax found me. He came over to nuzzle me, but missed and indignantly fell over with a thud. I laughed at his misfortune as I guided him over. Then he curled up in my lap and began to purr like an old engine.

That's when it hit me. That's when it finally felt real. Listening to my son's inhales and exhales in the bed behind me, with a warm cat purring in my lap and my wife, so pregnant with our second son, leaning against the door, smiling at me. I was finally home. That's when my dam broke.

Never in my whole life did I ever believe I would be so happy.

AFTERWORD

HARLAND W. RILEY
(May 14, 1940–June 21, 1996)

When the giant tumbled from the sky
Jack was too far away to see him fall
He saw a flash and counted slow
One Mississippi, two Mississippi, three
I am Jack Giantson
Mississippi, four
I traded our cow for magic beans Mississippi,
Five Mississippi, and for them tasted the strap
Six Planted and sown Mississippi,
I climbed the beanstalk
And, Seven kept the goose's Golden
eggs Mississippi, but
Eight,
We were almost friends
Mississippi,
When I said goodbye
Where the giant had fallen, Nine
To the ground, Mississippi
Flowers sprang from his blood
Thunder gave a report of Fe-Fi-Fo-Fum
And I strive to be a better man
To be a giant
But I can't keep cows
And beans don't seem so magic anymore

CHAPTER 40

June 2004—San Antonio, Texas

One story ends, another begins, life goes on.

Negotiations to name our soon-to-be-born baby boy continued for nearly two weeks more. Mostly just as I was finally falling asleep. Jo's negotiation tactics were tougher than all the merchants in Kuwait and Iraq. I lost almost every round.

Xander decided that the new baby should also be named Xander, but when I explained to him that having two Xanders in the house would make it hard to know who was being called or who was in trouble, he laughed and said, "Well, Daddy, that's easy. It would be him, of course."

After pondering the implications, he did suggest an alternative. He proclaimed in a loud, clear voice that the new baby should be called Xander 2, the Sequel. "Sequel" for short.

Xander didn't take the veto well.

My second son was born on June 28. Whereas Xander arrived early, his brother seemed to have no intention of leaving the womb. After many long walks through, around, above, and below Wilford Hall Medical Center, Jo's water finally broke. She was still arguing for baby names when they moved her to the delivery suite. She argued until her first major contractions, and then she agreed to a ceasefire. The anesthesiologist administered her epidural, and then she focused on getting our baby born.

Jo did a great job and delivered a beautiful baby boy.

After the nurses cleaned him up, I got to hold him. The first thing he did when he looked at me was scowl. I knew instantly he was my son. I chuckled, and he made content baby noises in my arms. I was in a different place than when I'd held our first boy, and I knew without a doubt that everything was going to be all right. Jodi was watching us, and when I placed him in her arms, she said, "We should call him Samuel. We'll start him off with Sam, and he can grow into the rest."

I thought that was perfect, so that's exactly what we did.

After getting back home, learning how to relax again was even harder than learning how to sleep through the night. I was always expecting . . . something. The baby couldn't sleep, either, so we had that in common, and we kept each other company. We fell into a comfortable rhythm, but I couldn't shake the feeling that I was waiting for . . . something. Maybe I was still waiting for the other shoe to fall. I was home and safe, but going from a war zone back to the mostly civil world was a harder thing than just moving from the city to the county. It shouldn't have been difficult, but it was. New familiar sights, different familiar sounds, better smells—different expectations. It was too quiet. There was a reasonable expectation that when I went to sleep I'd wake up the next morning. For a while, the silent nights were unnerving. Not a single gunshot sounded in the night until hunting season, and that was strangely comforting. I could tell, even in my sleep, that the shots were far enough away to not worry about.

There were things I had to remember that took some time for the still too sharp details to blunt. To sleep, I tried counting Mississippis, and then helicopter rotors, then sheep. Just when I was about to give up, the baby would cry, and I'd have something useful I could do.

The doctors at our transition briefings said that the first three months back might be hard. Not only was there the coming down from fear, adrenaline, shock, stress, noise, and the immediacy of everything, there was the reality that time had passed, I'd been gone, and families change while we're away. Not just us. A lot of marriages don't survive combat deployments. People get stressed, afraid, and lonely—so they take comfort where they can. I was lucky in that regard; Jo was more independent, and she managed to learn how to be a single parent while I was away, but she was also exhausted and ready for a break. It worked out for a while that I couldn't sleep—Jo finally got some rest. One day, I did sleep, and Jo let me. I slept for almost three straight days. I woke groggy and unsure of where I was, but refreshed. My mind and body had finally caught up with each other. I felt like the waiting was finally over. Jodi was nursing Sam. Xander was sitting at the table eating dessert and swinging his legs. Jo smiled and said, "Welcome back."

Xander laughed and said, "Sleepyhead."

Right now, baby Sam is sleeping, and the house is filled with the smells of fresh-brewed coffee, bread from the bakery, and fried bacon. I'm stretched out, sinking into the foam of our new bed, watching my wife sleep for just five minutes more. I'll try waking her up again soon, but I'm content to wait. The small foot pressed against the back of my head belongs to a little boy who snuck in bed to snuggle and then fell asleep. It's a perfect moment, and I'm in no rush to see it end.

My career began in intelligence analysis and operations. After a while, I specialized in communications, and I continued to support military, intelligence, and special missions for almost thirty years. Mother told us such vivid tales as children about "the" organization and about working undercover to preserve democracy. I remember, when I was little, really wanting to be a part of something that big someday. The irony of my growing up to work in the world of her stories isn't lost on me. Even though none of her tales were true, she did work out telecommuting years before anyone even had computers.

I don't believe my mother was evil, but she was ill, and she did bad things that hurt us. I think she loved me in her own way, and I don't believe that's a conceit or Stockholm syndrome. I remember when we were very small and she laughed and played with us. She was so happy before she grew sad. For years, there were occasional flickers of who she'd once been before that flame, regrettably, burned out. I wonder how different our lives might have been if the treatments we have today for bipolar disorders, depression, and schizophrenia had been available to her back then and she'd taken her meds. What happened happened. I'm at peace with it. I love my life. For better or worse, I wouldn't be me without her.

My father once told me that one definition of adulthood was surviving your childhood. My dad was a strict, sometimes harsh, occasionally brutal man. He had an infectious laugh. People loved to work for him, and he taught me many painful lessons. It's hard for me to think about the lessons my father taught me—what he taught and how he did it—and not wonder about the lessons I've taught my children. I've also been tough and strict with my boys, but I've tried hard to temper it. When Xander was a young teenager, he once told me, with all his passion and sincerity, "You know, you really put the 'dick' in 'dictator,' Dad." In those moments, it's hard to stay serious and stern. It was funny, but laughing would have only made things worse. So, I responded with the truth.

"You're right. I'm glad you finally noticed. Yes, I do. And now you're grounded for another day . . . Want to make it three?"

He responded like most young teenagers in the moment: like I'd just ripped out his soul. "Ahhh. You just don't get it, Dad. I hate you." Followed by a retreat of stamping feet and slamming doors. Now I'm watching him make small mistakes and pick himself up and grow into a fine young man. It's frustrating and exciting. Most times, I can see the train wreck coming, and I want to save him the pain, but I know I can't. He wants to make his own choices, and he has a fine moral compass. All I can do is dust him off after he stands back up and point him in the right direction. Occasionally, he even asks for my advice. I live for those moments. In between, I sometimes ponder what and how my father taught me and what and how I try to teach my boys. No one gets it right all the time, and every dad and kid is different.

I taught my boys how to fish instead of hunt.

In Iraq, my dad's lessons, as miserable as they were, saved my life. How do you weigh and measure that? Even though I hated his methods and was angry with him for years, those lessons helped get me home to the family I love. He's still the gruff, salty voice of my conscience.

I think he would have liked my boys.

We captured Saddam Hussein during my first tour in Iraq, and he was executed during my wife's last tour there, hanged until dead on December 30, 2006, at the first light of a cold and partly cloudy sunrise.

We prepared for the worst: uprising, coordinated attacks, synchronized bombings, the short-sighted anarchy that envelops an armed, ecstatic mob. There were a few incidents and deaths, but most Iraqis celebrated. It was the end of an era, and there was hope that there could finally be something better. It was bigger than the Super Bowl. The monster was dead.

Saddam, the dictator, was no more. He went out, surprisingly composed, with a whimper and one wet snap. The word spread fast across Iraq.

My experience in Iraq was brief, as was my time in Kuwait and Saudi Arabia, but I won't soon forget the people I met and what I've seen. Some of it still doesn't make sense, and I don't know if it ever will, but that's OK. The world's a big place. There's still a lot to do and see, and I still believe even one person can make a difference. I've seen enough to have a little faith.

January 2008—Camp Victory, Baghdad

I met John one last time in Baghdad, some years after the events depicted in this memoir. I was a major, and my new duties took me all over Iraq. He'd secured one of the villas across from the Al Faw Palace, and, on the anniversary of Lucy's death, I grilled steaks, and we had Iraqi pastries and coffee for dessert. John was excited that there was finally a decent digital version of the complete Beatles, and I listened to "Lucy in the Sky with Diamonds" and "While My Guitar Gently Weeps" echo off the stone.

We stayed up all night, sitting on the roof watching the lights and reflections of the Al Faw as helicopters patrolled in the distance, catching up and drinking until we couldn't stand.

We still had our Saint Christopher medals, and I know Lu heard our toasts to her, to the future, and to life. We're still here, and she's still watching over us, I know it.

I never had a guardian angel before, but there are times I can almost feel her there.

The next day, John showed me around the Perfume Palace complex, just down the road from the Al Faw, and offered me a pretty good job at a new venture he was starting up that would have nearly tripled my pay. As tempting as it was, I showed him a picture of my family and talked about how much I loved Jo and how big the boys were getting. He already knew my answer was no.

I told him my goal was for Jo and me both to retire as lieutenant colonels and that then I wanted to be a writer. More than anything, I want a quiet life, with my family, and the luxury of time with them. I hadn't expected to live long enough to see thirty. I was going to do what I wanted with any bonus days I had coming.

John grunted. Then he poured us another drink, and after swirling his ice for a bit, he said, "I can't get in the way of that. So, here's to you and Jo. And to getting out. I won't say retirement because that sounds too much like goodbye."

We clinked glasses, and I told John I was thinking about writing a memoir about the early parts of my life and career. When I told him the story, he didn't hesitate a moment or caution me against it like I thought he might. He jumped out of his chair, grabbed both sides of my head, and said, "Yes. You have to do it." His only stipulation, aside from security issues, was that I make him a villain. Then he went on to quote from Shakespeare's *Richard III*: "And thus I clothe my naked villany with odd old ends stol'n out of holy writ, and seem a saint when most I play the devil."

When I said he most likely wouldn't be a villain in the final cut, John replied:

"Well, we'll see. There's still some time."

ACKNOWLEDGMENTS

I'd like to thank Chris Armor, my brother from another mother and a true friend. After I retired from the air force, he dragged me into the Mont Blanc store and bought me a ridiculously good pen. Then he said, "Keep this on your desk, and use it. You're a writer. Never forget." Sometimes all you need is one person to really believe in you.

I owe my parents a debt for the gift of life and for teaching me how hard life could be if I were unprepared.

Sarah, thank you for showing me a big and wonderful world. Sally, you'll never know how much you mean to me. You kept me together when I had no idea how to do it myself.

And Patty and Adri, thank you for caring about me when I didn't.

This book wouldn't have been possible without the approval of the Office of the Director of National Intelligence and the organizations I've worked for, and with, who let me share this story about some of my favorite people who truly made a difference in this twisted, terrifyingly awesome world.

Each book has its own journey, and mine is better for the love and attention it received from a small army of believers and experts. I'd like to thank my first readers—Mike Ryan, Linda Channel, and Dawn Palmer—for their enthusiasm, encouragement, and comments. My editors: Kristen Hamilton, Hallie Raymond, and Mike Towle, who showed me a different, better way to tell this story.

Finally, I'd like to thank Tom Reale for his enthusiasm and faith in this story and all the amazing folks at Brown Books who navigated the million details of publishing to bring *Baghdaddy* to market.

ABOUT THE AUTHOR

Bill Riley is a writer and retired US Air Force lieutenant colonel with interests in space exploration, coffee roasting, global communication, intelligence activities, and ancient ruins. Bill was an intelligence analyst during the Cold War. Later, he specialized in strategy and communications. During his career,  he's worked with intelligence and special operations professionals from every service, virtually every intelligence agency, and several friendly foreign governments.

Bill's deployments took him through combat zones across the Middle East where he played significant roles in Kuwait and Iraq, supported joint coalition operations, and helped nations rebuild after wars. He was the first US electronic warfare officer in Iraq for Operation Iraqi Freedom, he led the air force's largest network operations and security center, and he was the first cyberspace operations officer to receive the Air Force Combat Action Medal.

He holds degrees in literature, public administration, and strategic leadership, and he is a graduate of Air Command and Staff College and the Air Force Space Command Vigilant Look program.

Bill lives in Idaho, just outside Boise, with his wife and two sons.